DISCARDED

DISCOURSES

Peak-Load Pricing

Peak-Load Pricing

European Lessons for U.S. Energy Policy

Bridger M. Mitchell
Willard G. Manning, Jr.
Jan Paul Acton

A Rand Corporation Research Study

Ballinger Publishing Company • Cambridge, Massachusetts
A Subsidiary of J.B. Lippincott Company

 This book is printed on recycled paper.

Copyright © 1978 by The Rand Corporation. All rights reserved. No part of this publication may be reproduced, stored in a retrieval system, or transmitted in any form or by any means, electronic mechanical photocopy, recording or otherwise, without the prior written consent of the publisher.

International Standard Book Number: 0-88410-670-5

Library of Congress Catalog Card Number: 77-27897

Printed in the United States of America

Library of Congress Cataloging in Publication Data

Mitchell, Bridger M.
  Peak-load pricing

  Bibliography: p. 221
  Includes index.
    1. Electric utilities—Rates. 2. Electric utilities—United States—Rates. 3. Electric utilities—Europe—Rates. 4. Peak load—Economic aspects. I. Manning, Willard G., joint author. II. Acton, Jan Paul, joint author. III. Title.
HD9685.A2M5   338.4'3   77-27897
ISBN 0-88410-670-5

For Katherine, Erika, and Helen.

Contents

List of Figures	xiii
List of Tables	xvii
Preface	xix
Acknowledgments	xxi

Part I
Electricity Rates and Energy Efficiency   1

Chapter 1
Electricity and U.S. Energy Policy   3

National Energy Policy	3
Conservation	4
The Role of Prices	5
The Electricity Sector	6
Structure of the Industry	6
The Determination of Electricity Rates	7
U.S. Rate Structures	9
Declining-Block Rates	10
Industrial and Commercial Rates	13
Criticisms	15
New Rate Structures	16
The Load Curve	16

Peak-Load Pricing	18
Marginal-Cost Pricing	18
Reform of Electricity Rate Structures	19
Summary	21

Chapter 2
Basic Economics of Electricity Supply — 23

The Nature of Electricity Costs	23
Generation and Distribution	24
Energy and Capacity	24
A Simple Model	25
Storage	28
The Role of Marginal Costs	30
The Marginal Costs of Generation	30
Marginal Costs of Distribution	33
Summary	36

Chapter 3
The Design of Rate Structures — 37

The Theory of Peak-Load Pricing	38
The Basic Model	38
More General Models	40
Engineering Models	41
Marginal-Cost Pricing	42
Economies of Scale	44
Inflation	46
Short-Run Versus Long-Run Marginal Costs	47
Methods of Modulating the Load Curve	48
Rate Incentives	48
Load Management	49
Summary	49

Part II
The European Experience: A Quantitative Study of Utilities in Six Countries — 51

Chapter 4
The Structure of European Electricity Tariffs — 53

The Variety of Rate Structures	53
Differences in System Characteristics	56

Shortages and Interruptible Loads	58
Detailed Characteristics of European Rate Structures	59
Norway	60
Sweden	62
France	65
The Structure of the Green Tariff	66
The Residential Tariff	74
England and Wales	75
The Wholesale Tariff	75
High-Voltage Tariffs	77
The Residential Tariff	77
West Germany	80
High-Voltage Tariffs	80
Low-Voltage Tariffs	83
Finland	84
Summary	86

Chapter 5
The Response of European Industries to Peak-load Tariffs   89

France	90
Idealized Load Response	90
Examples of Response in Specific Industries	90
Self-Generation	100
Interruptible Customers	104
Other Industries	104
England and Wales	107
Load Response in Specific Industries	108
Potential Peak Warnings (PPWs)	112
Sweden	113
Norway	116
Finland	117
Summary	118

Chapter 6
Residential Tariffs and Load Management in Europe   121

Modulating the System Load Curve	121
Load-Management Considerations	122
England and Wales	124
Storage Heating	124
Shifted Load	125
West Germany	128
Storage Heating	128

Avoiding Distribution Peaks ... 128
France ... 133
Finland, Norway, and Sweden ... 133
Summary ... 136

Chapter 7
Assessing the European Experience ... 137

Effect of Peak-Load Pricing on Capacity Requirements ... 137
   France ... 138
   England and Wales ... 142
   West Germany ... 142
Shifting Peaks ... 143
   Theoretical Solution ... 144
   Evidence of Shifting Peaks ... 145
Does Nationalization Make a Difference? ... 146
Summary ... 147

Part III
Peak-Load Pricing for the United States ... 149

Chapter 8
Peak-Load Pricing for Industry ... 151

Potential Industrial Response to Peak-Load Pricing ... 152
Industrial Adaptation over Time to Peak-Load Tariffs ... 154
   Factors Affecting Adaptation ... 154
   Adaptation to a Stylized Tariff ... 155
Data and Methodology ... 164
   Applicability ... 164
   Conservative Nature of the Calculations ... 166
   Data Used ... 166
   Methods of Calculating Response to Peak-Load Pricing ... 168
The National Effect of Peak-Load Pricing ... 173
   Industrial Use of Peak-Period Electricity ... 173
   Impact of Time-of-Day Pricing on Seventeen Industries ... 174
   Impact on Other Industries ... 175
   National Savings from Peak-Load Pricing ... 176
   Initial Response to the First U.S. Peak-Load Rates ... 180
Related Changes in Electricity Usage ... 185
   Cogeneration of Electricity ... 186
   Interruptible Tariffs ... 187
Summary ... 188

Chapter 9
Rate Reform for Commercial and Residential Customers — 191

Information Requirements — 192
The British Experiment — 194
    Experimental Tariffs — 194
    Results — 194
    Evaluation — 196
The First U.S. Experiments — 198
The Los Angeles Experiment — 198
    Time-Invariant and Seasonal Tariffs — 200
    Time-of-Day Tariffs — 200
Summary — 202

Chapter 10
The Transition to Peak-Load Pricing in the United States — 203

Electricity Pricing and Energy Policy — 203
    Increases in Efficiency — 204
    Summary of the European Experience — 205
Introducing New Rate Structures in the United States — 206
    Industrial Tariff Reform — 206
    Commercial and Residential Tariff Reform — 206
Some Necessary Research — 207
    Marginal-Cost Structures — 207
    Interconnection — 208
    Cogeneration — 209
The Outlook for Peak-Load Pricing — 210
    Regulatory Complications — 210
    Other Constraints — 211
Phasing-In New Rate Structures — 211

Appendix
French and British High-Voltage Electricity Tariffs — 213

French Tariffs — 213
English and Welsh Tariffs — 217

Bibliography — 221

Index — 237

About the Authors — 247

Selected Rand Books — 249

List of Figures

1	U.S. Rate Structure Process	8
2	European Rate Structure Process	8
3	Declining-Block Tariff	10
4	Daily System Load Curve	17
5	A Simple Model with Three Generating Technologies	26
6	Load Shift From Peak to Shoulder Hours	28
7	Illustrative Power System Diagram	34
8	Load Curve	39
9	Average Cost Pricing	39
10	Marginal Cost Pricing	39
11	Illustrative Utility Load Curves	39
12	French Daily Load Curve for a Representative January Workday, 1952, before the Introduction of the Green Tariff	66
13	Kilowatt-Hour Charges in the French Green Tariff, 1975, for Service at Medium Voltages	68
14	Rate Curves for the Four Principal Versions of the French Green Tariff	72
15	British Annual Daily Load Shape, 1960/61	76
16	The Potential Effect of the French Green Tariff on Industrial Loads	91
17	Winter Load Curves for a French Cement Plant	92
18	Midweek Load Curves for a French Cement Plant in Four Seasons of the Year	93
19	Winter Weekday Load Curve for a Sample from the French Cement Industry	94
20	Winter Load Curves for a French Ferro-alloy Plant	95

xiii

xiv List of Figures

21	Winter Load Curves for a French Ferro-alloy Plant	96
22	Winter Weekday Load Curve for a Sample from the French Electrometallurgy Industry	96
23	Winter Weekday Load Curve for a Sample from the French Electrochemical Industry	97
24	Winter Load Curves for Liquid and Gas Transportation	98
25	Winter Load Curves for a French Cold Storage Plant	100
26	Winter Load Curves for a French Commercial Meat and Fish Supplier	101
27	Winter Load Curves for a French Water Purification Plant	101
28	Winter Load Curves for a French Raw Materials and Fuel Supply Firm	101
29	Winter Load Curves for a French Financial Institution	102
30	Winter and Summer Load Curves for a French Petroleum Refinery with Self-Generation	103
31	Winter Load Curves for a French Electrochemical Firm with Self-Generation	105
32	Classification of Load Curves of French High-Voltage Industrial Customers	106
33	Load Curves for an English Cement Plant	108
34	Winter Load Curves for an English Petroleum Refinery	109
35	Average Winter Weekday Load Curve for the Chemical and Allied Industries in England and Wales	111
36	Average Winter Weekday Load Curve for the Brick, Pottery, Glass, and Cement Industries in England and Wales	112
37	Load Curve for an English Steel Company during a Potential Peak Warning	114
38	Response to Potential Peak Warnings (PPWs) by a Sample of British Industrial Customers	115
39	Winter Load Curves for a Sample of Finnish Industrial Customers	118
40	Daily Pattern of Electricity Consumption in English Homes with Different Methods of Space Heating	127
41	West German Network Load Curves on Days of Peak Demand, 1964 and 1974	129
42	System and Residential Load Curves for Hamburg	130
43	Load Patterns in West German Storage Heating Systems	131
44	Load Curves for French Residential Customers on the Single Tariff	134
45	Load Curves for French Residential Customers on the Double Tariff	135
46	French Daily Load Curves for Representative January Workdays	138
47	Change in French Load Duration Curves over 20 years	140
48	British Daily Load Curves, Annual Average, 1960/61 and 1972/73	143
49	West German Network Load Curves on Days of Peak Demand 1964 and 1974	144

List of Figures xv

50	Case 1: Initial Single-Shift Operation in which Labor Costs Are Small	157
51	Case 2: 24-Hour Operation in which Labor Costs Are Small and a Minimum Level of Electricity is Required	158
52	Case 3: Initial Single-Shift Operation in which Labor Costs are Significant	160
53	Case 4: Initial Single-Shift Operation in which Labor Costs Are Significant; Optimal Shifting Leaves Peak Use Above Off-Peak Use	161
54	Case 5: Three-Shift Operation in which Capital Costs Are Significant	163
55	Matrix Illustrating How Alternative Assumptions about French and U.S. Load Changes Yield Four Methods of Calculating Load Response in the United States	168
56	Percentage Reduction in Peak-Period Energy Estimated by Method 1	170
57	Percentage Reduction in Peak-Period Energy Estimated by Method 4	171
58	California Cement Firm before and after the Introduction of Peak-Load Rates	182
59	California Chemical Plant before and after the Introduction of Peak-Load Rates	183
60	California Paper Products Firm before and after the Introduction of Peak-Load Rates	184
61	California Shopping and Office Complex before and after the Introduction of Peak-Load Rates	185
62	Response of 130 Large California Electricity Consumers to the Introduction of Peak-Load Rates	186
63	Time-of-Day and Control-Group Load Curves in the British Experiment, Average Winter Weekday Loads, 1969/70	197
64	Energy (kwh) Charges in the French Green Tariff, 1975	215
65	Load Curve for a Hypothetical Area Board	218

List of Tables

1	The U.S. Electricity Supply Industry, 1975	6
2	Representative U.S. Residential Rate Structures	11
3	Representative U.S. Industrial and Commercial Rate Structures	14
4	Pattern of Marginal Generating Costs, by Type of Generating System	33
5	Representative High-Voltage Tariffs in Several European Utilities	54
6	Electricity Production and Installed Generating Capacity in Europe and the United States	57
7	Norwegian High-Voltage Tariffs, 1975	60
8	Norwegian Residential Tariffs, 1975	61
9	Swedish State Power Board High-Voltage Tariffs, 1976	63
10	Stockholm Energiverk High-Voltage Tariffs, 1975	64
11	Swedish State Power Board Residential Tariffs, Central Sweden, 1976	64
12	Stockholm Energiverk Residential Tariffs, 1975	65
13	General Tariff Version of the Green Tariff, 1976	69
14	The Green Tariff at High and Medium Voltages, General Tariff Version, 1976	70
15	Versions of the Green Tariff, 1976	73
16	French Residential Tariffs, July 1974	75
17	Midlands Electricity Board Maximum Demand Tariff, 1976	78
18	Energy Charges under Optional Time-of-Day Tariff for Industrial Customers in England and Wales, 1976	78
19	South Eastern Electricity Board Domestic Tariffs, 1976	79
20	Medium-Voltage Tariffs in Westphalia, West Germany	81
21	Terms of a Special Contract for a West German Cement Plant	82

22	Peak Periods of Special Electricity Contracts for West German Steel Firms	83
23	Special Contract for Interruptible Power Supplied to a West German Acetylene Firm	83
24	West German Residential Tariffs, 1976	84
25	Terms of Special Agreement for Storage Heating, Westphalia, 1975	84
26	Finnish State Power Board High-Voltage Tariffs, 1973	85
27	Helsinki Electricity Works Tariffs, 1977	86
28	Summary of Industrial Responses to Peak-Load Tariffs	119
29	Comparative Energy Charges in England and Wales, 1965	125
30	Percent of Annual Electricity Consumption During Off-Peak Hours in English and Welsh Households	126
31	Examples of Staggered Charging Periods for Storage Heating in Hamburg	132
32	Subscribed Power under the Green Tariff, December 1974	142
33	Comparison of Peak Season Time-of-Day Rates in France and California	165
34	Annual Electricity Use in U.S. Manufacturing Industries	167
35	Projected Effects of Time-of-Day Pricing on Annual Electricity Use in U.S. Manufacturing Industries	176
36	National Effects of Peak-Load Pricing for U.S. Manufacturing Industries	178
37	Rate Structures for the Largest PG&E Customers	181
38	Estimated Potential for Generating By-product Electricity in U.S. Industry	187
39	Peak-Load Tariffs in the British Experiment	195
40	Changes in Electricity Consumption in the British Experiment	195
41	U.S. Residential Time-of-Day Experiments	199
42	Time-Invariant and Seasonal Tariffs in the Los Angeles Experiment	201
43	Time-of-Day Tariffs in the Los Angeles Experiment	201
44	Subscribed Power Coefficients for the Green Tariff	216
45	Green Tariff at Medium Voltage, 1976	216
46	Green Tariff at High Voltages, 1976	217
47	Central Electricity Generating Board Bulk Supply Tariff, 1976/77	219

Preface

Several research projects at The Rand Corporation are investigating the economic basis for more effective public policy in the electricity sector. This book is an outgrowth of those projects. At the time of the 1973/74 oil embargo we began a study of the effectiveness of appeals to the public for conservation of energy, backed by emergency municipal ordinances, to curtail electricity use in Los Angeles.

At about the same time we began an analysis of the determinants of residential demand for alternative forms of energy under existing rate structures, concentrating especially on separating short- and long-run adjustments to price changes and studying the distributional and regulatory implications of alternative public policies. The following year we launched a joint investigation with the Los Angeles Department of Water and Power into the desirability of new electricity rate structures for U.S. utilities; the principal feature of this extensive 5-year project is a social experiment designed to test a variety of time-of-day, seasonal, and flat electricity rates for residential customers. Partial support for the study was provided by the Federal Energy Administration.

The lack of experience of U.S. utilities with peak-load rate structures has made it desirable to augment experimental methods with data from abroad in order to assess the prospects for peak-load pricing in the United States. In 1975 and 1976, the project for the L.A. Department of Water and Power as well as research for the California Energy Resources Conservation and Development Commission made it possible for us to visit utilities, government agencies, and industrial firms in six European countries. From data assembled in these interviews we developed quantitative estimates of the potential effectiveness of peak-load pricing in California industries. At the request of the White House energy staff we extended these calculations to all U.S. industry with the assistance of funding from an Energy Resources and Development Administration project.

Although we have published technical reports and papers on several aspects of this research,[1] there has been no comprehensive evaluation of peak-load pricing in the electricity sector. It is our hope that this volume will help fill that gap. Our goal has been to provide an integrated presentation of the theory of peak-load pricing, its practical application in European electricity utilities, and its implications for U.S. energy policy.

In Part I the role of electricity pricing in national energy policy is examined, and the economic principles that should form the foundation for electricity rate structures are postulated. After describing the salient features of traditional methods of pricing electricity in the United States, as well as proposals for reform, we investigate the pattern of costs in different types of utilities. We then explain how rate structures can be designed to reflect the features of a utility's marginal costs.

Part II is devoted to a detailed examination of current practice of cost analysis and rate design in European utilities. First, a review of the principal electricity tariffs in England and Wales, Finland, France, Norway, Sweden, and West Germany is presented. Succeeding chapters contain a quantitative investigation of how effective peak-load pricing is in shifting the electrical usage of industrial and residential customers, and an assessment is given of the changes in system load and capacity needed.

Part III concentrates on U.S. conditions and the opportunities for increasing efficiency through peak-load pricing. In the case of U.S. industrial customers, we project the potential changes in electrical loads, energy resources, and capacity requirements that could be expected from nationwide adoption of peak-load rates. For residential customers a systematic program of experimentation and assessment of benefits and costs is needed before a nationwide change in residential rates is undertaken. Several experiments designed to test new rate structures for residential customers that can provide the basis for such an assessment are then reviewed. The book concludes with a summary of the policy issues that face the United States in reforming electricity rate structures and the prospects for putting peak-load pricing into practice.

1. See Acton and Mowill (1976); Acton, Mitchell, and Mowill (1976); Manning, Mitchell, and Acton (1976); Mitchell, Manning, and Acton (1977); Acton, Manning, and Mitchell (1977); and Mitchell and Acton (1977). The last cited report is copyrighted by The Rand Corporation.

Acknowledgments

Our research has been immeasurably assisted by experts and scholars in Europe and the United States who have made unique quantitative data available for inclusion in this volume. We especially thank Madame Y. Pioger of Electricité de France, and T.A. Boley and J.G. Boggis of the Electricity Council of London.

Many other engineers, economists, and managers in electric utilities, private industry, and government have also contributed to this research and reviewed earlier drafts. We would particularly like to acknowledge the assistance of Y. Balasko, L. Bergman, S. Falck-Jørgensen, M. Francony, D. Jung, O. Koenig, K. Lönngren, J. Lorgeou, R. Orson, A. Puromäki, A. Robin, E. Skalsky, F.L. Taylor, H. Trenkler, G. Vatten, I. Vogelsang, P.E. Watts, and W. Wendt in Europe; and A. Beringsmith, C. Cicchetti, P. Joskow, P. Kleindorfer, D. McKay, M. Moore, and D. Whitney in the United States. The dedication of our Rand associates David Gold, Heather Hanunian, and Ed Woo made possible the computations reported in Chapter 8.

No researcher finishes a manuscript without incurring a lasting debt for secretarial and editorial assistance. We especially appreciate the good cheer with which Mollye Merideth, Chris Char, Frayda Seigal, Helen Seifert, and Sheila Winckelmann have managed our typing chores, and Becky Goodman, Sid Seamans (at Ballinger) and Dorothy Stewart have improved the content and style of several portions of the text.

The Los Angeles Department of Water and Power, the California Energy Resources Conservation and Development Commission, and the Energy Resources Development Administration have funded research on which this book is based. A portion of the work for the Department of Water and Power has been supported by the Federal Energy Administration. Corporate funds of The Rand

Corporation and a grant from the National Science Foundation provided the opportunity to draw these materials together into a single, integrated volume, and B. Mitchell's contributions to the completion of this book were undertaken while he was a Research Fellow of the International Institute of Management and the recipient of a German Marshall Fund fellowship. We are indebted to all of these institutions for their support.

Bridger M. Mitchell	Willard G. Manning, Jr.
	Jan Paul Acton
Berlin	Santa Monica

Part I

Electricity Rates and Energy Efficiency

Peak-load pricing is a familiar concept to U.S. consumers who place long-distance telephone calls at premium rates during business hours, take night-coach airplane flights, or rent automobiles at weekend discounts. Yet their electricity is almost always sold at a single price, day or night, the year round, even though the costs of producing electrical energy vary according to regular hourly and seasonal patterns.

Worldwide concern for the cost and availability of energy and the environmental complications associated with growing energy consumption make a critical examination of electricity use of pressing importance. Peak-load pricing—charging higher rates during hours and seasons of highest demand—can potentially help to harmonize the interest of present consumers, future generations, and the utilities. Charging higher rates at peak periods encourages the conservation of energy at those times when the greatest fuel and capital resources are required to produce it; setting reduced off-peak rates encourages energy uses to be shifted to periods when excess capacity is available and fuels costs are frequently lower.

Public concern to preserve the quality of the environment has increasingly affected planning and construction of electricity generating plants. Fortunately, the net effect of peak-load pricing would have beneficial environmental as well as economic effects. More efficient use of generating capacity will mean that fewer plants are required to satisfy a given total demand for electrical energy. Shifts in demand away from peak hours will increase the proportion of energy supplied by those units that are most efficient in converting fossil fuels into electricity.

Peak-load pricing in this way increases the efficiency with which energy is used and reduces the need for costly investments in new generating capacity.

Furthermore, it can contribute to a utility's financial stability by producing changes in revenue that are commensurate with the changes in a utility's incremental costs as usage of electricity varies. Peak-load pricing also serves the generally accepted regulatory principle of making rates match cost of service as closely as practicable. In so doing, greater fairness is introduced into the rates, since customers whose costs of service are greater than average pay higher electricity bills and those with less expensive patterns of consumption pay lower bills.

Chapters 1-3 present a description of the role of the electricity sector in the context of U.S. energy policy. The conventional method of pricing electricity is critically reviewed, the central importance of prices in achieving an effective energy policy is examined, and the way in which U.S. electricity rate practices could be reformed by the adoption of peak-load pricing and other efficient rate structures is indicated. Then, in order to establish a cost-based foundation for designing new rate structures, the basic economic factors involved in supplying electricity are reviewed.

Chapter 1

Electricity and U.S. Energy Policy

NATIONAL ENERGY POLICY

The hour-long waits in automobiles to purchase gasoline during the 1973/74 Arab oil embargo jolted the U.S. public and created an awareness of the central role of energy in the economy. Consumers were abruptly forced to recognize the nation's dependence on foreign sources of oil, and they experienced the disruptive effects that result from being cut off from energy supplies by political events or natural disasters.

The first attempts to understand future energy conditions were dominated by the notion of a "shortage" in world supplies of crude oil, natural gas, coal, and uranium, which are continually being depleted and cannot effectively be renewed. Over time, even if the demand for energy were not growing, one could expect nonrenewable supplies to be eventually exhausted. However, as more and more people become aware of this potential shortage, it will generate higher market prices, stimulate the search for new energy reserves, promote the development of less energy-intensive methods of production, and encourage industrial economies to shift from their traditional dependence on oil to greater reliance on newer technologies for using coal, nuclear, solar, and other forms of energy.

A coherent public policy toward the role of energy in the U.S. economy has been slow to develop. The federal government's first reactions to the oil embargo were to impose restrictions on uses of energy, establish price controls, and proclaim a goal of achieving independence from foreign energy supplies. But sober analysis has exposed the stop-gap nature of many of the first policy decisions and revealed that there is no possibility of rapidly achieving energy independence. To moderate energy usage and bring forth new supplies, higher energy prices are essential. Although the economic adjustment to higher prices is often painful for consumers, it is ultimately less disruptive than the outright shortages that occur when prices are persistently held below cost. Thus, following the initial period of crisis, consumers in the United States have become accustomed to paying substantially more for gasoline and heating oil, whereas the long-standing policy of price control for natural gas has resulted in recent winter shortages that have caused serious hardship and economic dislocation in several regions of the country.

In 1977 the new Carter administration introduced complex legislation that would establish a strategic oil reserve, bring energy prices into line with replacement costs, tax automobile and gasoline usage to reduce demand, and subsidize the development of new coal and solar energy technologies. In the electricity sector the administration proposed that utilities be required to offer peak-load rates for electricity to encourage more efficient uses of both energy and generating capacity. These proposals reinforced investigations in electricity pricing already in progress in several state regulatory commissions and congressional committees.

Increasingly, policymakers and the public are perceiving that existing energy resources can be used more effectively if the price of energy consumed accurately reflects the cost of the resources used.

Conservation

Discussions of energy policy frequently emphasize the importance of conservation. Particularly in the electricity sector, widely publicized appeals have succeeded in persuading consumers to save energy. For example, businesses and households have found that moderately lower standards of illumination and heating are quite tolerable.[1] Just as the repair of a leaky faucet halts a waste of water, these changes, to the extent they are enduring, represent a continuing savings of energy.

But once the readily made adjustments in thermostat settings and lightbulbs have been achieved, what is the further role of conservation as an energy policy, and how much conservation is desirable? Should the growth of electricity consumption be slowed to 5 percent per year, or to zero growth, or should electricity use actually be reduced to make more oil available for transportation and other uses? Should the nation instead attempt to achieve an equal level of saving in all energy sectors? To ask these questions exposes the need for a standard for weighing the gains and losses such policies would entail; without such a yardstick, energy policy must be arbitrary.

An assessment of conservation measures on the basis of economic criteria

---

1. In their analysis of the electricity curtailment ordinance in Los Angeles, Acton, Graubard, and Weinschrott (1974) found that commercial customers reduced their use of electricity by almost 30 percent during a 4-month period and by about half that amount after the ordinance was suspended. Most of these savings were due to adjustments in lighting.

provides an objective and consistent method of examining alternative energy policies. Although it might appear that energy is essential to all economic activities, in fact the amount of energy used in the economy is ultimately determined by its cost relative to the costs of labor, capital, and raw materials. Furthermore, the choice of the type of fuel used for climate control, transportation, and the heating and cooling of liquids and gases is based largely on the comparative cost, performance, and convenience of different fuels. Equally important, energy costs, through the market prices for fuel, influence the design of consumer appliances, construction standards, and the specifications for industrial equipment.

The Role of Prices

Prices play a central role in determining how much energy the country uses. In an efficient economy market prices are signals of values, sending information in two directions—to purchasers and to suppliers. To purchasers the price of a commodity expresses the minimum payment its producers must receive to repay their costs of production and provide a return to their invested capital. And to suppliers the price measures how much customers are willing to give up to consume that good. The signaling function of prices can be exceedingly important in promoting the efficient use of society's scarce resources.

If a market is competitive—so that there are a reasonably large number of both sellers and buyers—the market price will generally be approximately equal to *marginal cost,* which is the extra cost incurred by the seller in producing an additional unit of output. When this occurs, the value to consumers of the last unit produced—that is, the price consumers must pay—is equal to the value of the resources that its production requires—that is, the marginal cost. Competitive markets and marginal-cost pricing thus ensure that resources are used effectively to satisfy consumer needs.[2]

Because electricity is not sold in competitive markets, its price is not necessarily set in a fashion that will ensure the efficient use of resources. Electric utilities are monopolists whose closest competitors are the suppliers of other fuels. Facing only indirect competition, utilities have the power to set market prices that need not correspond to marginal costs.

This market power is, however, limited by state regulatory commissions who must approve electricity tariffs and who attempt to ensure that the utilities earn a normal, but not excessive, profit for their owners. Regulatory practice in the United States has historically been directed to ensuring that the *average* price level set by a utility has corresponded to its average costs. However, commissions have allowed the utilities wide latitude to determine the *structure* of their rates— the particular pattern of charges to a group of customers of various services. As a result U.S. rate structures for electricity are not closely related to the structure of marginal costs and do not ensure efficient energy use.

2. There are, however, important exceptions when externalities such as environmental pollution are involved.

THE ELECTRICITY SECTOR

More effective use of electricity will be of primary importance to the development of any national energy policy for the United States. Several factors account for the electricity sector's key role.

First, electricity occupies a central position in an industrial economy. In the United States the production of electricity annually consumes over one-fourth (28 percent) of all primary energy. In 1975 the value of this energy delivered to final users in business and at home was $47 billion—about $220 per person.

Second, a growing national interest in maintaining the quality of the environment has fostered opposition to the construction of power plants of all types—hydroelectric plants that would endanger wildlife habitats or destroy wilderness areas, coal plants whose emissions could increase atmospheric pollution, and nuclear plants that pose an awesome but highly improbable threat of radioactive contamination. As the public has perceived the social costs of expanded generating capacity and recognized the increased rate at which nonrenewable energy sources are being depleted, various interest groups have sought to slow or halt the growth in U.S. electricity production, which had averaged 7 percent until the early 1970s.

Finally, the rise of electricity prices caused by sharply higher utility payments for oil has had a rapid and widespread impact on consumers' pocketbooks. Less than two years after the oil embargo, households in the Northeast found themselves paying several hundred dollars more a year for electricity. Across the country, higher utility bills and gasoline prices have brought home to the U.S. consumer the reality of a more costly energy economy.

Structure of the Industry

In the United States electricity is produced and sold by both public and private organizations (see Table 1). Privately owned firms, financed by shareholders'

Table 1. The U.S. Electricity Supply Industry, 1975

Organization Type	Revenue (billions)[a]	Energy Produced (billions kwh)[b]	Generating Capacity (million kw)[c]
Investor Owned Companies	$41.9	1486	398
Municipal Companies	—[d]	82	29
Federal Organizations	—[d]	221	50
Cooperatives and others	—[d]	127	29
Total	$46.9	1916	505

[a] Edison Electric Institute, *Statistical Yearbook of the Electric Utility Industry*, 1975, p. 43.
[b] Ibid., p. 18.
[c] Ibid., p. 6.
[d] Not available.

equity and publicly traded long-term bonds, supply 78 percent of the electricity sold to retail customers. However, in a number of cities municipally-owned companies are responsible for the distribution and, in a few cases, the generation of electricity. Power production by the federal government is confined to operation of the large multipurpose water projects that generate hydroelectricity and to the Tennessee Valley Authority.

Public policy aimed at the electricity sector is largely formed in the decisions of state and local agencies. State public utility commissions and other regulatory bodies are responsible for licensing plants and approving the tariffs of privately-owned utilities. City agencies generally govern the operation of municipal power companies. At the national level the role of the Federal Energy Regulatory Commission (formerly the Federal Power Commission) is limited to setting standards for electrical equipment and the regulation of the terms on which wholesale electricity is exchanged between power companies. This pattern of state-by-state policymaking has characterized the industry throughout most of its history. The Federal Power Act of 1935 does, however, allow the federal government to preempt state authority, and if an issue rises to the level of a national crisis the President and the Congress may intervene to establish new policies.

The Determination of Electricity Rates

In the United States the state regulatory commissions have traditionally confined their attention to the total revenue a utility was expected to receive from its rate structure, and attempted to ensure that the firm earned a reasonable, but not excessive, return on its invested capital. Broadly speaking, as indicated in Figure 1, these commissions have approached the subject of electricity tariffs in terms of: (1) determining what historically-incurred costs are allowable; (2) allocating these costs to major classes of customers; (3) setting an allowable rate of return on total invested capital; and then (4) permitting utilities to adjust the average level of rates to recover these costs. State commissions have, until recently, declined to involve themselves in the *structure* of electricity rates. Given this latitude, the utilities have determined the classification of customers and designed rate structures that would stabilize revenues and be competitive with alternative sources of energy.

In contrast to this U.S. practice, European utilities have generally followed a different approach to the design of electricity tariffs. As shown in Figure 2, the European practice generally begins with an analysis of the marginal costs of generating and transmitting power at the highest voltages. Next, the basic rate structure is established to reflect both the time pattern and the level of these costs, and is applied to sales to both wholesale and high-voltage consumers. These rates are then augmented by the costs of distributing power at successively lower voltages, and the basic rate structure is simplified to reduce metering and administrative costs. Rather than establish separate tariffs for different classes of customers (such as commercial or industrial) based on the mean characteristics

8 Electricity Rates and Energy Efficiency

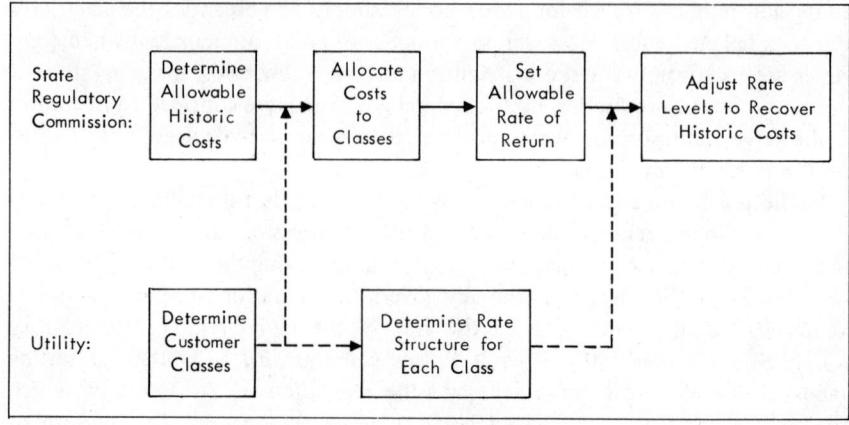

Figure 1. U.S. Rate Structure Process

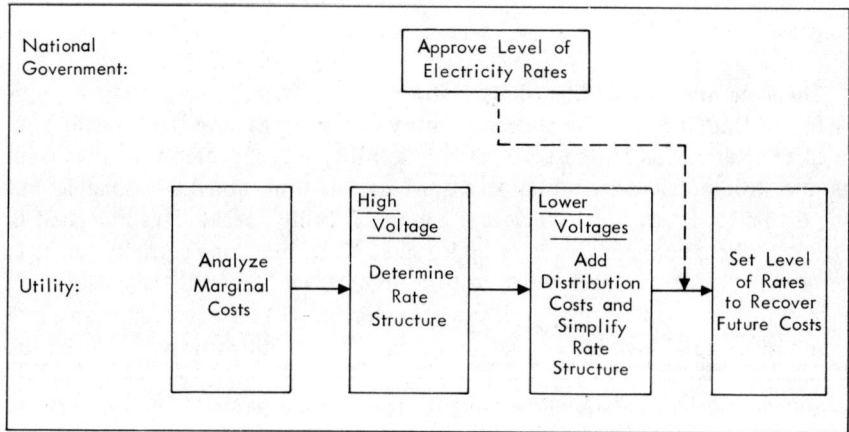

Figure 2. European Rate Structure Process

of each class, European utilities tend to make a given tariff available to all customers who are supplied at the same voltage level, and to allow users to choose, from among several options, the particular rate structure most suitable for an individual's pattern of use. Finally, an overall level of the rate structure is established to recover expected future costs, rather than the historic level of total costs as is used in the United States. The role of national public authorities in Europe is chiefly to approve the overall level of electricity rates.

U.S. RATE STRUCTURES

In terms of cost, the most important physical characteristics of electricity are the *amount* of energy supplied, the *rate* at which it is consumed, and the *potential* at which it is delivered. The amount of electricity used by a customer is ordinarily measured in *kilowatt-hours* (kwh), while the rate of consumption at any moment is measured in *kilowatts* (kw).[3] By analogy with a water system, the number of kilowatt-hours of electricity used by a household corresponds to the number of gallons of water it consumes, while the kilowatt rate at which it uses power is comparable to the speed with which water flows out of the pipe. The third factor, electrical potential, is measured in *volts,* and is analogous to the water pressure in the pipe supplying the house. For ordinary residential circuits, U.S. utilities have standardized on 110 volts, with 220 volt circuits used for electric stoves, clothes driers, and other appliances. Industrial customers receive power at voltages that vary according to their requirements.[4]

The term *electricity rate* is most commonly used to mean the price charged per unit of electricity consumed. The *rate structure* signifies the full set of prices charged for different units of electricity consumed by one customer; for instance, there may be a lower price for any electricity consumed in excess of a given quantity each month, or different prices for the quantities of electricity used at different hours of the day.

In regulatory usage, the *electricity tariff* means both the rate structure and all terms and conditions that are associated with it. The complete tariff for residential customers, for example, would specify the frequency with which the customer will receive a bill; the right of the utility to install, repair, and read the electricity meter; and so forth. In this book, however, we adopt the customary economic practice of using the word tariff as a synonym for rate structure.

In setting their rates, utilities indirectly determine how much electricity will be consumed in the economy, because the amount of electricity each customer uses will depend in part on the price that person must pay. The fundamental economic law of demand states that for any normal good or service, the quantity consumed will vary inversely with price charged.

Prices play a further role in the electricity sector. Utilities must make decisions to replace aging generating units and to expand their total capacity long in advance of the time when new units will first supply power, and these investments are based on forecasts of the quantity of consumption of 5 to 20 years in the future. Until very recently, utilities generally assumed that the historic rate of growth would continue unchanged. But now, with sharply higher electricity prices, the rate of growth of electricity usage has dropped and less additional capacity is needed. Further changes in electricity prices will undoubtedly further

---

3. Large rates of consumption are measured in megawatts (1 MW = 1,000kw).
4. Higher voltages are measured in kilovolts (1 kv = 1000 volts).

alter the growth of electricity usage and thus the need for new generating units. Pricing policy—including peak-load pricing—will therefore interact with the need for new investment.

Declining—Block Rates

The declining-block rate structure is the most widely used residential electricity tariff in the United States. As shown in Figure 3, the price of one unit of electricity, a kilowatt-hour, is highest for the first units consumed in a month,[5] after which it declines in a series of steps to lower and lower levels. Thus the price of the last kilowatt-hour used in a month, the *marginal price,* depends on the total amount of electricity used by the customer. In addition to declining-block rates, residential tariffs also frequently include a fixed monthly customer charge, a minimum billing amount, or both; this amount is collected regardless of the quantity of electricity consumed.

The effect of the declining-block tariff is to provide volume discounts that reward the use of large quantities of electricity with a lower average and marginal price. Several typical rate structures are given in Table 2. Although the declining-block rate structure is found in virtually all U.S. utilities, the *levels* of residential electricity rates differ substantially across the country because of the

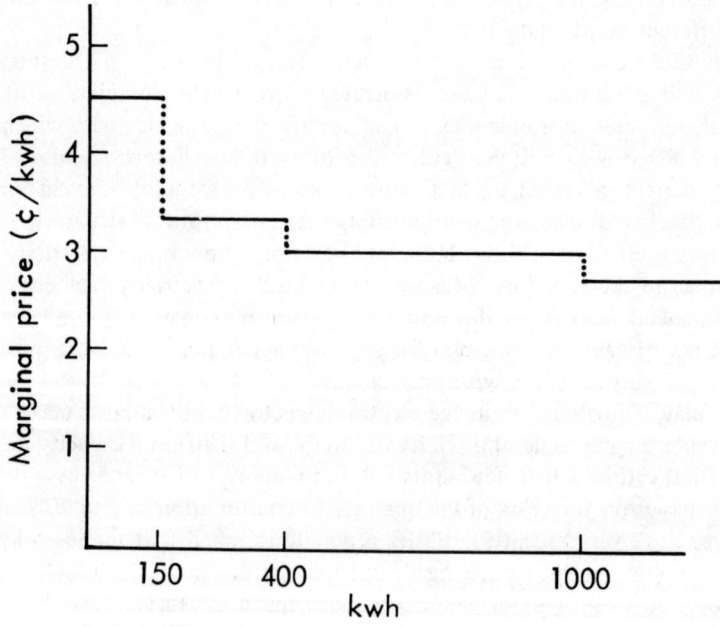

Figure 3. Declining-Block Tariff

5. Many U.S. utilities use a two-month billing period.

Table 2. Representative U.S. Residential Rate Structures[a]

City and Utility	Rate Class	Customer Charge ($ per month)	Energy Charge in ¢/kwh/month (block range, kwh/month, in parentheses)			
			First Block	Second Block	Third Block	Fourth Block
New York City (Consolidated Edison)	SC1	3.27	0 (0–10)	7.22 (10+)	—	—
Los Angeles (Department of Water & Power)	D1	1.50	4.44 (0–150)	3.23 (150–400)	2.95 (400–1000)	2.72 (1000+)
Tennessee Valley Authority	R2	2.50 (minimum bill)	4.57 (0–75)	3.52 (75–225)	2.30 (225–500)	1.94 (500+)
Detroit (Detroit Edison)	D1	2.40	3.78 (0–500)	3.98 (500–1000)	4.18 (1000+)	—
Cincinnati (Cincinnati Gas and Electric)	RS-IG	2.00	5.89 (0–40)	4.38 (40–80)	3.37 (80–220)	3.17[b] (200–1000)

Source: Utility rate offices.
[a]Rates in effect in July 1976. Includes average 1976 fuel-adjustment, except New York (July value only) and Detroit (April-December only). Taxes not included.
[b]Above 1000 kwh/month the energy charge is 1.92¢/kwh/month.

major differences in the average cost of supply. For example, in January 1976, average rates for 500 kwh per month varied from 0.9¢ kwh in TVA areas to 7¢ kwh in New York City.[6]

The Origin of Declining-Block Rates. Several factors have contributed to the widespread use of declining-block electricity rates by U.S. utilities. All monopolists have a natural incentive to arrange their marketing practices so as to maximize profits. One explanation for the prevalance of the declining-block rate structure is that volume discounts allow utilities to discriminate effectively between large and small users. Such discrimination will increase total profits if small users are relatively insensitive to price and high-volume users have more price-elastic demands.[7] Although empirical support for this belief is not entirely well established, it is plausible that households that use electricity primarily for lighting and a refrigerator are less affected by a high price than are other consumers who use substantial amounts of energy for heating, cooking, and laundry. For the latter households, other fuels—such as natural gas or heating oil—offer a competitive alternative to electricity, particularly when its price is high.

A second historical explanation for the declining-block rate structure is based on the expanding market for residential appliances. Electricity was first used for lighting. Later, electric cooking was introduced, followed by electric heating, and then by television and air conditioning. For some years the consequent growth in monthly electricity use per home was accompanied by a diversification of the peak residential load; cooking times tended to occur earlier in the evening than maximum lighting demands, air conditioning increased usage in the off-peak summer season, and so forth. As a result the power company could supply additional electricity without having to increase proportionately the capacity for generating and distributing electricity, which must be large enough to meet peak demand. Thus, because of the patterns of use of the additional electricity, utilities could at that time afford to sell incremental kilowatt-hours at a lower price that reflected the savings in the costs of capacity.

A third explanation for declining-block rates can be found in the fact that each utility has important *fixed costs*—for the service line from the pole to the meter, and for metering and billing—that must be met even if the customer uses no electricity whatsoever. Some of these costs are recovered in the rate structure by a separate customer charge the consumer must pay every month even when no electricity has been used. However, in many utilities only a portion of the fixed costs are collected by customer charges; the remainder is recovered by increasing the price per kilowatt-hour, and the largest increases are applied to the

---

6. *Federal Power Commission Rate Book,* June 1976.
7. The demand for a product is *elastic* if a price reduction causes consumers to increase the quantity they purchase to such an extent that the total revenue (price × quantity) increases. Demand is *inelastic* if a lesser increase in purchases occurs and total revenue falls. If the quantity consumed does not vary at all, demand is *totally inelastic.*

first units consumed per month to ensure that nearly all consumers will contribute significantly to the fixed costs.

Electric utilities have frequently benefited from *economies of scale* that enabled them to reduce the marginal costs of the last kilowatt-hour they supplied by increasing the total amount of electricity they generate. Until the late 1960s many U.S. utilities were able to realize such economies by constructing larger, more efficient generating units. The utilities have often argued that declining-block rates are justified because they encourage greater consumption and cause larger generating plants to be built, making possible lower unit costs. But this line of reasoning is valid only under particular demand conditions. If all households always consumed the same amount of electricity per month, a declining-block rate structure could be used to reflect accurately such economies of scale. In this case the incentives to all consumers would be identical, and the increased consumption by each of them would result in an expansion of the electricity system and lower long-run marginal costs.

In fact, however, consumers are far from equal—one household may use 100 kwh per month while another uses 1000 or more. Since the same declining-block rate structure is offered to all customers, small users will face the highest prices. The declining-block rate structure will in this way promote increased consumption by large users and inhibit greater consumption by small users. If the utility is, in fact, able to lower unit costs by increasing its total production, then greater consumption by any user is equally important. Only if the electricity demand of large users is demonstrably more price-elastic than that of smaller consumers can a declining-block rate structure be justified in terms of a reduction in unit costs made possible by a larger generating system.

Industrial and Commercial Rates

If the declining-block residential tariff is ubiquitous, the two-part, or "Hopkinson," rate is almost as widely used for billing U.S. industrial and commercial customers. This two-part rate structure has a separate charge for the consumer's maximum demand—his highest rate of power use (measured in kilowatts)—in addition to a declining-block rate for quantity of energy consumed per month (measured in kilowatt-hours). The maximum demand charge applies to the highest rate at which a customer uses power during any short (15- or 30-minute) period in the month, regardless of the hour at which the maximum occurs. In some cases the charge applies to the maximum attained in a 12-month, rather than 1-month, period, and declining-block rates are frequently used for the maximum-demand charge. Examples of several U.S. industrial and commercial rate structures are shown in Table 3.

In the marketing strategy practiced by U.S. electric utilities, both the residential and the industrial-commercial rate structures have been an important tool in promoting the growth of electricity usage. By charging consumers at the lowest per-unit rates for the last kilowatt-hours of electricity they consume, the

Table 3. Representative U.S. Industrial and Commercial Rate Structures[a]

City and Utility	Rate Class	Customer Charge or Minimum Bill	Maximum Demand Charge per kw/month (block range in kw)	Energy Charge per kwh (block range in kwh)
New York City Consolidated Edison	SC4	$99.70/mo (minimum bill)	$9.97 (0–100) 8.53 (100–300) 7.90 (300–10,000) 7.46 (10,000–25,000) 6.48 (25,000+)	4.73¢ (0–40,000) 4.01 (40,000–150,000) 3.84 (150,000+)
Los Angeles Department of Water and Power	A-1	$2.29 to 3.82/mo (customer charge) Minimum bill = service charge + $1.36 × max. kw during last 12 months	$0 (0–20) $.28 (20+ of max. kw last 12 months)	5.21¢ (0–1,000) 4.17 (1,000–3,000) 3.45[b] (3,000–7,200) 2.21[b] (7,200–16,400) 1.50 (16,400+)
Tennessee Valley Authority	C	Minimum bill = kw charge for max. kw last 12 months	$2.01 (0–75,000) 1.91 (75,000+)	0.91¢ (0–20,000,000) .88 (20,000,000+)

Source: Utility rate offices.
[a]Rates in effect in July 1976. Energy charge includes 1976 average fuel-adjustment except New York; July value used for Consolidated Edison.
[b]Tariff has a block extender. To the energy-charge bracket add 110 kwh for each kw of maximum demand last 12 months; if between 20.1 and 300 kw maximum demand, add 80 kwh/kw beyond 300 kw.

utilities have aggressively marketed new uses of power and diminished the attractiveness of competing fuels. At the same time, by allocating a large proportion of their total costs to charges for the initial blocks of kilowatt-hours and for maximum demand, the utilities have effectively prevented variations in commercial and industrial business activity or weather-induced changes in residential demand from causing large fluctuations in their total revenues.

Criticisms

From several sides critics have attacked these traditional methods of selling electricity, and they have called for a basic reexamination and revision of the structure of electricity rates. Consumers perceive that the declining-block tariff rewards the consumption of large amounts of energy by offering quantity discounts. Promoting increased energy use offends public opinion at a time when low-cost energy sources are in short supply, and when the economies of scale in generation that may have once provided some justification for the present rate structure have largely been exhausted. Moreover, electricity rates are widely perceived to be unfair, requiring the small user to pay more; this impression is fostered not only by the declining-block structure but also by comparisons of the average price charged for electricity supplied to different classes of users.[8]

A more fundamental criticism of U.S. rate practice is its use of a single price per kilowatt-hour at all hours throughout the year, despite the fact that the costs of electricity vary by the hour and season in which it is supplied. This one-price philosophy necessarily implies that consumers who use peak-hour electricity pay less than its full cost and are being subsidized by those who use electricity at the less expensive off-peak hours. In U.S. rate practice the absence of price signals that reflect the time-related costs of electricity means that energy is inefficiently used. A reform of electricity rate structures therefore offers significant opportunities for increased energy efficiency in the U.S. economy.

The first systematic examinations of current rate structures by public policy-making bodies were undertaken in generic rate cases before the public utility commissions in Wisconsin, New York, and California in the early 1970s.[9] These hearings have resulted in commission orders requiring utilities to devise peak-load tariffs under which the price of electricity varies according to the time of day or the month in which it is used.

Interest in increased energy efficiency has also led government agencies and some utilities to begin investigating the benefits to be gained from techniques for managing and shifting electrical loads. Some of these studies are designed to test or demonstrate the feasibility of a particular technology, such as remote control

---

8. As discussed in the next chapter, however, there are important added costs of supplying electricity at household voltages that account for at least some of the differences between average rates for residential and industrial customers.
9. The *Madison Gas and Electric* case began in 1972. Generic cases in several states began shortly after the oil embargo of 1973–74.

of electricity loads by electronic signals or the use of storage units for space heating. Others focus on measuring the effectiveness of peak-load pricing in persuading customers to modify conventional patterns of using electricity. This research is intended to provide new data from which to assess the impact of such pricing schemes on consumer budgets, environmental objectives, and energy requirements, as well as to measure in quantitative terms the contribution of peak-load pricing to greater economic efficiency.

NEW RATE STRUCTURES

The proposals for new rate structures examined in this book have in common the use of electricity prices to signal the actual marginal costs of energy. These costs are not constant, but vary principally because of the need to supply different quantities of power at various times of the day or year. Cost-based rate structures will therefore reflect the state of the aggregate load on an electric utility system, as well as the incremental costs of delivering power to different locations and at different voltages.

The Load Curve

The utility system load curve is obtained by plotting on a time axis the total amount of electricity demanded by all of a utility's customers at a given moment. The most frequently used diagram is the daily load curve, which shows continuous changes in load over a 24-hour period (see Figure 4). Weekly, monthly, and annual curves are also relevant to establishing variations in seasonal and weekend requirements. Analysis of system load curves by utility engineers has established that, for any particular utility, the timing of peak demands follows regular patterns.

The system load curve provides an approximate but highly useful indicator of the pattern of marginal costs of supplying electricity. At the time of the system peak demand (for example, at 3 p.m. in Figure 4), the use of generating and distributing capacity is at a maximum; in periods of substantially lower demand, some of this capacity is partly or totally idle. Furthermore, since the generating plants that are used during the peak period frequently include fuel-intensive peaking units, the marginal running costs of meeting additional load at that time will be higher than during off-peak periods, when only the more fuel-efficient units are needed. Thus, in a system that relies primarily on various types of thermal plants (nuclear, coal, oil, or gas) to generate electricity, peaks in the load curve are systematically associated with both increased capacity costs and higher running costs than are encountered in periods of lesser demand.[10]

10. Above-average operating costs may also exist on days of lesser demand if some capacity is unavailable, for instance, because of forced outage or scheduled maintenance. Since planned maintenance can be undertaken during months of lesser demand, the seasonal variation in marginal costs in a predominantly thermal system is usually considerably less than the daily variation.

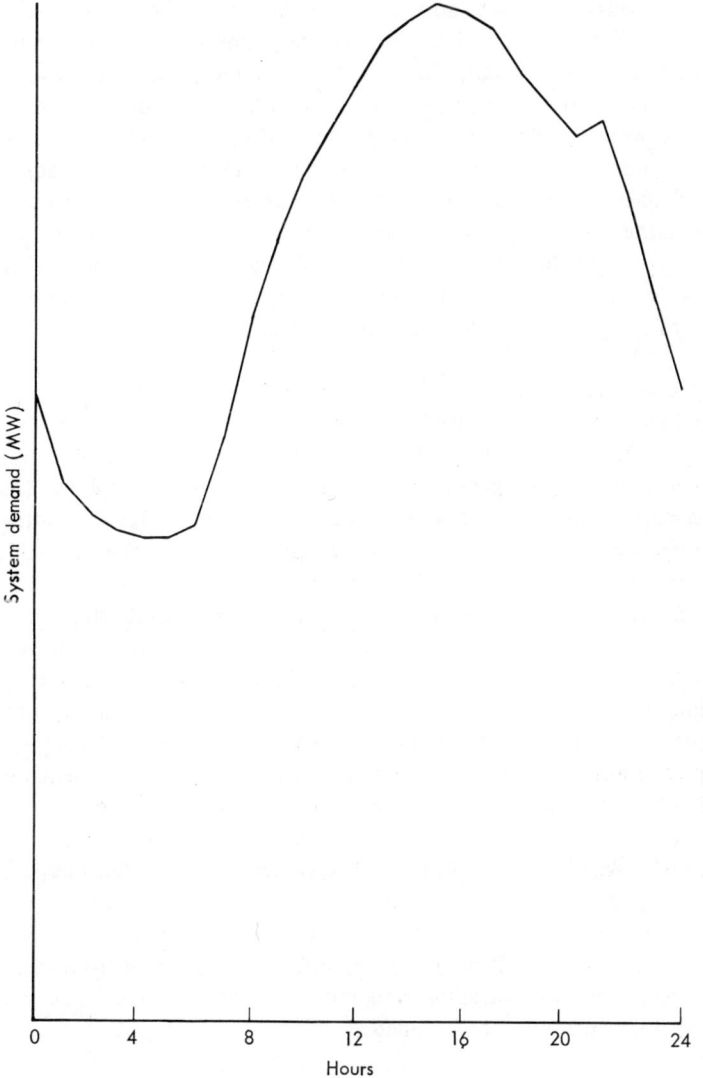

Figure 4. Daily System Load Curve

The availability of hydroelectric generating resources modifies this relationship between the load curve and the marginal costs of the system. Hydroelectric facilities permit the utility to reserve energy in the form of impounded water and to smooth out variations in system loads by modulating the rate at which water is released for generation. In a totally hydroelectric system, only a small fraction of the capital costs of generating capacity—for turbines and penstocks— varies directly with the maximum load, so that despite large hourly differences in system loads, there is relatively little variation in the costs of meeting demands at different hours. Furthermore, the running costs in a hydroelectric system are extremely small. These factors combine to make the capacity costs of the reservoir and of transmission and distribution facilities of much greater relative importance. As a result, significant savings are possible if demand peaks can be avoided in all segments of the *distribution* system. In largely hydroelectric utilities, therefore, it is the load curves of individual groups of consumers, rather than the system load curve, that signify important variations in marginal costs. Furthermore, seasonal variations in demand take on greater importance, since reservoir storage capacity must be sufficient to supply the total amount of energy demanded during the dry season.

Peak-Load Pricing

Peak-load pricing of electricity means selling electricity under a rate structure that reflects the *pattern* of variation in marginal costs. This pattern will vary according to the specific conditions of the utility supplying the power. In most parts of the United States—those areas served by predominantly thermal generating systems—a *time-of-day* rate structure, in which the price of a unit of electricity varies according to the height of the system daily load curve, will be appropriate. Also, some *seasonal* variation in these rates will usually be justified. For example, in a system in which maximum loads occur during the summer because of heavy air-conditioning demands, rates for the summer season might be established at both a higher level and for more hours each day than during the winter season. In areas of the country that are served largely by hydroelectric generating systems and normally experience their peak demands during the winter, purely seasonal rates may be the appropriate form of peak-load pricing.

Although peak-load pricing is a relatively new and untested means of selling electricity in the United States, peak-load rate structures have been widely used in European electric utilities for several decades. In Part II the design of peak-load tariffs in Europe will be analyzed, and the success that utilities there have had in using such rate structures to reduce peak loads and achieve increased economic efficiency will be examined.

Marginal-Cost Pricing

Marginal-cost pricing in its purest form would set the price of each unit of electricity at exactly the incremental cost of its supply at every moment; electricity prices would therefore reflect the *level* as well as the pattern of marginal costs. Such an idealized rate structure would not generally improve social well-being, because of its high implementation costs and its effect on total revenue.

This "pure" marginal-cost pricing scheme would require that prices vary almost hourly and also differ among many groups of customers. Some simplification of the complex structure of marginal costs is necessary in order to limit the expense and complications of measuring and billing for electricity usage. A practical marginal-cost rate structure will represent a compromise between a highly detailed tariff and major costs of billing. Its pattern of prices would follow only the principal pattern of variation in marginal costs and thus be a form of peak-load pricing.

By long-standing practice the rates of U.S. utilities have been based on the historically incurred costs of constructing generating units and distribution systems, and the level of electricity rates is set according to the level of costs at the time these components were built. But the costs of expanding an electricity system can change due to inflation as well as changes in the relative prices of fuels used to generate electricity. Today, replacement costs are considerably higher than the historic costs of the equipment in service.

Unrestrained marginal-cost pricing of electricity would set the level of electricity rates equal to the current costs of producing additional kilowatt-hours. The adoption of marginal-cost pricing in light of current costs would therefore result in sizable increases in the present electricity bills and windfall revenue gains to the utilities.[11] Such rates have been proposed by electricity rate reform groups in hearings before a number of state regulatory commissions. While marginal-cost prices would have the advantage of informing consumers of the true current cost of supplying energy, and would in this way encourage efficient choices in the marketplace, it is not surprising that these proposals have met with widespread objection by some intervenors and regulatory bodies.

It is possible, however, to pursue a modified form marginal-cost pricing of electricity. Marginal costs can be used as the basis for determining the *structure* of electricity rates. The *level* of the rate structure can then be set as nearly equal to marginal costs as possible, subject to the limitation that the overall level of revenues does not exceed a given amount—for example, current expenses and a fair rate of return on historic investment costs. Such a "second-best" pricing strategy can achieve many of the improvements in economic efficiency sought by proponents of rate reform, and yet retain the traditional regulatory tests for the reasonableness of a monopolist's revenues and profits.

Reform of Electricity Rate Structures

The movement to change the structure of U.S. electricity rates has grown to encompass environmental groups, consumer representatives, federal energy agencies, members of Congress, and the President. Rate reform has joined the construction of nuclear reactors as a leading matter of public debate confronting the electric power industry.

The utilities, at first reluctant to consider changes in their traditional pricing

11. In principle, price levels could be set equal to marginal costs and lump-sum rebates paid to consumers to offset these distributive effects. However, regulatory bodies do not have the fiscal authority to effect such transfers outside the rate structure, and they have historically been reluctant to order ex post lump-sum rebates to customers.

methods, have begun to examine the implication of rate structure reform at the urging of state regulatory commissions. Proposals for new rate structures include the replacement of the current declining-block rate structure by either flat or inverted rates, by time-of-day rates and seasonal forms of peak-load pricing, and by full marginal-cost pricing.

Rate reform proposals can be evaluated according to their effects on the efficiency with which energy and other scarce resources are used and according to the fairness or equity with which the costs of energy are distributed among customers. Appropriate electricity rates can encourage greater efficiency, both within the electricity sector and throughout the economy. Rate structures based on the pattern of a utility's marginal costs will encourage consumers to adjust the timing of their use of electricity and increase the effectiveness with which fuels, capital, and personnel are combined to supply that electricity. Of equal importance, they will promote desirable social choices between alternative sources of energy—encouraging consumers and planners to select the most efficient method for heating a room, cooking a meal, or operating an industrial process. Moreover, throughout the economy, cost-based electricity rate structures will encourage the substitution of additional capital equipment for energy where such investments are indeed economically justified.

In a society that aims to promote individual well-being, the distributive effects of new price structures should utlimately be appraised in terms of the values of its individual members. One widely accepted principle for allocating economic resources is that the users of a service should pay their own way, bearing the costs of the resources they consume. Electricity rate structures based on marginal costs satisfy this principle and correspond to the price structure that would arise if electricity could be produced and sold in competitive markets. However, a different and often conflicting principle is that the rate structures of public utilities should serve as a means of social taxation, to shift at least some of the cost burden from one group to another. This is the central objective of interest groups proposing rate structure changes that would create permanent subsidies for selected types of consumers.

Throughout this book we will examine the performance of electricity rate structures in terms of their effectiveness in promoting the efficient use of economic resources. This emphasis reflects our view as economists that the correct role of a well-functioning price structure is to signal to consumers the true costs of the resources their consumption requires and that consumers should be free to decide for themselves what goods and services they will have. Rather than relying on public utilities and their regulators, society can better accomplish the task of achieving a just distribution of income—no less important a goal than resource efficiency—by modifying federal and state fiscal programs (income, sales, and property taxes) and transfer mechanisms (unemployment, welfare, and service benefits programs). The case for relying on fiscal policy instruments to accomplish distributional goals is twofold: it is efficient to separate the objectives of efficiency and distribution and make the latter the central goal of specialized programs; and it is more effective to transfer generalized purchasing power from one group of customers to another in the form of income rather than specific commodities (such as electricity).

SUMMARY

Over a quarter of the nation's annual consumption of primary energy is used to produce electricity. Public concern to conserve energy resources and to prevent environmental degradation have focused attention on the role of prices in encouraging an appropriate level of electricity consumption. In a well-functioning energy market, prices signal the value of the resources that must be used to make more electricity available, and also indicate the value consumers place on additional consumption.

In the United States electricity is produced predominantly by privately owned utilities whose prices are regulated by public utility commissions. Historically the commissions have endeavored to limit a utility's rate of profit by controlling the average price of electricity. Free to determine the structure of electricity rates, the utilities have traditionally sold power under declining-block rates that provide volume discounts and promote increased energy consumption.

Recent U.S. discussion has focused on new peak-load rate structures. The proposed rates would employ the signalling function of prices to indicate more accurately the time-dependent costs of supplying electricity. For many utilities the system load curve provides a reasonable indication of the variation in the marginal cost of supplying power. Although the specific cost patterns will depend on the particular circumstances of each system, the highest costs occur during hourly and seasonal periods of peak demand when the maximum generating and distributing capacity is required and fuel-intensive power plants are in use.

Peak-load pricing means selling electricity under a rate structure that reflects the pattern of variation in marginal costs. Marginal-cost pricing, in purest form, would set the price of each unit of electricity at its incremental cost of supply at every moment, so that prices would signal the level as well as the pattern of marginal costs. Today, because of general inflation and changes in the relative prices of fuel, marginal-cost pricing of electricity would require that the average level of electricity rates be substantially increased to reflect the current cost of replacing existing generating units. A modified version of marginal-cost pricing can, however, form the basis for designing a peak load rate structure: the pattern of marginal costs can first be used to determine the structure of electricity rates, and then standard regulatory procedures can be followed to establish the total amount of revenue to be collected and thereby the level of those rates.

Throughout this book peak-load pricing is evaluated in terms of its effects on the efficiency with which energy and other scarce resources are used in the economy. The adoption of peak-load rates in the United States would distribute the cost of supplying electricity according to the principle that consumers should pay their own way, ensuring that each consumer bears the incremental cost of providing energy at the time it is consumed. The fundamental costs of supplying electricity and how those costs vary over time is examined in Chapter 2.

✳ *Chapter 2*

Basic Economics of Electricity Supply

As a basic carrier for useful energy, electricity possesses a versatility unequaled in an extremely wide variety of applications. In terms of physical properties, the essential characteristics of electricity are the same, regardless of when it is consumed. Despite this physical uniformity, the value to consumers of a unit of electricity is not the same at all hours. Since electricity, once generated, cannot easily be stored, its value varies more or less directly with the level of human activity, the need for climate control, and the level of industrial activity. The costs of supplying electricity also vary over the course of a 24-hour period, as well as over the days of the week and according to the season of the year. In this chapter the basic economic factors that are involved in electricity supply will be examined, with particular attention paid to time-related variations in costs.

THE NATURE OF ELECTRICITY COSTS

The functions of supplying electricity can be broadly grouped into two major activities: generating power at different times of the day or week, and delivering power at specified voltages to individual customers through the transmission and distribution systems. These activities require a substantial investment in fixed capital, and, in most utilities, a major expenditure of fossil fuels.

Prudent management of an electric utility requires that its engineers anticipate the growth and periodic variation in the demands of its customers, and that it then constructs and operates the power system so as to ensure a reliable level of service at the least cost. Uncertainty about the levels of demand, the functioning of power system equipment, and the periodicity of demand make this a difficult optimization problem. An extensive electrical engineering literature is devoted to its solution.[1] Today nearly all large utilities routinely use computer-supported mathematical programming models to guide daily and weekly operating decisions and to simulate the effects of alternative investment and utilization strategies.

Generation and Distribution

The costs of generating power are collective costs, common to all customers, in the sense that the same increase in total generating costs will result from an increase in the system load regardless of the identity of the customer who causes it. In contrast, the costs of distributing electricity to a particular customer are somewhat specific to individual demands. To reach the consumer, power must flow through a network of conductors and transformers. As the electricity moves farther from the point of generation and approaches the individual user, the network becomes more segmented, until at the consumer's premises the distribution capacity exists solely to serve that one customer. The costs of distribution are therefore a mixture of costs shared among users who take power from the same segment of the network, and of individual costs determined entirely by the requirements of the specific customer being served.

The distinction between generation cost and distribution cost cannot always be so sharply drawn. In fact the capacity of high-voltage transmission lines that interconnect power plants and large areas of consumption is closely related to the capacity requirements for generation, and few, if any, customers are served directly from these lines. For this reason the costs of transmission are usually analyzed as a component of the costs of generating it.

Energy and Capacity

The cost of supplying electricity may be conceptually divided into the cost of resources used to provide *energy*—the quantity of electricity consumed per unit of time, measured in kilowatt-hours (kwh)—and the cost of resources used to provide *capacity*—the maximum instantaneous amount of energy that can be supplied at any one moment, measured in kilowatts (kw). Both the energy and the capacity costs vary hourly and seasonally.

Capacity is needed in all stages of producing and providing electricity—for generating power from the energy contained in falling water, the combustion of fossil fuels, or nuclear reactions; for the transmission of electricity from the generators to the general area of consumption; and for the distribution of power at useful voltages to final users. For a given level of reliability, the utility is required at all times to supply whatever amount of electricity its customers demand. If the peak load can be reduced, less generation, transmission, and distribution capacity is needed to maintain reliable service. Because capital costs per kilowatt of capacity are significant, a reduction in peak-hour or peak-season

1. See, for example, Berrie (1967); Bessiere and Massé (1964); Lindquist (1962); and Scherer (1977).

demand is an opportunity for substantial savings in the invested capital required to supply electricity.

Although capital costs often constitute the greatest portion of the total costs of producing electricity, the cost of labor and the cost of the fuel consumed are also important. Moreover, the technology available for producing electricity makes it possible to choose one of several different mixes of capital, labor, and fuel to produce the same quantity of electricity. The opportunities for trading off lower capital costs for higher fuel expenses are greatest in power generation, although some possibilities for substitution also exist at other stages of production. Based on construction costs prevailing in 1977, nuclear generating plants have extremely high capital costs—on the order of $1000 per kw of effective capacity—but the running costs of the fuel they consume are only about 0.1 to 0.3¢ per kwh.[2] In contrast, gas turbine generators have much lower capacity costs, about $200 per kw, but consume large quantities of fuel and incur running costs of about 3 to 5¢ per kwh.[3] In general, the total costs of supplying the electricity demanded over the course of a year can be minimized by having a *combination* of generating plants of different types—some baseload capacity in the form of nuclear or coal-fired units that run continuously, and some intermediate and peaking capacity in the form of oil- and gas-fired units that can be turned on and off to meet variations in total load.

A Simple Model

To illustrate the trade-off between capital and running costs with a very simple model, we may suppose that only three basic generating technologies are available—a baseload (for example, nuclear or coal) plant, with an annual capital cost of c_1 per kw of capacity and a constant running cost of r_1 per kwh of electricity generated; an intermediate (for instance, oil-fired) plant, with somewhat lower capital costs c_2 but higher running costs r_2; and a peaking plant (say a gas turbine) with the lowest capital costs c_3 and the greatest running cost r_3.[4] In Figure 5(a) each straight line represents the total annual cost per kilowatt of capacity of constructing and operating a plant of one type for any number of hours during the year. The vertical intercept gives the annual fixed cost per kw of capacity, while the slope is equal to the running cost per kwh. From an examination of the curve, it is clear that of the three technologies available, one will always have the lowest total cost of supplying electricity for a given number of hours per year. For example, if the consumption of electricity exceeds h_2 hours per year, power can be supplied most cheaply by a baseload plant.

The desirability of employing a combination of different types of generating

---

2. Nuclear Energy Policy Study Group (1977), ch. 3.
3. These running costs are based on the artificially low price of natural gas resulting from current U.S. gas price controls. Higher costs would be observed in unregulated situations.
4. The basic model may be found, for example, in Turvey (1968) or Crew and Kleindorfer (1976).

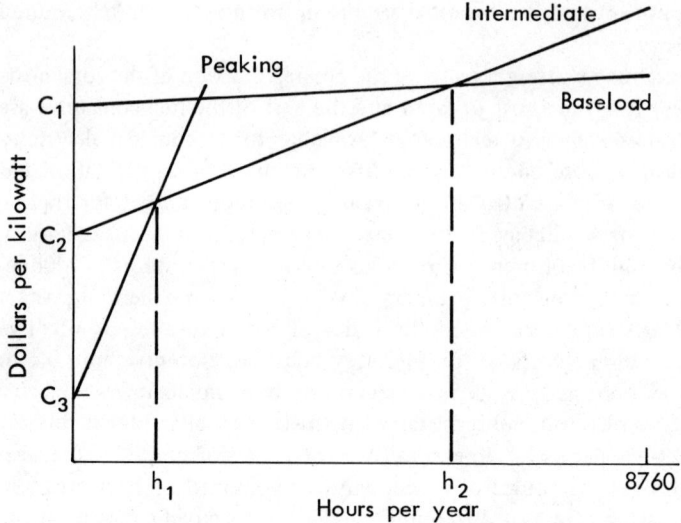

Figure 5a. Total Costs per Kilowatt

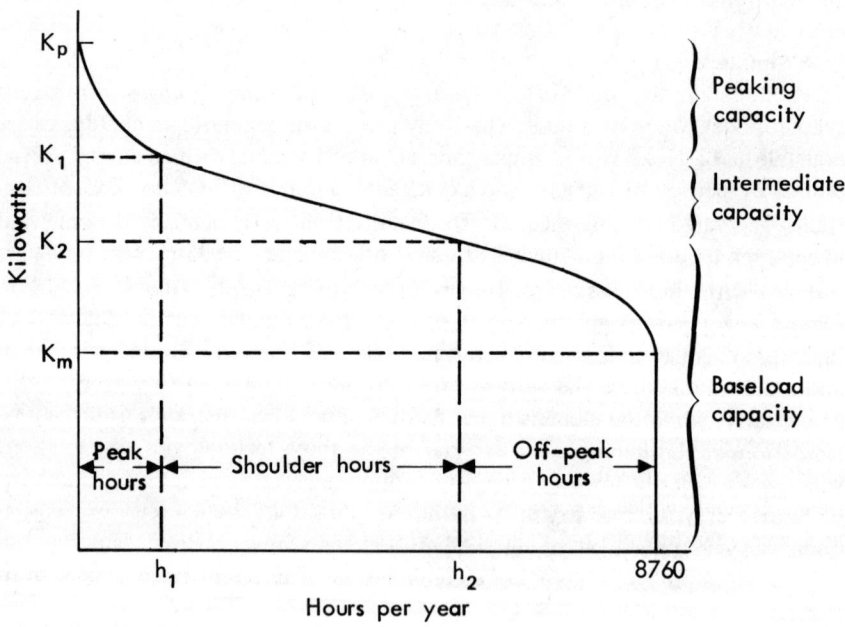

Figure 5b. Load Duration Curve

Figure 5. A Simple Model with Three Generating Technologies

plants is due to the fact that the amount of electricity demanded is not constant. Figure 5(b) shows the amount of electricity demanded for different lengths of time, measured in number of hours per year. This graph, termed the *load duration curve,* can be derived from each of the daily load curves throughout the year. It indicates, for example, that the annual peak load of K_p kilowatts will occur for only a very few hours, and that the minimum load K_m occurs every hour of the year. Combining the information in both diagrams, we can see that the least costly method of satisfying demands of h_2 or more hours per year is to use a baseload plant, with K_2 kilowatts of capacity. For demands above K_2 kilowatts that last between h_1 and h_2 hours per year, the intermediate plant is least costly to build and operate; incremental loads of this duration total $K_1 - K_2$ kilowatts. And the optimal amount of peaking capacity, to service loads of less than h_1 hours, is $K_p - K_1$.

This representation of a power system is, of course, highly simplified. It assumes, for example, that costs are the same for any given number of annual hours of consumption, whether that consumption occurs one hour every weekday or continuously for 10 summer weeks. And it neglects the uncertain availability of generating units created by the risks of forced outages and the random variations in demand created by weather and other factors.

Despite its simplicity the model provides a key insight into the economics of electricity supply. In its investment strategy the typical utility will construct a mix of baseload, intermediate, and peaking generating units to minimize the total costs of meeting its customers' loads. And in daily operation of the power system, the dispatcher will minimize the short-run operating costs of meeting hourly loads by using first the unit with the lowest running cost and then adding units in the order of their fuel efficiencies.

A reduction in the peak load of the system—from K_p to K'_p in Figure 6—accompanied by a shift of some of that load to hours when there is lower demand, will reduce total costs. As an illustration, suppose that the load is shifted to hours of the year when the total load does not exceed K_1; in Figure 6 this shifted load is represented by the shaded areas. Two types of cost savings result. The first is due to an increase in short-run operating efficiency achieved when the shifted kilowatt-hours are generated by the more efficient intermediate generating unit that requires less fuel than a peaking plant. The cost savings per kwh is equal to $r_3 - r_2$, the difference in the running costs of a peaking and an intermediate plant, which is exactly the difference between the short-run marginal costs of generating electricity in the two periods. The second type of cost saving will be realized from modifications of the utility's construction schedule. Over time, a permanent shift in the system load will permit the utility to alter its mix of generating units, in this illustration by reducing its peaking-unit capacity and enabling it to save on capital costs. The total saving in both running and capital costs represents the reduction in long-run marginal costs.

The simple model also makes clear that the marginal costs of supplying addi-

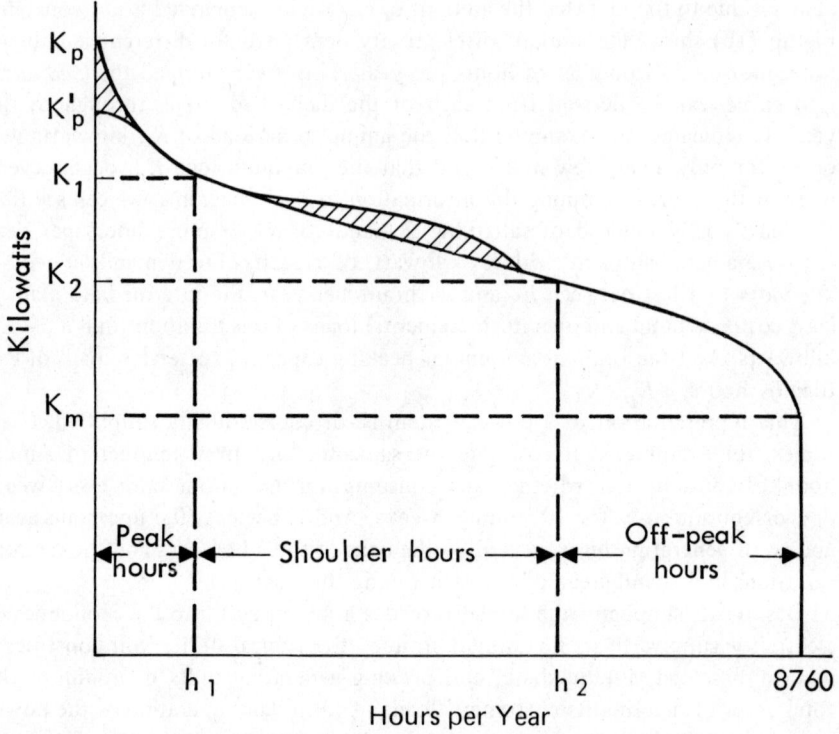

Figure 6. Load Shift From Peak to Shoulder Hours

tional electricity will generally vary with the level of system demand. In this model the year can be divided into a peak period (the h_1 hours when demand exceeds K_1); the shoulder period (the $h_2 - h_1$ hours when demand is greater than K_2 but less than K_1); and the off-peak period (hours when demand is less than K_2). The short-run marginal costs of generating added power in these periods are r_3, r_2, and r_1, respectively.

The pricing implications of these costs now become clearer. A dichotomy between a single price for capacity and another for energy cannot correctly reflect this marginal-cost structure. The maximum-demand tariff commonly used for U.S. industrial and commercial customers—with time-invariant rates for maximum demand (kw) and energy consumed (kwh)—is therefore unable to provide reliable price signals of the true generation costs of additional loads.

Storage

If electricity were a completely perishable resource, there would be no possibility of making productive use of idle capacity in off-peak hours. Suppose, however, that a costless storage medium (a perfect battery) were available in which unused electricity could be held in inventory. With such a device the utility could operate its baseload generating units at a constant level 24 hours a day, meeting the variations in the load curve by storing up excess energy in slack periods and using it to supplement that generated at peak hours. Storage, then, would effectively solve the peak-load problem at the generation stage. However, if the storage battery were located at the generating site, the size of the transmission and distribution network would still have to be sufficiently large to meet peak demands and would be partly idle at other times. Of course, if storage could be accomplished at the site of final consumption, a uniform load, equal to virtually 100 percent of capacity, could be generated and delivered at all times.

Only imperfect and costly storage media are available. Dams permit water to be stored in reservoirs and released to generating turbines at the time power is demanded. Because water-driven turbines can be started, stopped, and adjusted very rapidly, hydroelectricity is especially attractive for modulating the quantity of electricity generated in step with variations in the system load. Naturally occurring sources of elevated water can be supplemented by pumping water uphill to a reservoir and recycling it through turbines at periods of peak demand. Such pumped-storage is cost effective (even though some energy is consumed in the pumping process) when low running-cost electricity, generated from baseload units with excess capacity, is available to power the pumps during off-peak periods.[5] Finally, individual customers, as well as utilities, have a variety of possibilities of storing the energy provided by electricity, principally by heating or cooling a storage medium and drawing on the energy at the time it is needed.

Because all storage technologies are costly, the desirability of using pumped-storage or storage heating is an economic question. Such investments involve trading off the increased capital costs of the storage media for the reduced operating costs they make possible. Utilities have incentives to reduce their total costs and to invest in storage technologies, rather than in peak generating units, when it is less costly to substitute such investments for the construction of additional peaking capacity.[6] The utilities' customers, however, have no comparable incentive to invest in cost-saving equipment unless the terms under which they are supplied power induce them to economize on peak-period electricity and increase consumption in the off-peak hours. The structure of electricity tariffs, therefore, is of fundamental importance in encouraging customers to invest in load-shifting technologies.

Whether it will be advantageous for the utility or its customers, or both, to undertake storage and load-shifting investments will depend on the specific

---

5. Impounded water is by far the most common type of storage used by utilities. However, a variety of new methods is under investigation, which include the use of compressed gas, large flywheels, and batteries of advanced design.

6. The nature of rate-of-return regulation, which gives utilities an incentive to choose capital-intensive methods of production, may increase the attractiveness of storage facilities over less capital-intensive alternatives. See Averch and Johnson (1962).

supply circumstances of the utility and the demand characteristics of the customers; no general answer is possible. It is therefore especially important that the signals provided to consumers—the prices for electricity at different periods of consumption—accurately reflect the marginal costs to the utility of supplying additional power at those times. If, by modulating their loads, customers can reduce their electricity bills under such tariffs by more than the costs of inconvenience and additional investment, a net saving of resources will result.

THE ROLE OF MARGINAL COSTS

As indicated earlier, a power system—if it is optimally designed—will meet its customers' demands for electricity at a specified level of reliability and quality of service at minimum total costs. It is, however, the *marginal* cost of supplying electricity—the increment to total system cost of producing and delivering an additional unit of output under specified circumstances—that is central to establishing the conditions for efficient *use* of electricity. Although some uses of electricity are valued very highly by most consumers and exceed the cost of supplying the electricity, other uses are less valuable, and the quantity consumed for these secondary uses will depend importantly on the price charged by the utility. In order to make efficient economic use of scarce resources, electricity consumption should be encouraged when its valuation by consumers exceeds the added cost of production, and consumption should be discouraged whenever the costs of producing additional electricity exceed the added benefits to consumers. This balancing of added benefits with added costs is most readily achieved by establishing electricity prices equal to the marginal costs of supplying electricity and relying on the decentralized, self-interested, marketplace decisions of consumers to equalize benefits and costs at the margin.

The determination of marginal costs in any particular power system is a complex undertaking. Since marginal costs depend on the sources of primary energy used to generate power, the costs of other factor inputs, and the pattern of demand for electricity, the optimization models used to minimize the utility's total costs can be of substantial value in quantifying the changes in costs resulting from specified increments in demand.[7] A detailed exploration of the analysis of marginal costs in a power system lies beyond the scope of this book. The remainder of this chapter will be confined to an outline of the major qualitative characteristics responsible for differences in marginal costs.[8]

Marginal Costs of Generation

The economics of generating electric power depend in great part on the generating resources available to the utility system. These resources may be broadly

---

7. In a mathematical program to minimize the total cost of meeting a given load curve, the solution values for the Kuhn-Tucker multipliers may be interpreted as the marginal costs of output supplied in each period.

8. The reader who wishes to pursue the subject may profitably consult the volumes by Nelson (1964); Scherer (1977); Turvey (1968); and Turvey and Anderson (1977).

grouped into two types of units: (1) *thermal* generating units—including coal, oil, or natural-gas combustion units, as well as nuclear plants—that develop high-pressure steam used to drive turbines; and (2) *hydroelectric* generating units, which are driven by falling water.

For a given load curve, extreme differences in marginal costs are found in a comparison of all-hydroelectric systems and all-thermal systems. In fact, most electric utilities have a mixture of both types of generation and will therefore exhibit an intermediate level and pattern of marginal costs.

Thermal Systems. Systems that are composed entirely of thermal generating plants correspond most nearly to the simple models found in the theoretical economic literature on peak-load pricing. In an all-thermal system, storage of electricity by the utility is generally not feasible, so that aggregate generating capacity must be sufficient to meet the annual peak demand.[9] Furthermore, for a typical daily load curve in which there is a substantial difference between minimum and maximum demand, the optimal system will consist of a mix of baseload, cycling, and peaking plants, each with a different ratio of capital to operating costs. As demand rises toward its peak level of the day, the use of fuel-intensive plants will increase; as a result, running costs will vary directly with the level of the system load curve.

In order to supply customers with reliable levels of electricity, a utility must maintain excess capacity to guard against unforeseen outages of power-system equipment or unexpected increases in load. Utility systems in the United States are generally designed to limit the risk of a power shortage to a predetermined level, most commonly measured by the loss-of-load probability. Higher loads during peak hours of the year greatly increase the probability of a shortage, while increased demands in off-peak hours have only a small effect on the security of supply.[10] In all-thermal systems the peak period is usually determined by the shape of the weekday load curve during the year's three or four months of extreme temperature (either summer or winter), and the peak period is typically a small number of hours per day. In such systems the cost of maintaining a given standard of reliability will depend principally on the cost of adding capacity to meet demand during the peak period.

Seasonal variations in consumer loads account for important variations in the annual pattern of marginal costs in thermal systems. In the off-peak season there is a high probability that the system will have excess capacity during the entire day, and during this season the differences in marginal costs between the peak-load hours and the off-peak hours are due primarily to variations in running costs, which may be relatively small. In contrast, the difference in long run

---

9. New technologies, such as underground storage of compressed air, may permit all-thermal systems to augment their resources in a manner similar to the pumped-storage of water.

10. See Caille and Lhermitte (1971); Balasko (1974); and Vardi, Zahavi and Adi-Itzhak (1977).

marginal costs between the summer and winter seasons is due primarily to the need to provide capacity for the peak season. This amount, however, is generally less extreme than might be suggested by the seasonal difference in customers' loads, because the utility can schedule plant maintenance during the months of reduced demand.

Hydroelectric Systems. Systems that are entirely supplied by hydroelectricity are characterized by quite different patterns of marginal costs. In "run-of-the-river" installations, power is generated by using naturally falling water when it is available. Most hydroelectric plants, however, impound water in a reservoir. By withholding the release of water until a later hour, the utility is effectively able to store "electricity" costlessly over the course of a day. Therefore, in sharp contrast to the rise and fall of marginal running costs with the daily load cycle in thermal systems, there is little daily variation in marginal running costs in hydroelectric systems.

Hydroelectric systems are, however, strongly affected by the seasonal availability of runoff water and are limited by the amount of water that can be stored from the wet season to the dry season. The primary constraint on supplying all of the electricity that is demanded is the aggregate amount of water that can be stored—a limit on total energy—whereas in a thermal system the constraint is the maximum rate at which electricity can be supplied—a limit on *maximum demand* or power.[11] (Of course, capacity to meet the daily peak-demand can also be a limiting factor in a hydroelectric system, but the capacity-related costs for turbines and penstocks are a relatively small proportion of its total generating costs.) This means that the marginal cost of supplying an additional kilowatt-hour during the dry season will include the cost of marginally expanding storage capacity. Furthermore, variations in annual precipitation create a risk of an energy shortage during the dry months. So when prices are based on marginal costs, the peak pricing period in a purely hydroelectric system will extend over the several months of the dry season, in contrast to the peak period of several hours daily in a purely thermal system.

Mixed Systems. Mixed thermal-hydroelectric systems are common in the United States and in many parts of Europe. Hydroelectric resources enable utilities to store energy over at least some part of the daily load cycle and to smooth out sharp peaks in the system load curve. As compared with the pattern of costs in all-thermal systems, in a mixed system marginal costs are highest for a longer daily period, but the variation in the level of marginal generating costs over the course of the day is more limited. When naturally occurring hydroelectric resources are supplemented by pumped-storage plants, the daily variation in costs will be further limited. Mixed thermal-hydroelectric systems will typically have at least some seasonal variation in marginal costs, although if wet months coin-

11. See Morlat (1964).

cide with—or immediately precede—seasonal peaks in the system load, that variation may be small.

Interconnection. Nearly all utility systems have the possibility of importing and exporting power (although many systems try to equalize net imports and exports over the year). Since the economic gains from buying and selling electricity between utilities tend to be largest between quite dissimilar systems, it is not surprising that, when external resources are accounted for, most utilities are mixed thermal-hydroelectric systems. For example, the Norwegian hydroelectric system interchanges power with the mixed system in Sweden, and has constructed a cable to the all-thermal system in Denmark. Similarly, England's all-thermal system has a transchannel cable to exchange power with France's mixed system. In West Germany, a network of thermal utilities exchanges power with neighboring hydroelectric facilities in Austria, Switzerland, and France. In the United States, regional pools connect utilities with excess base capacity to those with excess peaking capacity, and many utilities are connected into large federal hydroelectric projects.

Summary. The division of generating systems into all-thermal, all-hydroelectric, and mixed thermal-hydroelectric cases provides a qualitative indication of the pattern of marginal generating costs in each type of system. The general structure of a peak-load tariff based on marginal costs will follow this same pattern. In Table 4 we summarize the daily and seasonal variations in marginal generating cost, as well as the period of highest marginal cost, that are characteristic of each type of system. In addition to these characteristics, which are predominantly determined by the nature of the generating system, a given type of system may be either winter- or summer-peaking, according to the seasonal pattern of demand.

Marginal Costs of Distribution

In order to reach the consumer, electricity must flow from the point of generation through a distribution network. This is shown schematically in Figure 7. The costs of distributing electricity from the point of its generation to the cus-

Table 4. Pattern of Marginal Generating Costs by Type of Generating System

Marginal Generating Cost Characteristics	Type of System		
	All-Thermal	Thermal-Hydro	All-Hydro
Daily variation	Extreme	Moderate	None
Seasonal variation	Generally small	Moderate	Pronounced
Period of peak	A few hours daily	A long daily period	All hours of the dry season or dry years

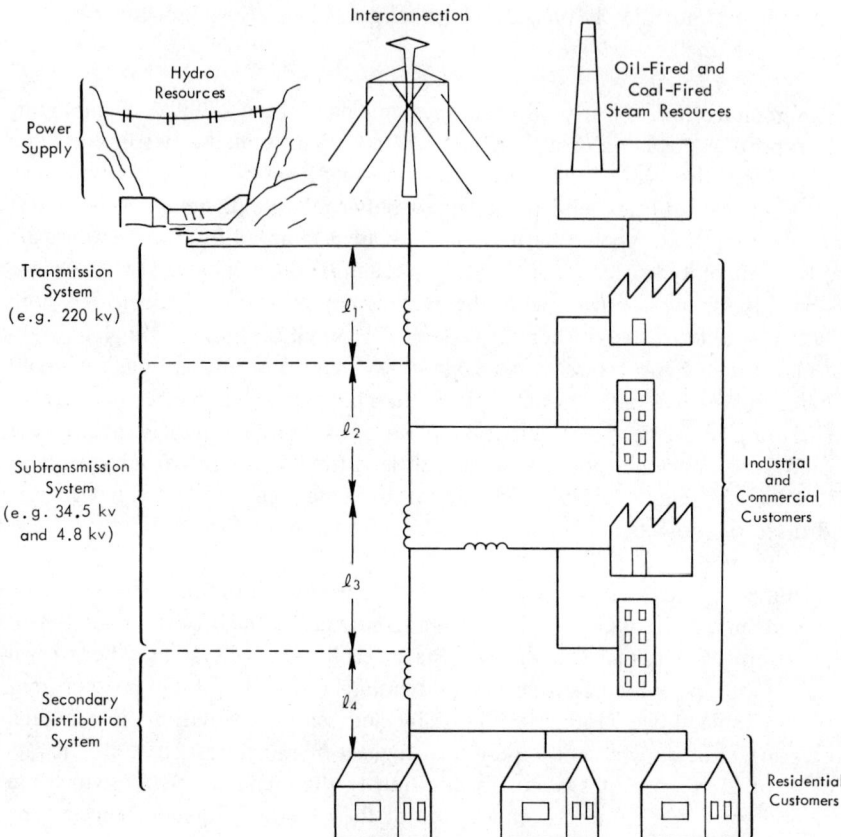

Figure 7. Illustrative Power System Diagram

tomer consist of the additional marginal running costs that result from energy lost when power moves through the network, and the fixed costs associated with installing and maintaining cables, transformers, circuit-breakers, and associated equipment.

Energy losses are similar to shipping costs: they increase with the distance of the customer from the generating source and the number of stages of transformation through which the electricity must pass before it has been reduced to the voltage at which the customer takes delivery. In fact, the rate of loss increases when the amount of electricity flowing through a distribution link approaches the link's capacity. In ratemaking practice, however, calculations of marginal costs resulting from distribution losses are usually based on the average value of losses for each segment of the network between the generation point and the customer. These losses can be represented by a series of multipliers, l_i, calculated as the ratio of energy input to energy output over link i, that are necessarily greater than 1.0 in value. The costs of supplying a customer are then calculated by scaling up the generation costs by the product of the multipliers for the links over which that customer's electricity is delivered. This cascading effect means that at any given time of the day the marginal energy costs increase in a regular fashion at lower and lower voltages.

To analyze the long-run marginal costs associated with the capacity of a distribution system, statistical factors that are not encountered in analyzing the costs of generating electricity must be examined. Each link in the distribution system must be constructed to meet the maximum quantity of electricity flowing through it. However, as one follows the network from the source of generation to an individual customer, each link becomes increasingly "individualized," serving only those customers who are downstream of it. At the final link, the capacity of the service leading to the customer's meter is completely determined by that one customer's requirements.

In general, the peak demand on any link can be calculated by aggregating for each period the demands of the "downstream" customers. The *period* in which this particular link's peak demand occurs will be determined by the time at which its aggregate demand is maximal, and it will not necessarily coincide with the peak period for the entire system.[12]

The difficulty of constructing a rate structure that will reflect accurately the marginal costs of generating *and distributing* electricity can now be appreciated. In some sections of the network, generation and distribution link peaks may closely coincide, while in other segments the distribution link peaks are likely to occur at different hours. To supply power to most customers, furthermore, the capacity of several types of links is required, and each of these links may have a different peak period. The marginal costs of supplying electricity can therefore vary in quite complex patterns over the daily and annual cycle.

One practical method of designing a tariff to reflect the marginal costs of distribution is to establish a charge based on the peak demand of the individual customer rather than on the energy that customer consumes in each period. The statistical relationship between the maximum demand on a link and the sum of the individual peak demands will depend on the *diversity* of the loads of individual customers. For representative groups of customers, load studies can measure the variability of individual load curves and the correlation of individual peak demands with the demand on the link. When these relationships follow a regular pattern, tariffs that include charges for the individual customer's maximum demand in kilowatts can provide reasonable approximations to marginal distribution costs.[13]

---

12. See Boiteux and Stasi (1964).
13. The load study measurements from which these calculations are made also provide essential information for determining distribution-link capacity. For the very largest consumers, a separate distribution link is frequently required, and in this case demand charges can reflect the exact marginal costs imposed by the customer.

SUMMARY

To supply electricity, a utility must use generators to convert primary energy into high-voltage electricity, which it then transforms to lower voltages and distributes to individual customers. Both the generation and the distribution system must have sufficient capacity to supply the maximum amount of power demanded at any time.

Because the maximum load occurs only a few hours per year, the utility can supply electricity most cheaply by using a mixture of generating units with varying ratios of capital costs to running costs. Typically, a utility with thermal generating plants will have base-load, intermediate, and peaking units, each with successively higher running costs per kilowatt-hour. In the short run the marginal costs of supplying an additional kilowatt-hour of electricity will be given by the running cost of the least efficient unit in use; marginal costs will vary directly with the height of the system load curve and be greatest at the time of the peak load. Storage of energy can reduce the cost of meeting the variations in electrical load over time and enable a utility to increase energy supplied at peak hours.

The pattern of marginal costs of generating electricity depends largely on the generating resources available. In thermal systems the marginal costs vary widely during a 24-hour period, and follow the general pattern of the system load curve. In hydroelectric systems, marginal costs are higher in the dry months of the year, but there is essentially no variation over the course of the day. Mixed thermal-hydroelectric systems have both daily and seasonal variations in their marginal costs.

Unlike the costs of generation, the marginal costs of distributing power depend on the location of the consumer in the network. Industrial customers supplied at high voltages are served most cheaply. To supply customers who are farthest from the source of generation—households and small businesses served at low voltages—requires relatively greater amounts of distributing plant and results in larger losses of energy in transmission. Moreover, each link of the distribution system must have the capacity of the maximum demand of the subset of customers that it serves. The fact that this peak may occur at a different time from the peak load on the generating facilities complicates the analysis of incremental costs and the design of peak-load rate structures.

The electricity rates paid by a utility's customers recover the cost of supplying electricity and provide price incentives that affect how consumers use electricity. Chapter 3 considers how rate structures can be designed to reflect the most important feature of the pattern of marginal costs in an electric utility.

Chapter 3

The Design of Rate Structures

Electricity prices serve three fundamental economic purposes: (1) they raise revenues to pay the costs of supplying electricity; (2) they distribute these costs to the utility's customers; and (3) they create financial incentives that align production and consumption decisions.

Broadly speaking, the *level* of electricity rates will determine the revenues earned by the utility and how much a customer ends up paying per year for the electricity used, while the *structure* of rates will serve the incentive function, signaling the types of uses of power and the hours and months in which the utility wishes to encourage or to limit consumption.[1]

A peak-load tariff or rate structure is one in which the marginal price of electricity is higher during the period of the peak load on the utility system, rather than being uniform at all hours of the year.[2] As we have seen in the previous chapter, this period may be a few hours each day (in an all-thermal system) or as much as several months in duration (in an all-hydro system).

There are several methods that can be used to establish the actual prices charged for a unit of electricity in each rating period of a peak-load tariff. From a theoretical point of view, the most appealing approach is to set price equal to marginal cost in each period. In that way the rate structure will signal to consumers exactly the incremental resources needed to supply added power and permit individual consumers to equate benefits and costs of energy usage. However, other cost calculations may be used. For example, peak-load rates could be

---

1. The overall level of electricity rates will also exert an incentive effect on electricity consumption by influencing the consumer's choice of energy-using equipment and appliances.

2. As noted earlier, capacity shortages and high marginal costs can occur at times other than when the system load is at its peak; for example, when available capacity is reduced by scheduled maintenance of plants. Hereafter, we use the term peak-load tariff to encompass both demand- and supply-induced variations in marginal cost.

based on the variation in average costs between periods, or on the historic costs of operating the available generating units in different periods and seasons. To the extent that these rates differ from marginal costs and induce different levels of electricity usage, they will cause some loss in economic efficiency. Because U.S. utilities are not well-acquainted with procedures for calculating marginal costs, it may be initially necessary to rely on such methods to develop peak-load tariffs in the United States. Nevertheless, so long as the new rates are closer to rates based on marginal costs, it is almost certain that such changes will increase overall efficiency.[3]

By basing tariffs on economic principles, utilities and regulatory agencies can design electricity rate structures to promote greater energy efficiency. In this chapter the theory of peak-load pricing is reviewed, the major principles of setting prices on the basis of marginal costs are examined, and the methods of modulating a utility's load curve are surveyed.

THE THEORY OF PEAK-LOAD PRICING

The economic literature on peak-load pricing has focused primarily on those variations in marginal costs that are associated with the *generation* of electricity, rather than with its *transmission, transformation,* and *distribution.*

Two fundamental types of economic analysis can be distinguished in this literature. The first, found in papers on economic theory, begins by casting the characteristics of the electricity market into abstract and often highly simplified form.

The Basic Model

The economic theory of peak-load pricing originates in the seminal papers of Boiteux (1949) and Steiner (1957). As applied to electricity, the Boiteux-Steiner model in its basic form postulates that throughout the year there is a uniform rate of demand, or load, in each of two 12-hour periods, shown as day and night in Figure 8. A single technology is available for generating power. Each

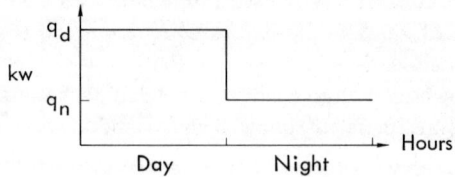

Figure 8. Load Curve

---

3. A benefit-cost comparison is needed to assure that the administrative and metering costs of new tariffs do not eliminate the efficiency gains. This issue, as it applies to different groups of customers, is covered in Part III.

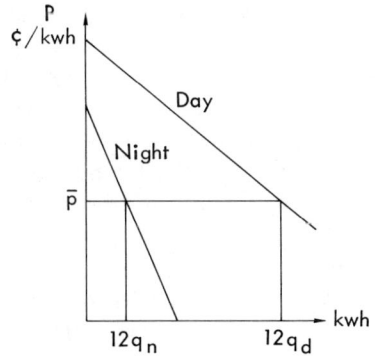
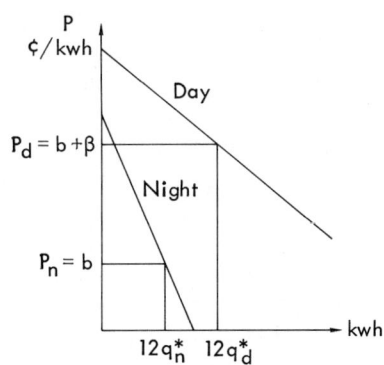

Figure 9. Average Cost Pricing   **Figure 10.** Marginal Cost Pricing

kilowatt-hour of electricity requires the expenditure of b dollars for running costs—fuel and other operating expenses. In addition, the generating unit must have a capacity equal to the maximum demand. Such capacity requires capital expenditure at an annual rate of c dollars per kilowatt, or $\beta = c/(12 \times 365)$ dollars per kilowatt for each hour of peak-period use.

The levels of demand in each period are assumed to vary inversely with the price of electricity in that period, and to be independent of the price in the other period. Thus, there are two economic *demand curves* for the quantities of day ($12q_d$) and night ($12q_n$) electricity in Figure 9. In this model the marginal cost per unit of output at night (the off-peak period) is the running cost b, since the production of additional electricity will require more fuel, but no additional capacity. In the peak period, however, any expansion of output will require that new capacity be added, so that the daytime marginal cost is $b + \beta$ per unit of output.

If a single price per kilowatt-hour is to apply in both periods—day and night—and the utility is allowed to recover costs but not make excess profit, then—as shown in Figure 9—an average price $\bar{p}$ must be set equal to the average cost per kilowatt-hour, and consumers will demand $12q_d$ kwh during the day and $12q_n$ at night.[4]

If, however, prices are set equal to marginal costs in each period, the equilibrium quantities of electricity produced and consumed will be the amounts $12q_d^*$ and $12q_n^*$ shown in Figure 10. In contrast to the single-price case, the day price is higher and therefore less capacity is necessary. This market equilibrium is the

---

4. The value of the average price is found by solving the equation for total revenue = total costs: $\bar{p}q_d(\bar{p}) + \bar{p}q_n(\bar{p}) = (b + \beta)q_d(\bar{p}) + bq_n(\bar{p})$, in which $q_i(p)$ is the demand function for period i.

optimal pricing solution in the following sense. Of all the possible pairs of day and night prices, the prices equal to marginal costs maximize the difference between the value that consumers place on the amount of electricity they use and the cost of its production. This difference is the economic surplus that is realized by having electricity available to the community. Marginal-cost pricing ensures that in each period productive resources will be used to supply electricity up to—but no further than—the point at which the value of the last unit of electricity consumed is just equal to the cost of its supply.

It is worth noting that in this model the peak-load pricing solution of setting prices equal to marginal costs automatically collects revenues that are just equal to total costs. The reason is that the last kilowatt-hour of energy or the last kilowatt of capacity is exactly as expensive as the first, so that the size of the generating plant can be expanded at constant returns to scale.

Like all models, the Boiteux-Steiner paradigm is a simplification that does some violence to reality. Its virtue is the clarity with which it links the design of the optimal rate structure—two rating periods with separate prices, each equal to marginal costs—to the structure of the costs of production and to the demand (load) conditions facing the utility.

More General Models

The economic theory of peak-load pricing expressed in this basic model has been substantially extended and made more realistic in several directions. More recent papers have generalized the demand assumptions to provide for any number of rating periods of arbitrary length (Williamson 1966), and to accommodate variations in load within rating periods (Dansby 1975; Wenders 1976). A number of authors have addressed the potential complication raised by a "shifting peak," in which the establishment of a higher peak-period price would reduce the peak-period demand sufficiently, or shift it into another period, so that the off-peak period would become the new peak period (Bailey and White 1974; Boiteux 1949; Hirschleifer 1958). And extensive efforts have been made to expand the analysis to encompass stochastic variations in demand—the major papers are Balasko (1974); Brown and Johnson (1969); Crew and Kleindorfer (1978); Panzar and Sibley (1977); and Sherman and Visscher (1978).

The model has also been generalized to encompass more realistic supply conditions for electricity. As noted in Chapter 2, electric utilities can minimize total costs by simultaneously using several generating technologies to meet their total load. Activity analysis models that incorporate this feature have been developed by Crew and Kleindorfer (1976); Turvey (1968a, b); and Wenders (1976). By working with models incorporating continuous production coefficients, rather than fixed proportions of capital and fuel, Boiteux (1949) and Panzar (1976) have incorporated the nonlinear response of generating units to level of production. Further realism has been introduced by considering models incorporating economies of scale (Mohring 1970) and storage (Gravelle 1976; Nguyen 1976).

As the theoretical economic models have grown more realistic, their normative prescriptions have become increasingly qualified and are not easily summarized. The optimal prices for each period must now incorporate considerations of expected shortages, the long-run substitution of capital for fuel, and constraints that ensure that revenues will cover costs. In many of these more general models, the optimal prices require that the off-peak as well as peak-period prices include some elements of capacity costs.

Engineering Models

The second type of economic analysis found in the literature involves engineering-economic models that are used by electric utilities to minimize their overall costs of supplying power. Characteristically the literature on such models is grounded in a wealth of detail about the complexities of real-world markets and power systems.[5] On the demand side these models represent consumer demands by continuous daily, weekly, and monthly *load curves* (Figure 11a). These demands are then reduced to an annual *load duration* curve (Figure 11b), which shows the number of hours that demand is at, or exceeds, any specified level. On the supply side these models permit the utility system to minimize short-run operating costs and to make long-run investment decisions that minimize discounted total costs.

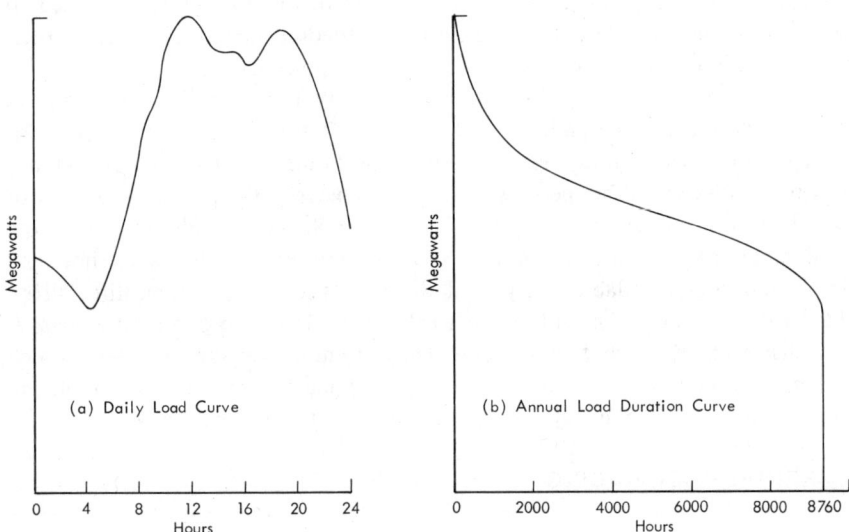

Figure 11. Illustrative Utility Load Curves

5. See, for example, Berrie (1968); Kirchmayer (1958); Lindquist (1962); Little (1955); and Morlat (1964).

In daily and weekly operation, "economic dispatching" models rank available generating units in order of increasing operating cost, and enable the dispatcher to equalize short-run marginal costs across units in operation. In their most developed form these models, using mathematical programming, also optimize the commitment of units to production, the scheduling of maintenance, and the use of hydroelectric resources. To guide their long-run planning, utilities rely on investment-decision models that can select new generating units from a wide spectrum of generating technologies having varying proportions of capital and running costs and different scales of output. Historical data on variations in loads and forced outages are used to simulate the probabilities of failure to meet the load demanded at each hour of the year, and capacity is constructed to meet a specified standard of reliability.

Although the models of electrical engineering and economic theory have provided substantial guidance to the design of electricity rate structures, there are a number of theoretical problems that have not been fully worked out. In an electric power system, marginal costs vary almost continuously, both over time and across customers. In practice, only a few distinct rating periods are used for pricing electricity, and theoretical advances are needed to determine the optimal number of rating periods that should be used. Closely related to this topic is the use of several peak-load tariffs, among which the consumer is allowed to select. Research into the benefits of optional tariffs, and how they are best designed, is just beginning.[6] Finally, the costs of distributing (as opposed to generating) electricity are rarely included in theoretical models, despite their importance in the total capacity constraint of the power system.[7]

In practice, the design of peak-load electricity tariffs in European utilities can be understood as a blending of ideas from both strands of this literature. For example, European utilities aggregate the 8760 hours of annual production into only a few distinct rating periods. A rigorous analysis of the optimal number of rating periods and the hours at which they should begin and end would be a formidable task. The utilities in fact embrace the objective that rates should be simple and understandable. They limit themselves to no more than three different price *levels* over the 24-hour or weekly period, and to one or two *periods* at which each of those prices obtain. They attempt to make each period such that marginal costs of generation are roughly equal during the hours it encompasses, and to reflect the major temporal patterns of consumer loads.

MARGINAL-COST PRICING

At the beginning of this chapter the three economic functions of electricity rates were spelled out: (1) to raise revenues; (2) to distribute costs to consumers; and

---

6. See Faulhaber and Panzar (1977), Panzar (1976), Willig and Bailey (1977), Sibley, Goldman, and Leland (1977), and Dansby (1977).

7. The papers by personnel at Electricité de France are an exception.

(3) to provide incentives for efficient consumption and production. The optimal rate structure will be the one in which the rating periods are determined by the major temporal variations in marginal costs, and the price of electricity in each period is equal to that period's marginal cost of supply. Of all the possible tariffs, this rate structure will encourage the most efficient use of scarce economic resources. Economists attach great importance to this efficiency property, and for good reason. In the U.S. electrical sector, for example, a 10 percent increase in efficiency would mean a savings of nearly $5 billion a year.

Efficiency incentives are, however, but one of the three purposes served by electricity rates, and a rate structure based strictly on marginal costs may conflict with other goals. The clearest case occurs if, for any reason, society wishes to distribute the burden of electricity costs in a fashion that does not accord closely with the principle that each consumer pay all, but no more than, the costs of the additional resources that individual's consumption requires. While this is the established principle by which nearly all private economic goods and services—food, clothing, entertainment, and so forth—are exchanged in the U.S. economy, the principle has at times been modified in the case of utility services and other goods that are subject to public regulation.

As a matter of policy, regulatory or legislative bodies may tilt rate structures to favor certain groups, and impose the additional costs of these cross-subsidies on other consumers. For example, proposals for "lifeline" tariffs are of this form. Such tariffs are characterized by an inverted-block rate structure in which a price below average cost is set for the first block of kilowatt-hours used per month, with higher rates for subsequent blocks. Lifeline tariffs, according to their proponents, are intended to subsidize low-income households or reduce rates below cost for consumers who use small quantities of electricity. A second example of a departure from the principle of marginal-cost pricing has been the use of value-of-service pricing. Under this rationale, utilities have charged higher prices to customers with inelastic demands and lower prices to other customers, such as those with ready alternative sources of energy, whose demands are more sensitive to price.

A conflict between the goal of economic efficiency and the desire to achieve a particular distributional effect is a conflict of social priorities or values, and for this reason economic science can be of only limited help in making a policy choice. It is, however, important to recall that other instruments of public policy are available to ease the burden of the costs of utility service on selected groups, the most powerful of which are the tax and transfer mechanisms of the federal government. If desired, the electricity costs of low-income or other consumer groups judged to be deserving can be eased or offset by reduced income tax rates or even by the establishment of earmarked payments for specific commodities. For example, a program of energy stamps, using a mechanism similar to the food stamp program, could be established to provide targeted energy subsidies to specific groups of the population.

As noted in Chapter 1, there are persuasive arguments for separating the distributive and allocative functions of economic policy. The consideration of economic equity is appropriately centralized in the nation's tax and transfer policies, while allocative efficiency is most readily achieved by pricing individual commodities in terms of their resource costs.

The other potential conflict in goals that would arise from using marginal-cost pricing would occur if such rates were to raise an amount of revenue different from what is needed to pay the total costs of running the electric utility. We have seen that in the simple Boiteux-Steiner model of peak-load tariffs no such conflict need arise—prices equal to marginal cost raise just enough revenue to repay total costs, with no excess profit. But in general there is no assurance that this result will be obtained. Pricing is complicated by the existence of economies of scale, inflation, and a disequilibrium between short-run and long-run marginal costs.

Economies of Scale

The technology of producing many public utility services is such that, in the absence of inflation, the average cost of one unit of service—a telephone call or a kilowatt-hour—is reduced if the total number of units produced is increased. Such economies of scale are most clearly seen in the distribution of electricity, where, for example, a doubling of the amount of electricity consumed does not require doubling the costs of poles, cables, and transformers needed to deliver the power. Until recently, similar scale economies could also be achieved by building larger and hence more efficient generation units. While these possibilities may now be nearly exhausted, the total costs of generating and delivering power to the final consumer are undoubtedly subject to a moderate degree of scale economies. The importance of this fact is that—when calculated in current prices—the marginal costs of supplying additional kilowatt-hours will tend to be less than the average costs. Therefore, prices equal to marginal costs will produce *too little* revenue, and a deficit will result.

There are two methods available to deal with the potential deficit. First, rates can be set equal to marginal costs and the deficit covered by a subsidy payment from another source, such as central taxation or perhaps profits earned by a publicly owned firm in another industry. This solution, which preserves the goal of efficient electricity prices, has lost a good deal of its theoretical appeal in recent years. It is now recognized that imposing such taxes for extraneous reasons will result in inefficiencies elsewhere in the economy, distorting the supply of capital and labor.[8] It is also clear that managerial control of public subsidy programs itself uses up resources, which can be economized by requiring that utilities be self-financing.

If deficits from marginal-cost pricing are not to be covered by external funds,

8. See, for example, Baumol and Bradford (1970).

then the only recourse is to raise the average level of rates to the level of average costs. Satisfaction of this budget constraint necessarily means some departure from the optimal marginal-cost prices. But since a peak-load tariff will have several rating periods with different prices, there are many possible combinations of rates that will cover costs. Accepting the budget constraint as a requirement, one may ask: What is the *second-best* pricing rule—the rate structure that introduces the least inefficiency while still allowing the utility to cover all its costs?

The answer to this question is derived in the theory of second-best, or quasi-optimal, pricing. Beginning from trial prices equal to marginal costs, prices should be increased the most for those services that have the least elastic demands, and should be increased least for those with the most elastic demands. If, for example, a two-period peak-load tariff based on marginal costs would incur a deficit, and if it were the case that the peak demand is less sensitive to price than demand in the off-peak period, then both prices should be raised, but with the peak price being increased by a greater percentage. As an alternative to raising prices during *periods* of inelastic demand, the greatest percentage increases could instead be applied to the rates of *users* with inelastic demands,[9] or to the inelastic *segments* of a block rate structure. For instance, either the fixed customer charge or the first block of a rate structure could be increased to meet a deficit while leaving the marginal price facing most consumers at the level of marginal costs.[10]

The optimal second-best solution is reached when the relative price deviation from marginal cost for each service is inversely proportional to the elasticity of demand for that service. These so-called *Ramsey prices* (after Frank Ramsey [1927], who first established their efficiency properties) are desirable because they eliminate the deficit by introducing the minimum amount of distortion in resource use. A large price mark-up is applied to the service for which there is little change in consumption; this raises a good deal of additional revenue and yet produces only a small distortion in the optimal consumption amount. The smallest mark-up is applied to the service that is most sensitive to price; therefore a large reduction in usage is avoided.

If marginal cost-pricing were to produce a revenue surplus, rather than a deficit, the optimal second-best pricing rule would again be given by the Ramsey rule. In this case, the price of the least elastic service should be *reduced* by the greatest percentage amount, and the prices of more elastic services would be reduced by proportionately smaller quantities.

---

9. This principle is similar in spirit to value-of-service pricing, but it is applied with an explicit knowledge of the price elasticity of demand.

10. See Acton, Mitchell, and Mowill (1976). Such inframarginal adjustments will have minimal effects on electricity use except when the change in the total bill causes, in the long run, an important shift in appliances or equipment to another fuel.

Inflation

Until now we have implicitly assumed that prices remain the same over time. In such a world, the marginal cost of supplying more electricity is the same today as it was when the utility's first generating plant was built. But present-day economies are subject to persistent, but uncertain, rates of general inflation, and the costs of supplying electricity are no exception. In designing electricity rate structures the problematic questions are then: At what input prices should marginal costs be calculated? And what measure of total costs must be covered by revenues?

Inflation complicates the calculation of costs associated with long-lived capital assets—which account for a large proportion of the total costs of supplying electricity. The one-time investment costs of a generating plant or distribution system are annualized by applying a depreciation rate to the original cost of the asset. Over the lifetime of the asset the total depreciation charges are intended to recover its total cost, so that funds will be on hand to replace the physical equipment. (Of course, these funds may have been borrowed or raised from equity investors at the outset, in which case revenue from depreciation charges has been used to repay the loan and pay dividends to shareholders.) Provided that prices have remained stable, the asset can be replaced by using the accumulated depreciation funds, and no change in revenues is required. If, however, prices have been rising, it may now cost substantially more to replace the equipment. Unless the depreciation charge has included an amount for rising prices, insufficient funds will be available. In this case electricity rates must be raised and maintained at a higher level when the replacement occurs; the necessary funds would be financed by borrowing, to be repaid by the higher rates.

Regulatory practice in the United States generally calculates allowable total costs on the basis of *historic* costs, using depreciation rates that do not incorporate inflationary adjustments. In this situation prices equal to the marginal costs—calculated using current prices for replacing capital equipment—may result in *higher* revenues than the allowable total costs calculated on the basis of earlier prices. Thus a revenue surplus may occur even though economies of scale mean that marginal-cost prices would not fully cover total costs calculated at current prices. Indeed, much of the debate before state regulatory commissions in recent generic rate cases has focused on methods of adjusting *downward* the provisional rates based on marginal cost.

In terms of public policy, two choices are available. Rates can be brought into line with historic costs, thus accepting the conventional measure of allowable historic costs. This procedure allows the established mechanisms of regulatory audit and overview to continue unchanged, but it defers to the future the full adjust-to the level of costs that now exists. As plants are replaced, periodic rate increases will be needed. The alternative is to recalculate total costs at replacement prices and thus bring electricity rates into line with current conditions all at once. The additional revenues can be set aside in a reserve and paid out when plant and equipment are replaced. In this way no additional revenues will be needed at that time. This latter policy would require a large initial increase in average rates, but would eliminate the inefficiency induced by pricing electricity below its replacement cost.

The discussion thus far has been limited to capital costs. But current expenses are also subject to inflation. Many U.S. utilities now incorporate into their rate structures adjustments for changes in the prices of at least some current inputs. A fuel-adjustment clause often provides for an automatic increase or decrease in the authorized rate per kilowatt-hour, based on the average cost of fuel purchased or burned. Thus a portion of the rate structure, on the average, very nearly reflects current costs. However, increases in fuel costs will not generally exert a proportionate effect on rates in the different time periods of a peak-load tariff, and marginal-cost prices keyed to replacement costs should, in principle, be adjusted separately for each rating period. This difference is likely, however, to be of relatively minor importance except when large changes in fuel prices, such as followed the oil embargo of 1974, occur.

Short-Run Versus Long-Run Marginal Costs

Short-run marginal costs are the increase in total costs incurred to increase output by one unit, when no change in the quantity and type of plant and equipment is possible. Implicitly, much of the discussion of marginal costs in this chapter has referred to short-run marginal costs. But over time, capital equipment can be rescaled to provide for increased output, and the incremental costs that incorporate such adjustments in plant and equipment are long-run marginal costs. The relationship of short- and long-run marginal costs in an optimally designed system has been well established in the economics literature.[11] The utility will choose its capital stock and mix of technologies so that short-run marginal costs—inclusive of the opportunity costs resulting from the limited capacity that is available—are equal to long-run marginal costs at the designed level of output. Price can therefore be set equal to either measure of marginal cost to achieve economic efficiency.

Basic changes in relative factor prices for fuel and capacity raise, however, a third fundamental problem of tariff adjustment. Major additions to electric power systems must be planned 5 to 10 years in advance of the date at which they will first go into operation. For many reasons, actual conditions frequently depart from those anticipated when a system is designed. The most important examples are due to unforeseen changes in fuel prices, shortages of rainfall (in hydroelectric systems), unexpected outages, and performance of the equipment that is different from what was anticipated.

In recent years electric utilities on both sides of the Atlantic have been operating in a more-or-less continuous state of disequilibrium; a plant mix that was optimal for an era of low prices for oil and natural gas is now very costly to

11. See, for example, Boiteux (1949); Steiner (1957); and Turvey (1968a).

operate. In this type of disequilibrium there is a conflict between pricing at short-run marginal costs and pricing at long-run marginal costs. Presently, short-run marginal costs—roughly speaking, the fuel costs of oil or gas used in thermal generating units—substantially exceed the long-run marginal costs that can eventually be attained by shifting the generating mix away from these high-priced fuels.

A fundamental disequilibrium of this sort poses a dilemma: If prices are kept at the level of long-run marginal costs in order to preserve some degree of rate stability and encourage consumers to base electricity-using investments on future electricity costs, the utility will be forced to sell electricity at less than what it currently costs to supply it at the margin, and the economy will incur short-term efficiency losses.[12] In practice, the utility systems reviewed in this study follow an intermediate course. Their rate policies emphasize the desirability of a stable, long-run price signal, but when a major change in factor prices occurs electricity rates are brought closer to current, short-run marginal costs so that total costs will continue to be covered.

METHODS OF MODULATING THE LOAD CURVE

A utility can influence its customers' loads, and thus the total system load curve, in two fundamental and interrelated ways. First, by providing financial inducements, most importantly through the rates charged for power at different periods of use, it can encourage its customers to alter what would be their habitual pattern of using electricity. Second, it can undertake more direct methods of altering some consumers' loads, including actual control of consumer equipment, as well as the promotion of types of appliances that produce a systematic shift of load to off-peak periods.

Rate Incentives

By establishing a rate structure in which the prices of using electricity correspond to the marginal costs of supply, a utility automatically provides strong financial encouragement to users to restrict their consumption at peak periods and to undertake greater uses at off-peak hours. Large consumers of electricity in industry and commerce have detailed knowledge of the peculiarities of their own production activities and are in the best position to determine whether to economize on their use of electricity and, if so, what changes in production practices or new investments are most effective. The essence of a rate structure

---

12. Prices equal to short-run marginal costs will be suboptimal if the consumers who purchase durables and who make investment decisions for industrial processes base their life-cycle cost comparisons of competing appliances and technologies at least partly on current electricity prices. At the same time, prices that are less than short-run marginal costs will induce some excessive short-run utilization of present equipment and appliances. We are not aware of an analysis of the pricing policy to be followed to achieve the optimal transition from disequilibrium to a new long-run equilibrium in this type of market.

based on marginal costs is its reliance on price signals to induce customers to make choices that are in their own and the utility's joint interest. These decisions are decentralized and taken by individual consumers; the utility's role is to set an appropriate rate structure, but not to involve itself further in changing consumers' loads.

Load Management

In contrast, active load-management strategies consist of direct involvement by the utility in the planning of consumer investments and in control of actual loads. Active load management is thus characterized by a significant amount of centralized planning and decisionmaking, and can take many forms. The utility may promote the purchase or conversion of appliances that alter the load curves of a group of consumers to achieve a shape more favorable to the utility's costs of production. It may encourage customers to install equipment capable of using an alternative source of fuel in addition to electricity, so that power can be interrupted without serious inconvenience to the customer. It may take over actual control of the power flowing to particular appliances—such as storage space-heaters and water heaters—that perform tasks that are not affected by short interruption of power or the precise hours of operation. Regardless of the specific technology, customers will generally not install appliances with more favorable load patterns or acquiesce in relinquishing control of their power supply unless it is financially advantageous for them to do so. Tariff policy therefore plays a key role in facilitating the carrying out of an active load-management program.

SUMMARY

The level of electricity rates determines the amount of revenues collected by a utility and the costs paid by its consumers, while the structure of rates signals the uses of power and periods in which the utility wishes to encourage consumption. By designing the structure of electricity rates to reflect the major variations in the cost of supplying electricity, utilities and regulatory agencies can achieve greater efficiency in the use of energy resources.

The theory of peak-load pricing originates with the basic two-period Boiteux-Steiner model in which electricity is produced at constant returns to scale by a single plant with separate costs of capacity and fuel. For this model the optimal rate structure consists of a peak-period price per kilowatt-hour equal to running costs plus capacity costs apportioned per unit of consumption, and an off-peak price equal simply to running costs. More general theoretical models derive the rate structure appropriate to more realistic conditions that encompass a variety of generating technologies, storage, economies of scale, and uncertainty about both supply reliability and demand. Engineering models of an electric utility's costs incorporate details of the individual system and are used to guide short-run operating decisions and to plan long-term expansion.

When appropriately designed, electricity rate structures can reflect the detailed patterns of marginal costs in an electric utility. In practice the rate structures of European utilities emphasize only the principal variations in system costs, and are limited to no more than three different price levels over a 24-hour-per-weekday period, and to at most two periods in which each price applies.

Prices equal to marginal costs will generally result in the most efficient allocation of economic resources. If such prices conflict with other objectives, such as subsidizing the consumption of particular consumers, society can more effectively accomplish a redistribution of income by general taxation and transfer programs than by distorting energy prices. However, the existence of economies of scale, inflation, and disequilibrium in fuel markets does require that in setting rates certain adjustments be made to the level of marginal costs. By incorporating information about customers' price elasticity of demand, these adjustments can be made in a fashion that preserves most of the efficiency gains of marginal-cost pricing.

Peak-load pricing enables a utility to achieve a more desirable system load curve in two ways. First, the rate structure influences the pattern of consumption of individual customers, encouraging them to shift their electricity uses to low-cost periods. Second, such rates provide the financial incentive for consumers to install appliances with more favorable load patterns and thus enable the utility to actively manage its load by promoting specific types of equipment.

Part I has established the importance electricity rates can play in encouraging the efficient use of energy in the United States, examined the basic economic conditions underlying the cost of supplying electricity, and described the principles for designing electricity rate structures that can achieve greater efficiency. In most utilities these factors require some form of peak-load pricing. Part II is devoted to a detailed examination of the experience that European utilities have accumulated with peak-load rate structures—how they were designed, the effects they have had on the use of electricity by industrial and residential consumers, and the benefits that have been realized.

Part II

The European Experience: A Quantitative Study of Utilities in Six Countries

In the United States it is customary for utilities to consider the load curves of their customers as fixed, exogenous demands and to limit their role to supplying the electricity needed to meet those demands at minimum overall cost. Many foreign utilities have a contrasting approach to pricing and load management. Historically, the costs of coal, oil, and natural gas—and therefore the prices of all forms of energy, including electricity—have been higher in most other industrial economies than in the United States. As a result, foreign utilities have taken a more active approach to customer loads: They have not accepted the existing load patterns as given, but have tried to reduce costs by actually shaping the system load. To this end they have provided price reductions to customers who shift their peak-load usage to lower-cost hours, or to those who have installed direct control systems for those uses of electricity most susceptible to interruption or scheduled operation.[1]

Many separate aspects of the accumulated experience of foreign utilities are of potential interest for U.S. energy policy. The lessons from foreign experience can be broadly categorized into two groups: (1) those related to the supply and pricing of electricity; and (2) those related to the demand for electricity. Of particular interest in the supply of electricity are European methods of planning and evaluating system expansion, of measuring marginal costs of supply, and of using marginal-cost analysis to design tariffs. With respect to the demand for electricity, important topics include changes in European industrial patterns of

---

1. The almost total absence of peak-load pricing in U.S. electric utilities contrasts sharply with the routine use of these pricing methods in other regulated U.S. industries, such as telephones and airlines. An economic explanation for this puzzling behavior lies beyond the scope of the present study. However, some U.S. electrical utilities have made use of special tariffs for interruptible power for certain residential or industrial customers; for examples, see Sherry (1975).

demand in response to peak-load tariffs and changes in the use and ownership of residential appliances due to energy prices that are generally higher than those found in the United States.

In this volume we are limited to describing only a few aspects of this extensive body of experience—the principal factors that determine the pattern of marginal costs of supplying electricity, the response of consumers to peak-load pricing, and the techniques of active load management. In Chapters 4–7 the principal peak-load rate structures in use in European utilities are discussed, and the relationship of these tariffs to the structure of marginal costs in each utility is classified. A detailed examination of the responses of industrial and residential customers to these time-related rate structures is then given. Finally, an assessment of the effectiveness of peak-load pricing in reducing European utilities' capacity requirements and increasing energy efficiency is provided.

Chapter 4

The Structure of European Electricity Tariffs

Tariff policy in European utilities is grounded in the fact that the prices in a rate structure convey information (signals) to consumers and influence their use of electricity. The fundamental principle that guides the design of tariffs in many electricity utilities in Europe is that rates should closely reflect the pattern of the utility system's marginal costs. Tariffs based on marginal-cost principles provide price signals for efficient energy use and ensure that over a period of time every group of customers will be charged the full costs of their electricity consumption.

THE VARIETY OF RATE STRUCTURES

Viewed against this general uniformity of tariff principles, electricity pricing and load-management practices in Europe show substantial heterogeneity. The characteristics of European tariffs range from a time-invariant, subscribed maximum-demand tariff in Norway, to season and time-of-day pricing in France and Great Britain. Some of the more direct load-management techniques include time-of-day interruptions in West Germany and Great Britain, seasonal interruptions in Norway and France, and in several countries the use of storage-heating devices controlled by the utility rather than by the customers. Table 5 displays the major characteristics of the tariffs for high-voltage customers in several European countries. Each country's rate structure will be examined in greater detail below.

The structure of the high voltage tariffs for large industrial consumers and for wholesale supply to distributing companies most closely matches the underlying structure of each utility's marginal costs. These rate structures have in common a charge for *maximum instantaneous demand*—the customer's peak rate of use of electricity measured in kilowatts; and a charge for *energy* consumed—the sum of

53

Table 5. Representative High-Voltage Tariffs in Several European Utilities

European Utility	Fixed Charge ($/yr)	Maximum Demand Charge (kw)		Energy Charge (kwh)	
		Price per Kilowatt ($)	Rating Period	Price per Kilowatt-hour (¢)	Rating Period
England (1976): Southeastern Electricity Board (>650 v)	2.86	5.66/mo	January		
		4.28/mo	December, February	2.03	7:30 a.m.–1:30 a.m.
		2.71/mo	November, March		
		0.70/mo	April–October	1.02	1:30 a.m.–7:30 a.m.
Finland (1977): Helsinki Electricity Works	1692	25.55/yr	November–February only	4.04	7 a.m.–10 p.m.
				3.01	10 p.m.–7 a.m.
France (1976): Electricité de France (60 kv, 90 kv)	—	20.30/yr	7 a.m.–9 a.m., 5 p.m.–7 p.m. November–February[a]	4.30	Same periods as those shown for demand charges.
		8.12/yr	6 a.m.–10 p.m. October–March[a,b]	2.58	
		4.06/yr	6 a.m.–10 p.m. April–September[a]	1.96	
		1.42/yr	10 p.m.–6 a.m. October–March, and all day Sunday	1.33	
		0.41/yr	10 p.m.–6 a.m. April–September and all day Sunday	1.27	

Table 5. Continued

Norway (1975): Water Resources and Electricity Board	—	15.55/yr	All year	0.59	October-April
				0.30	May-September
	—	13.61/yr	October-April only	0.59	October-April only
Sweden (1976): State Power Board (70 kv, 130 kv)	36,585	2.44/yr plus 25.61/yr	For 1-hr demand, all year For 6-hr demand, all year	0.53 0.71	September-April May-August
Sweden (1975): Stockholm Energy Works (100 kv)	36,585	17.07/yr	All year	1.39	7 a.m.-9 p.m. Monday-Friday
				0.95	All other hours

Note: Most tariffs are subject to value-added taxes and adjustments for changes in fuel and cost-of-living indexes. Rates in dollars are at exchange rates prevailing January 3, 1977.
[a]Except Sunday.
[b]Except during the hours 7-9 a.m. and 5-7 p.m. for November through February.

those demands over a period of time measured in kilowatt-hours. The charges for both maximum demand and energy may be varied over several periods of the day, week, or year. To recover the costs of long-term investments in electricity generating and distributing capacity, several utilities employ *subscribed demand* charges. Under this method of pricing, the customer subscribes for a period of several years to a maximum rate of electricity use and pays a monthly charge based on that predetermined level. By imposing penalty charges for electricity used in excess of the subscribed level, tariff provisions encourage careful scheduling and planning by consumers.

The degree of complexity of rate structures used in European utilities varies from one group of customers to another, and depends directly on the quantity of electricity supplied. For wholesale supply to distributing companies and for high-voltage deliveries to very large consumers, the expense of metering equipment that permits rates to be varied in step with changes in marginal costs is justified by the large absolute changes in load that such rates induce. At lower voltages the utilities employ a more simplified form of the basic rate structure that reflects only the most important elements of marginal costs. And for residential and many small commercial customers the costly process of metering maximum demand is frequently circumvented by applying a charge for the maximum capacity provided to the customer, measured by the size of that customer's main fuse or circuit-breaker, or by simply adding the capacity charge into the rate per kilowatt-hour.

Differences in System Characteristics

In large part the wide variations in European pricing and load-management practice stem from differences among countries in the generating resources and load patterns in their systems. Comparative statistics of electricity production and generating capacity for several national systems as well as for the entire United States are shown in Table 6. These differences in generating resources lead to important international variation in both the pricing and use of electricity. A striking illustration of these differences is that while England generates electricity from steam turbines, the municipal utility in Oslo, Norway, generates electricity from hydroelectric facilities and, during off-peak hours, sells it to industrial firms that use it to produce steam.

Because system characteristics vary significantly in Europe, the choice of the optimal pricing and load-management techniques will differ from country to country. Several important dimensions of variation are the time pattern of the costs of producing and distributing power, the time pattern of demand itself, and the nature of the shortages that can occur when supply is inadequate to meet demand. By examining these characteristics in specific European utilities, one can understand the sources of variation in tariffs and in load management in different systems.

The costs of generating and distributing electricity will vary by time of day or

Table 6. Electricity Production and Installed Generating Capacity in Europe and the United States

Utility System	Annual production (millions of kwh)	Installed Capacity (MW)	Generating Resources (MW)		
			Hydroelectric (%)	Thermal	
				Steam and Turbine (%)	Nuclear (%)
Norway (1975)[a]	77,578	16,727	99	1	0
Sweden (1975)[a]	79,224	22,819	56	33	11
Finland (1975)[a]	25,558	7,395	32	68	0
France (1975)[b]	178,514	48,286	37	56	6
England (1974/75)[c]	208,215	63,136	1	91	8
Germany (1974)[d]	311,710	70,120	7	88	5
United States (1975)[e]	2,001,488	524,513	13	79	8

[a]*Facts in Brief*, 1976, Nordel, Helsinki.
[b]*Statistique de la Production et de la Consommation 1975*, Electricité de France, Paris.
[c]*Statistical Yearbook 1974/75*, Central Electricity Generating Board, London.
[d]*Elektrizitätswirtschaft*, Vol. 24, No. 21, October 13, 1975, Vereinigung Deutscher Elektrizitätswerke, Frankfurt.
[e]*Statistical Yearbook of the Electric Utility Industry*, 1975, New York, Edison Electric Institute.

by season if the types of generating units in use vary over time. In Stockholm the steam generated in district heating plants and used to heat commercial and apartment buildings provides a source of nighttime electrical energy at low marginal cost, so that the local utility supplies power under a time-of-day tariff that has a low nighttime charge. The seasonal differentiation of the Norwegian and Swedish State Power Board tariffs reflects the fact that it is more costly to store water for winter use than to use it for run-of-the-river generation. In largely thermal systems, such as those in England and Wales, France, and West Germany, the use of only the most efficient plants during periods of low system load leads to both seasonal and time-of-day pricing and to active promotion of off-peak uses of electricity.

The magnitude, as well as the temporal pattern, of cost differences will influence the choice of tariff structure and load-management techniques. In Norway the daytime/nighttime cost differential is too small to make time-of-day residential tariffs worth the incremental metering costs they would create. In the mixed hydroelectric-thermal system of the Swedish State Power Board, diurnal cost differences are not great enough to make storage space-heating cost-effective for the residential consumer. In Stockholm, however, the cost differences are larger and justify storage water-heating but not storage space-heating. In England and Wales, France, and West Germany extensive reliance on thermal generation results in a marginal-cost structure that justifies time-of-day tariffs and makes it mutually advantageous to the consumer and the utility to use storage devices, despite the added capital costs for the consumer and incremental distributional and metering costs for the utility.

Shortages and Interruptible Loads

Because capacity is costly, utilities maintain a limited number of reserve generating units and limited excess distribution capacity. Forced outages of generating units and higher than expected demands create some risks of electricity shortage during the course of a year for all utility systems. The nature of such potential shortages depends on the characteristics of the system and affects the type of pricing and load-management techniques that are employed. During normal weekdays the periods of peak daily demand follow quite regular patterns. Seasonal patterns of demand are also predictable. Nevertheless, the amplitude of the system peak load does vary significantly from day to day. On most days there will be some excess capacity even at the peak hours, since sufficient capacity must be available to meet the very highest peak load of the year. However, by interrupting service to selected customers for minutes or hours at a time, several times a year, the utility can reduce the amount of capacity that must be maintained for only the very greatest level of demand. This ability to interrupt consumer loads can significantly augment the load management achieved through tariffs and storage appliances alone.

The tariffs under which interruptible power is sold constitute perhaps the purest form of peak-load pricing, because the peak prices apply to only those few hours per year for which a condition of actual shortage is almost certain. During those periods the price of electricity to interruptible customers is very high indeed, reflecting the opportunity cost of the additional capacity required to meet further increments in load.[1] For the remaining days of the year, when a capacity shortage does not threaten, the price during the peak-period hours is substantially lower but still above the price during off-peak hours. This difference between peak and off-peak hours reflects the corresponding difference in the running costs in these periods on days when adequate capacity is available.

In predominantly hydroelectric systems the major supply risk is a drought. If interruptions of supply are used to meet the shortage, they can be several weeks or months in duration and should occur only a few times in a century. In dry years, Norwegian utilities interrupt several industrial customers (such as the aluminum industry) for periods that may last several months. In France the national utility has long-term contracts with certain industrial clients, including the aluminum industry, to interrupt power for prolonged periods if a dry year should diminish the system's hydroelectric potential.

In largely thermal systems, electricity shortages are likely to be of shorter duration, usually coinciding with the daily peak-load period. In the almost

---

1. Under some tariffs, certain consumers may choose not to shut off their load, but instead to continue to use electricity and pay the peak price. Under other tariffs the customers' power is shut off by the utility, and they then—in effect—face an "infinite" price.

totally thermal British system, the generating authority can meet periods of sharply elevated short-run marginal costs by shedding more than 10 percent of the total industrial load on short notice through interruptible contracts. In contrast the predominantly thermal systems in West Germany tend to have fewer interruptible contracts because they benefit from interconnection with Swiss, French, and Austrian hydroelectric facilities.

In mixed hydro-thermal systems, shortages are less likely to occur than in systems that must rely predominantly on a single type of generation, since the chance of simultaneously incurring both an energy shortage in hydroelectric units and a capacity shortage in thermal generation is less than the probability of either of those events alone. Scotland relies on pumped-storage to reduce the risks of thermal capacity shortages and offers no generally available interruptible contract. With a combination of reservoir and pumped-storage hydroelectric units, the French have used short-term interruptible contracts to only a limited extent.

When the additional costs of metering and control are included, interruptible power is of interest to a relatively small number of customers and for a few selected end-uses of electricity. Still, interruptible power can be a potent load-management technique for reducing capacity costs and substituting for the reserve margins that must otherwise be maintained to guard against outages. The extent of utilities' actual control over interruptible loads varies. In some systems consumers' space heaters and water heaters can be interrupted by the system dispatcher. In others, the dispatcher uses advance warnings to selected large industrial customers, and customers respond voluntarily.

As this discussion has suggested, variations among countries in underlying cost conditions result in important differences in the specific structure and terms of European electricity tariffs. The construction of generation and distribution facilities so as to minimize the total costs of supplying power gives rise to a pattern of marginal costs specific to each electricity system. European utilities seek to further reduce their overall costs by requiring consumers to pay rates for electricity that reflect its marginal costs at the time that it is used and by actively promoting the purchase of appliances that lead to cost-effective shifts in load.

DETAILED CHARACTERISTICS OF EUROPEAN RATE STRUCTURES

In the rest of this chapter the major characteristics of the electricity tariffs of six countries will be reviewed, with particular attention given to the marginal cost conditions that underlie the establishment of the rate structure for high-voltage consumers. To highlight the principles of marginal cost tariffs and how they are applied in different systems, this review of rate structures is organized according to the basic nature of the generating system in each country. Norway, which has an all-hydroelectric system, is discussed first; followed, in order of their increasing reliance on thermal generation, by Sweden and France; then the all-thermal system in England and Wales is examined; and finally the chapter concludes with a brief discussion of tariffs in the mixed systems of West Germany and Finland.

NORWAY

The all-hydroelectric nature of Norway's power system, in which running costs are a negligible portion of the total costs at high voltage, determines the structure of Norwegian tariffs. The Norwegian Water Resources and Electricity Board (NVE) is the major supplier of high-voltage power. Through its operation of the national grid and its control of import and export sales, NVE's tariff policies determine the rates paid in most areas of the country. Retail distribution companies, which are usually municipally owned, sell low-voltage electricity to commercial and residential customers.

High-Voltage Tariffs. Table 7 shows the relatively simple terms of the Norwegian high-voltage tariffs, which are based on a subscribed demand charge and on only a small energy charge.[2] In most cases the demand charge does not depend on seasonal or time-of-day factors. Because of the availability of electricity generated from runoff water, energy charges are lower during the summer.

NVE provides for the contingency of a dry year by supplying some large industrial customers (such as aluminum and hydrogen producers) with power under contracts that permit interruption of service for several months. Interruptible power is priced at 75 percent of the secure-power price.

Table 7. Norwegian High-Voltage Tariffs, 1975

Utility	Subscribed Demand Charge ($/kw)	Energy Charge (¢/kwh)	
		Winter (October–April)	Summer (May–September)
Norwegian Water Resources and Electricity Board (NVE)			
Winter contract (October–April)	13.60	0.59	–
All-year Contract	15.55	0.59	0.30
Oslo Lysverker (load >10 kw)	38.88[a]	0.70	0.70

[a]Special contracts for power supplied to industrial and commercial boilers and water heaters exempt selected users from the demand charge between 7 p.m. and 7 a.m. from April 16 to October 15 if sufficient hydroelectric power is available.

2. All of the electricity rates appearing in this chapter are calculated at the exchange rates prevailing on January 3, 1977.

Residential Tariffs. At low voltage the Norwegian residential tariffs exemplify the importance of distribution costs in an all-hydroelectric system. In the absence of significant differences in generating costs by time of day, the utility's total costs can be minimized by flattening the load curves of individual customers in order to reduce the amount of distribution capacity that is required. The subscribed maximum-demand tariffs also reflect the costs at the generation level because of the high degree of coincidence between individual residential peak demands and the system peak, which occurs on early winter evenings when heating and cooking activities are at their maximum.

Under the load-rate tariff (Table 8), the typical homeowner in Olso subscribes for an annual load at a rate of $22.94 per subscribed kw per year. He pays 0.58¢ per kwh for energy consumed, but he is charged about four times that amount (2.29¢ per kwh) for each kilowatt-hour consumed when his rate of demand is in excess of the subscribed load. An optional ammeter is installed in the consumer's kitchen to indicate when demand is exceeding the subscribed rate and thus excess charges are being accumulated. This permits residential users to avoid higher payments by reducing their use of nonessential appliances.

Now that most of the readily usable hydroelectric sources have been developed, some Scandinavian utilities are planning to construct thermal generating facilities. These units will have significant running costs that will decrease the relative importance of the costs of distribution-system capacity. Oslo and several other Norwegian utilities are abandoning the domestic load-rate tariff for a more conventional declining-block rate structure (Table 8), which provides an incentive to economize on kilowatt-hours whenever electricity is used, rather than to economize on maximum kilowatt demand.

Table 8. Norwegian Residential Tariffs, Oslo Lysverker, 1975

Load-rate tariff	
Subscribed power	$22.94 per kw per year per household
Price per kwh	0.58¢, plus
	2.29¢ per kwh for consumption in excess of subscribed level
Block tariff	
Fixed charge	$22.94 per year per household
Price per kwh	1.38¢ for first 9000 kwh/yr, plus
	0.88¢ for additional kwh
Flat tariff	
Price per kwh	2.29¢

SWEDEN

Electricity in Sweden is produced and distributed by municipal and privately owned companies and by the State Power Board, which operates the national grid and accounts for almost one-half of the total energy generated. Although predominantly a hydroelectric system, Swedish utilities rely on thermal generation for about one-third of their energy output, and for this reason seasonal and time-of-day pricing is used more extensively in Sweden than in Norway.

High-Voltage Tariffs. The structure of the State Power Board tariff includes a customer charge, two demand charges, and a set of energy charges (Table 9). The first demand charge applies to the *subscribed* maximum rate of power to be used in any 1-hour period throughout the year. The second charge is levied on the maximum *actual* average rate of demand over any 6-hour period throughout the year. To record this usage a special meter integrates over each 6-hour period: midnight to 6 a.m., 1 a.m. to 7 a.m., and so on. If a subscriber is willing to pay the additional metering and administrative costs, the demand meter can be disconnected for the periods when the system load is low, such as during the summer and at nighttime during the winter.

Empirical studies of high-voltage customers in Sweden have established that the average demand during the 6 continuous hours of highest usage per month provides stable predictions of capacity requirements and effectively reflects the peak-load conditions on high-voltage segments of the distribution network. Because of the abundance of hydroelectric storage, the State Power Board has only small differences between day and nighttime marginal costs of energy, and these variations have been included in the 6-hour demand rate. This special 6-hour demand rate structure is, in effect, a time-of-day or peak-load tariff. The State Power Board's energy rates per kilowatt-hour vary by season, higher rates being in effect during the winter months (September-April) when water must be held in reservoir storage. The increased rates for both demand and energy at lower voltages reflect additional capacity costs and energy losses in the distribution and transformation system.

The tariffs of the retail distribution companies, and of some municipal power companies that generate a large proportion of their own energy, vary somewhat from the State Power Board's rate structure according to local circumstances. For example, the Stockholm Energiverk, a municipal utility, obtains a large proportion of its power from thermal generation. Some of this electricity is generated from conventional condensing units. In addition, the utility generates electricity from back-pressure units driven by steam from the district heating plants which supply commercial and residential buildings in central areas of the city. Stockholm has an explicit time-of-day tariff (Table 10) in which the kilowatt-hour rates are about one-third lower during the nighttime and weekend periods when excess back-pressure steam is available. The tariff also includes a 1-

Table 9. Swedish State Power Board High-Voltage Tariffs, 1976 (Central Sweden distribution area)

Tariff Type and Supply Voltage (kv)	Fixed Charge[a] ($/yr)	Demand Charges		Energy Charges[a,b] (¢/kwh)			
		For Subscribed Demand per kw_1/yr[a] ($)	For Actual Demand kw_6/yr[a] ($)	Peak (September– April)	Off-Peak May– August	Day (6 a.m.– 10 p.m.)	Night (10 p.m.– 6 a.m.)
N1 70 and 130	36.59	2.44	25.61	0.83	0.71	—	—
N2 20 and 40	6.10	3.05	32.93	0.85	0.73	—	—
N3 6 and 10[c]	0.29	4.27	37.80	0.98	0.85	—	—
D3 6 and 10	0.29	4.27	0	—	—	2.46	—
E3 6 and 10	0.24	4.27	0	2.34	2.34	—	0.98

Notes: kw_1 = 1-hour maximum demand; kw_6 = 6-hour maximum demand.

[a] All charges are marked up by $0.25 (K - 260 - 4 [\text{year} - 1972])$, where K = consumer price index.

[b] Price per kwh is adjusted by the fuel price index in ¢/kwh, $0.7(C-1)$ when $C > 70.1$, where C is a cost-of-fuel index.

[c] Consumers have a choice of second and third tariffs if they have a short duration load of less than 1000 hours.

Table 10. Stockholm Energiverk High-Voltage Tariffs, 1975

Voltage (kv)	Fixed Charge ($/yr)	1-Hour Maximum Demand Charge[a] ($/kw/yr)	Energy Charges[b] (¢/kwh)	
			Monday–Friday (7 a.m.–9 p.m.)	All Other Times
100	36,585	17.07	1.39	0.95
30	6098	19.51	1.61	1.00
10	293	21.95	1.83	1.12

[a] Average of four maximum monthly values, no more than one of which can be from May through August.

[b] Before taxes or fuel-adjustment clauses. Percentage markup equals $0.25 (K - 320)$, where K is the average consumer price index during January and February.

hour demand charge for the customer's maximum demand, regardless of when it occurs.

Residential Tariffs. The structure of Swedish tariffs for domestic consumers preserves the idea of a subscribed demand charge in the form of a rate scaled to the size of the main fuse amperage (see Tables 11 and 12). A flat rate per kilowatt-hour is levied for energy consumed. Households have a choice of several tariffs according to their load factor. In many areas an optional time-of-day rate is available for residences with storage space- or water-heating; in this tariff a fixed charge is included to recover additional metering costs.

Table 11. Swedish State Power Board Residential Tariffs, Central Sweden, 1976 (400 volts)

Tariff Type	Fixed Charge ($/yr)	Fuse Charge[a]	Energy Charges (¢/kwh)		
			All Hours	Peak 6 a.m.–10 p.m.	Off-Peak 10 p.m.–6 a.m.
E4[b] (normal residence)	–	S	3.05	–	–
M4[c] (typically, residences with electric heating)	–	2S	2.20	–	–
D4[b] (typically, residences with storage heating)	35.12	S	–	3.17	1.46

Source: *Electricity Tariff 1976* (Vattenfall, Sweden, 1976).

[a] *Fuse charge parameter (S)*
Main fuse amperage: 16 20 25 35 50 63 80 100 125 160 200
S ($/yr): 79 105 138 205 307 395 498 629 805 1054 1332

[b] Maximum fuse allowed is 200 amps.

[c] Maximum fuse allowed is 50 amps.

Table 12. Stockholm Energiverk Residential Tariffs, 1975

Tariff	Annual kwh Range	Fixed Charge ($/yr)	Fuse Charge[b]	Energy Charges (¢/kwh)[a]	
				Day (7 a.m.- 9 p.m.)	Night (9 p.m.- 7 a.m.)
Normal tariff					
Apartments	<4500	7.32	S	3.17	3.17
Other	<5040	17.56	S	3.17	3.17
Långtidstariff[c]					
Apartments	>4500	29.27	2.4S	2.68	2.68
Other	>5040	42.15	2.4S	2.68	2.68
Double tariff[d]	–	36.59	1.5S	3.17	1.46

[a]Includes 0.48¢/kwh tax. Peak rates apply seven days a week.
[b]*Fuse charge parameter S*
  Main fuse amperage: 25   35   50   63   80   100   125
  S ($/yr):   88   146 241 322 446 607   805

  Main fuse amperage: 160   200   250   300   400
  S ($/yr):   1127 1493 1932 2415 3476
[c]Typically has electric space heating.
[d]Typically has electric space and water heating.

FRANCE

Electricity in France is generated and distributed by Electricité de France (EdF), a single national utility that also establishes the terms of electricity tariffs. About two-thirds of the utility's generating capacity is composed of thermal units, and the balance is hydroelectric. In addition, the nationalized mines and railway, as well as some large privately owned firms, have substantial generating resources of their own.

In the early postwar years the recently nationalized electricity sector was concerned with the problems of operating and consolidating some 1200 small, privately owned power companies. At that time, each company had a different electricity tariff in effect, and the need to rationalize electricity pricing was recognized as urgent. Furthermore, by the early 1950s it was apparent that the electricity system was severely constrained by the total generating capacity available, and EdF officials searched for ways to reduce the demand for electricity during peak periods. These two factors led to a systematic review and reform of electricity pricing. By 1955, EdF had developed marginal-cost schedules, and in 1958 the Green Tariff –so-called because of the color of the cover of the brochure in which it first appeared—was first offered on an optional basis to high-voltage consumers. Ten years later the Green Tariff was made standard for all high-voltage consumers. Marginal-cost pricing was subsequently extended to low-voltage services in the form of the Universal Tariff, which became available in 1965 for residential and agricultural customers, and in 1972 for small commercial customers.[3]

The structure of EdF's tariffs—the timing of tariff periods and the method of charging for both energy and capacity—is uniform throughout the country. However, small regional differences in rate levels do exist to reflect variations in supply costs, to encourage the siting of industrial plants near low-cost sources of power, and to diversify the location of new industry.

The Structure of the Green Tariff

EdF is a winter-peaking system. As can be seen from Figure 12, the weekday demand during the coldest months of 1952 typically had two pronounced

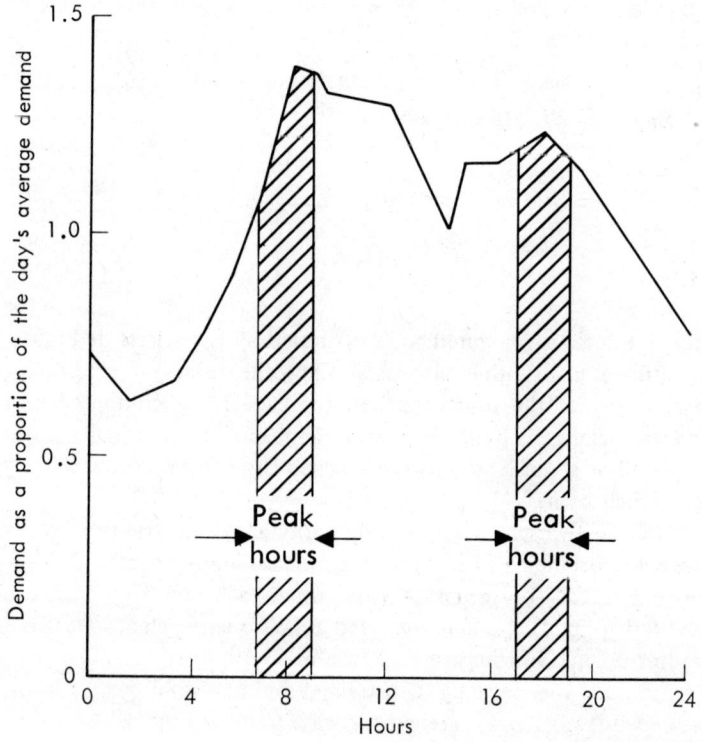

Source: Electricité de France.

Figure 12. French Daily Load Curve for a Representative January Workday, 1952, before the Introduction of the Green Tariff

3. See Requin and Lorgeou (1975).

peaks—at about 8 a.m. and 5 p.m. The shaded portions of the figure show the hours later designated as the peak pricing periods. An intermediate level of demand occurred at other daytime hours and during the early evening, and the lowest demand was registered after midnight. In the summer months, demand did not reach the same level, although the system load curve had similar but less pronounced morning and afternoon peaks.

Time Periods. The Green Tariff was structured to follow these major patterns of system demand and thus to reflect, approximately, the variations in the marginal cost of supplying customers with high-voltage power. The different tariff periods are defined in terms of the effect of increased demand on the requirement for additional generating capacity. *Peak hours* are those time periods when an additional megawatt of demand substantially increases the risk of an outage due to a shortage of capacity and thus, in the long run, requires that generating capacity be increased to maintain a given level of system reliability. The *shoulder hours* are considered to be the time periods when additions to system demand only somewhat increase the risk of capacity shortage. *Off-peak hours* are the time periods when increased demand on the system causes no increase in the probability of shortage.

The risk of a shortage of capacity is included directly in EdF calculations of marginal cost. When the system is optimally planned, the cost of increasing the capacity of the system by 1 kilowatt, net of any fuel saving achieved by this investment, will be equal to the expected cost of curtailed demand. EdF uses this relationship between investment cost and the risk of outage to define the curtailment cost per kilowatt. The expected marginal cost of supplying a kilowatt-hour in each time period is then the sum of the short-run marginal running cost when adequate capacity is available, plus the probability of a shortage times the curtailment cost.[4] Figure 13 illustrates the structure of the French Green Tariff in terms of the level of the rates per kilowatt-hour for service at medium voltage in the Bouches-du-Rhone department.

During the four coldest winter months, November through February, Electricité de France experiences it greatest demand and consequently has its highest operating costs and greatest risk of shortage (partly because some hydroelectric resources are unavailable). For these months there are three distinct periods:

Peak hours: 7 a.m. to 9 a.m. and 5 p.m. to 7 p.m., Monday through Saturday.
Shoulder hours: 6 a.m. to 10 p.m., except Sunday and peak hours.
Off-peak hours: 10 p.m. to 6 a.m. and all day Sunday.

Since running costs and risk of shortage are lower in the other eight months of the year, the Green Tariff introduces seasonal pricing in the months of

---

4. See Lhermitte and Caille (1971); and Balasko (1974).

68 The European Experience

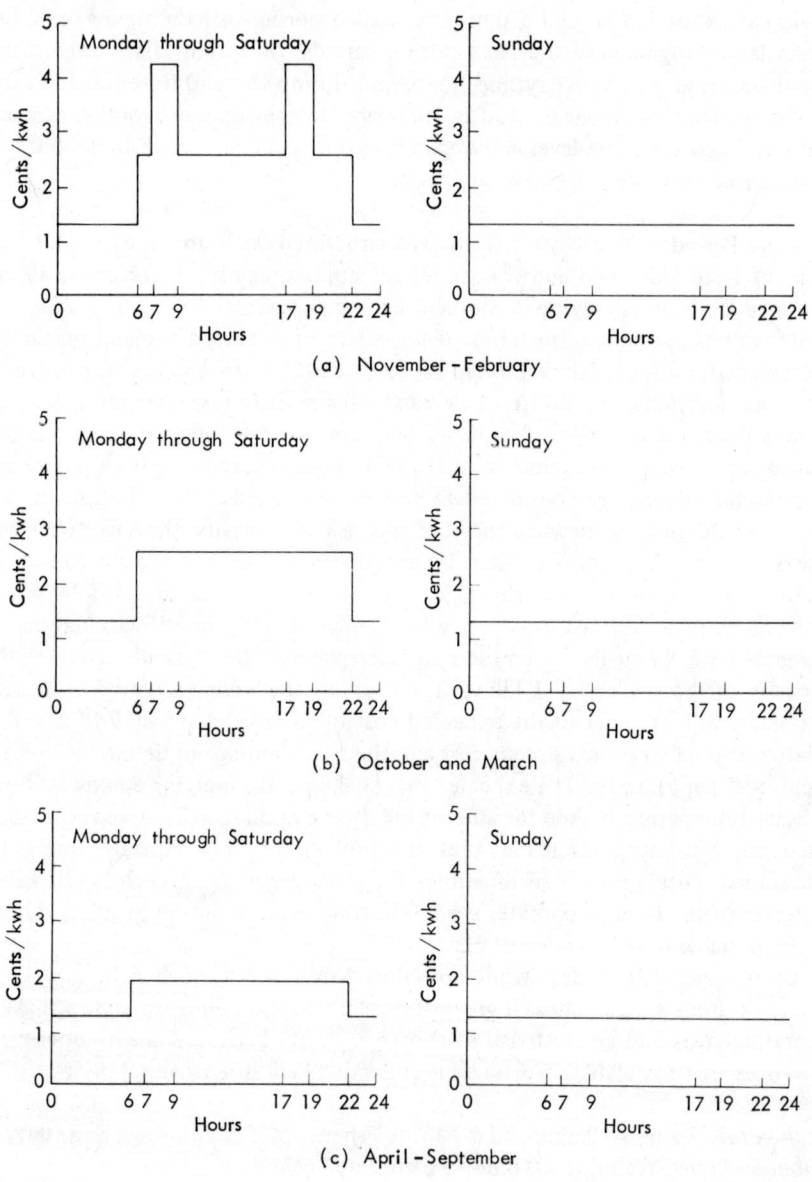

Source: Mitchell, Manning, and Acton (1977).

Figure 13. Kilowatt-Hour Charges in the French Green Tariff, 1975, for Service at Medium Voltages

October and March by eliminating the peak hours and charging at the winter shoulder rate for electricity consumed during the entire 6 a.m. to 10 p.m. period (except on Sunday), so that only shoulder and off-peak rates apply. And in the summer months (April through September), when running costs are even lower because of reduced demand and the availability of water from the spring runoff for hydroelectric facilities, only shoulder and off-peak hours of the day are differentiated; moreover, the summer shoulder and off-peak rates are less than winter rates. In all, the Green Tariff has five tariff periods: peak, shoulder, and off-peak in the winter; and shoulder and off-peak in the summer.

Subscribed Power Charges. In addition to facing different rates per kilowatt-hour for five separate periods, high-voltage consumers also pay for *subscribed demand*, and a consumer has the opportunity to subscribe to a different level of annual maximum demand (kilowatts) in each of the five tariff periods. The EdF rate structure uses the subscribed-demand charge to recover much of the capital costs associated with new generating equipment needed to meet demands in each of the five time periods, as well as to recover the entire costs of customer-specific capital investments.

Because the risk of shortage is significantly lower in the shoulder and off-peak hours, there is less need for additional capacity in these periods to maintain reliable service, and so the effective price per kilowatt of individual demand is successively lowered during those hours. As a result the subscribed-demand rates vary in parallel with the level of the energy price per kilowatt-hour. Table 13

Table 13. General Tariff Version of the Green Tariff, 1976 (Bouches-du-Rhone Department)[a]

	Prices[b] for Supply at 60 and 90 kv				
	Winter			Summer	
	Peak	Shoulder	Off-Peak	Shoulder	Off-Peak
Subscribed demand charge ($/kw/yr)	20.30	8.12	1.42	4.06	0.41
Energy charge (¢/kwh)	4.30	2.58	1.33	1.96	1.27

Source: Electricité de France.
[a]Calculated using rate of exchange prevailing on January 3, 1977.
[b]Prices exclude the 17.6 percent value-added tax. The amounts of power subscribed during shoulder periods must be at least the amount subscribed during the peak period, and the amounts subscribed during off-peak periods must be at least the amounts subscribed during shoulder periods.

shows this structure of the energy and subscribed-demand charges in the General Tariff, the version of the Green Tariff that covers about 85 percent of all high- and medium-voltage customers. The structure of the combined charges for energy and for subscribed demand provides a particularly strong incentive for customers to modulate their loads if they are able to do so.

The effective charge for subscribed demand in each period can be derived from the single rate that EdF charges per kilowatt of "reduced power," a measure equal to all of the power subscribed during the peak period plus fractional amounts of additional power (maximum demand) subscribed during shoulder and off-peak periods. The effect of the formula for calculating reduced power is to eliminate 93 percent of the demand charges for customers whose consumption occurs only in off-peak hours throughout the year and 98 percent of these charges if consumption is limited exclusively to summer off-peak hours.[5]

Voltage Levels. Under the Green Tariff, electricity is supplied at four basic voltage levels. As shown in Table 14, as the supply voltage is reduced, the energy charges increase in a regular fashion to reflect energy losses. The relatively greater mark-up at lower voltages during the peak hours incorporates an element of marginal capacity costs. Subscribed demand charges, shown in Table 14 as rates per kilowatt of reduced power, are increased to reflect the incremental capital costs of transforming electricity to lower voltages.

The Green Tariff contracts are for a 5-year term, and subscribed power levels apply for the duration of the contract. The long-term commitments to levels of subscribed power permit EdF to construct additional facilities as they are required and to assure revenue recovery for its investments.[6] A customer's sub-

Table 14. The Green Tariff at High and Medium Voltages, General Tariff Version, 1976[a]

Voltage (kv)	Subscribed Demand Charge for Reduced Power ($/kw/yr)	Energy Charges (¢/kwh)				
		Winter			Summer	
		Peak	Shoulder	Off-Peak	Shoulder	Off-Peak
220	20.30	3.32	2.01	1.32	1.92	1.26
150	20.30	3.71	2.24	1.32	1.93	1.26
60 to 90	20.30	4.30	2.58	1.33	1.96	1.27
5 to 30	26.06	6.25	3.40	1.40	2.16	1.33

Source: Electricité de France.
[a]Prices exclude the 17.6 percent value-added tax. High-voltage rates apply in the Bouches-du-Rhode department and are based on exchange rates prevailing January 3, 1977.

5. For further details, see the Appendix at the end of this book.
6. In certain instances (shipbuilding, for example), EdF will enter into a shorter contract if the customer pays an additional demand charge.

scribed level may be increased at any time, in which case the new subscribed power level then remains in effect for 5 years. If, in a given month, actual demand exceeds the customer's subscribed power, the excess is billed at the rate of 70 percent of the annual charge per subscribed kilowatt.[7] The effect is to penalize any overruns of subscribed power that occur more than one month in a year. If the customer exceeds subscribed power by a substantial margin, EdF will automatically increase the subscribed power level for that customer's contract. Furthermore, EdF maintains the right to install circuit-breakers that can cut off the customer's power when demand exceeds the subscribed level by 10 percent.

Versions of the Green Tariff. Four other versions of the Green Tariff are available to commercial and industrial customers served at high and medium voltages. The customers can select the most advantageous version. This choice is usually determined by the customer's annual load factor. In European utilities the load factor is typically measured by hours of utilization—which are equal to the customer's annual kilowatt-hours of consumption divided by annual maximum kilowatt demand—rather than by the equivalent ratio of average-demand to maximum-demand used in the United States. The five available versions of the Green Tariff are:

1. Very long utilization: over 5500 hr.
2. Make-up, or long utilization: 3500 to 5500 hr.
3. General: appropriate for most customers.
4. Short utilization: less than 700 or 800 hr.
5. Security, or emergency supply.[8]

Offering the customer a choice of tariffs is justified by the following line of reasoning. Assume, for simplicity, that there is only a single tariff period: the entire year. The curved line in Figure 14 shows that for a *given* maximum demand, the expected annual costs of supplying energy (kilowatt-hours) increase, but at a decreasing rate as the hours of use are increased, thereby reflecting the structure of costs at both the generation and distribution stages of supply. For a group of customers, these costs can be approximated by a tariff consisting of a fixed kilowatt charge (P_{kw}) and a kilowatt-hour rate (P_{kwh}). Each tariff, as shown in Figure 14, is then a straight line expressing the total payment per kilowatt of maximum demand. The intercept of the rate curve is the fixed kilowatt charge, and the slope of the rate curve is the kilowatt-hour rate. These prices are provisionally chosen so that the rate curve for a group of

---
7. Consumption is measured by multiple-register demand and energy meters. Demand is recorded as mean kilowatts over a 10-minute period.
8. The emergency tariff applies to standby electricity service for customers that generate their own electricity.

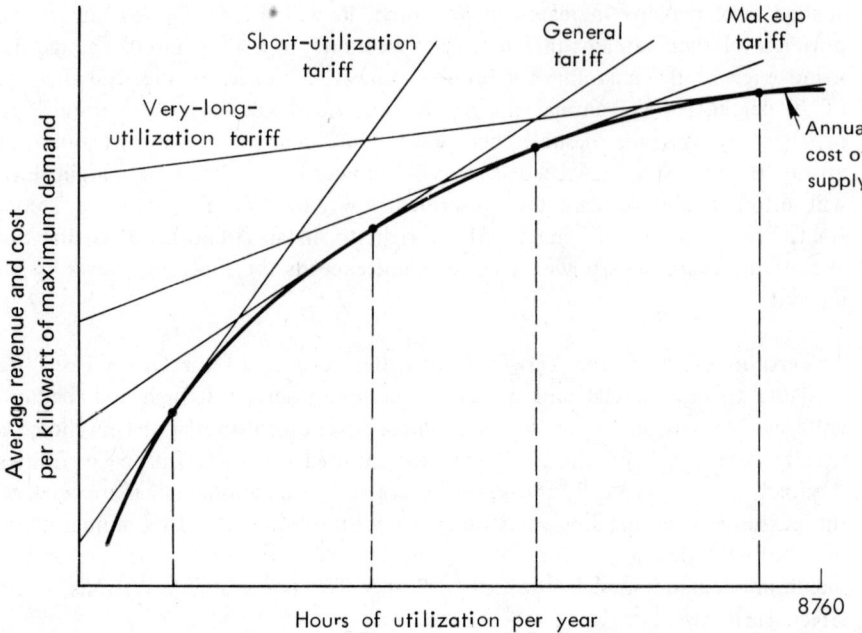

Figure 14. Rate Curves for the Four Principal Versions of the French Green Tariff

customers with similar hours of use is tangent to the annual-cost curve at the center or the distribution of customers scattered along the hours-of-use line.

In the Green Tariff there are four versions of such rate curves. As shown in Figure 14, as one moves to versions for longer hours of use, the kilowatt charge increases and the kilowatt-hour rate is reduced. Customers will rationally choose the version that offers them the lowest overall cost of electricity, and in this way they will automatically select the version that most closely approximates the marginal cost of their individual service. The structure of rates for the different versions of the Green Tariff are shown in Table 15 for supply at 60 and 90 kilovolts.[9]

[9] The appropriateness of offering several pairs of kilowatt and kilowatt-hour charges can be illustrated by considering the simplified case of a single rate that applies at all hours of the year. For a customer having a very high load factor, a 1-kw increase in maximum demand necessarily implies a 1-kw increase in system capacity (ignoring losses). At the same time, because this customer increases the system load evenly at all hours, it will be optimal to increase capacity by adding base load capacity rather than by expanding a cycling or peaking plant. As a result, this customer will impose a low running cost. Thus for customers with high load factors, a higher-than-average subscribed demand charge, coupled with a lower-than-average energy charge, will be appropriate.

In contrast, a 1-kw increase in the maximum demand of a customer having a low load factor results in only a fractional increase in the mathematical expectation of system maximum demand. Since it will be least costly to meet this increased load by expanding a peaking or cycling unit, running costs will be higher. For customers with low load factors, a lower demand charge—but a higher rate per kilowatt-hour—will be appropriate.

Table 15. Versions of the Green Tariff, 1976, at 60 and 90 kv[a]

Tariff Version	Sub-scribed Demand Charge ($ per kw)[b]	Energy Charges (¢ per kwh)				
		Winter			Summer	
		Peak	Shoulder	Off-Peak	Shoulder	Off-Peak
Very long utilization	60.54	1.67	1.67	1.19	1.29	1.14
Make-up	30.25	3.09	2.36	1.32	1.78	1.26
General	20.30	4.30	2.58	1.33	1.96	1.27
Short utilization	8.12	6.88	4.02	1.33	2.35	1.27
Emergency	12.18	6.88	4.02	1.33	2.35	1.27
Reactive Energy						
Surcharge (at all hours)			0.32		0.25	
Discount (at all hours)			0.13		0.10	

Source: Electricité de France.
[a]Rates apply in the Bouches-du-Rhone department and exclude the 17.6 percent value-added tax, at rates of exchange prevailing January 3, 1977.
[b]Charge for reduced power.

Rate Calculations. In practice the cost calculations are made for all five tariff periods of the Green Tariff, with the result that customers will be scattered above and below the mean annual cost curve because of differences among them in hours of use in each of the tariff periods. At each voltage level, EdF statistics on consumption measure the hours of use in each period, and analysts prepare a cost study to establish the generalized annual cost curve for each period. The provisional rates for demand and energy are then combined with the distribution of consumer-usage patterns to predict total revenues.

Once a provisional marginal-cost tariff has been calculated, its revenue yield is simulated and compared to total costs that include a specified yield on invested capital. Since there are increasing returns to scale in the distribution of electricity, and at least constant returns in its generation, this provisional tariff usually results in some revenue shortage in a period of stable factor prices.

Several methods of adjusting the rate structure have been used to make up the deficit that would result from strict marginal-cost pricing. For example, in the initial 1958 calculation, the Green Tariff was projected to have a 4 percent deficit. This revenue shortfall was removed by uniformly marking-up all price ratios for seasonal, time-of-day, and voltage differentials in the regions supplied by thermal generation. However, in 1968, when the preliminary calculations projected a 10 percent deficit, the utility shifted to nonuniform mark-ups and applied the greatest increases to the tariffs for customers with low load factors—that is, consumers who had a low ratio of average to maximum use of power over the day or year. This procedure effectively approximated the Ramsey second-best pricing rule of instituting the greatest departures of price from marginal cost for those consumers who, in EdF's belief, had the smallest price elasticity of demand.[10]

The Residential Tariff

At low voltage the Universal Tariff for French residential customers uses a fuse or circuit-breaker charge, which increases with the maximum current rating of the customer's service regardless of time of use. This charge replaces the subscribed-demand charge found in the Green Tariff, and eliminates the need for meters capable of measuring demand in each period. Because the installation or change of master fuses can only be done by the utility (they are in sealed boxes), EdF retains control of a customer's maximum demand and collects the revenue accruing from this charge.

Under the standard tariff (Table 16), a flat rate per kilowatt-hour applies to all uses of electricity, except that a higher rate in a small initial block is used to recover some fixed costs. This semblance of a declining-block rate structure is recognized as a departure from marginal-cost principles and was introduced for "social and psychological" reasons[11] to make the Universal Tariff appear more acceptable to low-volume users. Because more than 90 percent of EdF's residential customers use more electricity than that encompassed by the initial block, almost all consumers face a price for the marginal units of electricity that is based on marginal costs.

Time-of-Day Rates. Residential customers may choose the alternative "double tariff" and obtain off-peak energy between the hours of 10 p.m. and 6 a.m. at about one-half the standard rate by increasing their monthly fixed payments to cover the additional costs of a day/night meter. This time-of-day tariff has been found to be advantageous by some 2.7 million residential customers (about 18 percent of all customers on the Universal Tariff), principally those who have both storage space-heaters and water-heaters. A total yearly consumption of at least 800 kwh is generally needed to make the rate worthwhile to the customer.

Until 1973 a simplified version of the five-period Green Tariff was available to larger residential consumers on a pilot basis. Under this peak-load tariff, different rates per kilowatt-hour were charged during peak, shoulder, and off-peak periods, varying seasonally; a single subscribed-demand charge was levied, based on the size of the fuse or circuit-breaker. However, EdF discontinued this tariff when it found that the cost and complexity of metering outweighed the benefits. For residential customers having large loads (a subscribed demand of at least 24 kw), EdF has continued to make a tariff available that includes seasonally varying rates.

10. See Requin and Lorgeou (1975).
11. See Lorgeou (1976).

Table 16. French Residential Tariffs, July 1974[a]

Circuit-Breaker Size (kw)	Circuit Breaker Charge ($/Month)		Energy Charges (¢/kwh)		
	Regular Tariff	Peak/ Off-Peak Tariff	First Block	Regular Rate	Off-Peak Rate (10 p.m.–6 a.m.)
3	0.54	1.47	9.70 (1st 30 kwh)	3.00	1.42
6	1.28	2.40	9.56 (1st 40 kwh)	2.86	1.42
9	1.91	3.20	9.56 (1st 50 kwh)	2.86	1.42
12	8.01	9.45	–	2.86	1.42
18	12.01	13.77	–	2.80	1.42
24	–	20.29	–	2.80	1.42
30	–	26.82	–	2.80	1.42
36	–	33.35	–	2.80	1.42

Source: Electricité de France.
[a] Prices exclude the 17.6 percent value-added tax.

ENGLAND AND WALES

In England and Wales the generation and transmission of electricity is the responsibility of the nationalized Central Electricity Generating Board (CEGB), which supplies all wholesale energy to twelve local area boards under the terms of its Bulk Supply Tariff. Each area board is exclusively responsible for the distribution of electricity to industrial and residential customers in one geographic region.

The area boards establish their own tariffs based on the bulk rates at which they buy power from the CEGB and on their own local distribution and sales costs. Thus, in contrast to the uniform structure of the French national tariff, customers in England and Wales pay prices that are the result of regional decisionmaking. These rates are not widely different, because of the dominant effect of the wholesale tariff.

The Wholesale Tariff

The British winter-peaking system relies on thermal generating units of varying fuel efficiencies for nearly 100 percent of its supply. The system load curve prior to the introduction of time-of-day charges is given in Figure 15. The energy charges in the Bulk Supply Tariff attempt to reflect the daily variation in marginal costs that occur in an all-thermal system. The price per kilowatt-hour varies according to the time of day, with an off-peak rate in effect from midnight to 8 a.m., a shoulder rate that applies at most other hours, and a peak energy rate that takes effect during the two half-hours of the actual system peak demand each day.

76 The European Experience

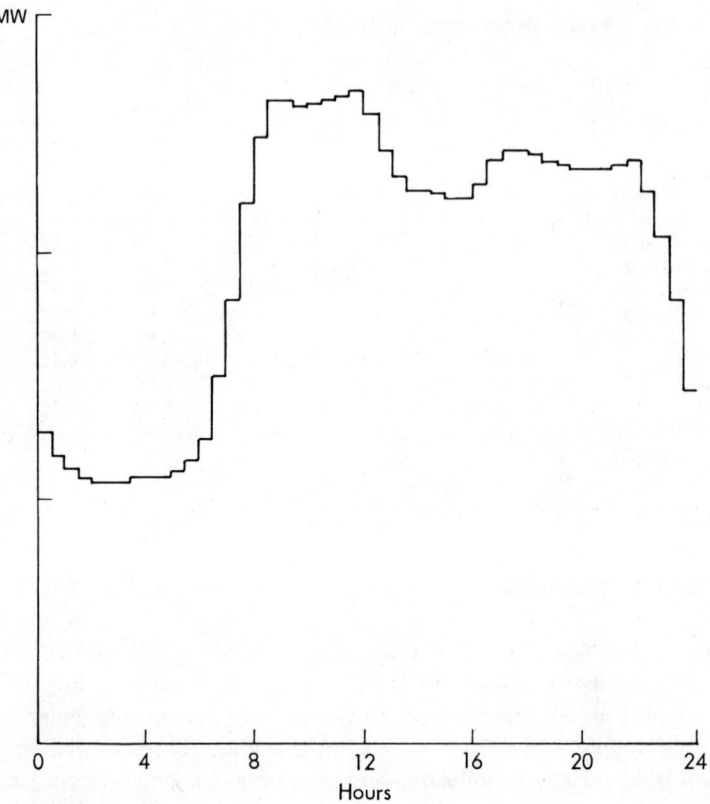

Source: Central Electricity Generating Board, "The Bulk Supply Tariff," Abridged Version, January 1975.

Figure 15. British Annual Daily Load Shape, 1960/61

Capacity charges are levied according to a complex formula that reflects both demand at the time of generating system's peak as well as the area board's own peak demand. Area boards pay a basic demand charge, which is a rate per kilowatt of the area board's average demand at the time the national system is operating at 90 percent of its maximum annual demand, and a peaking-capacity charge (or rebate), which is proportional to the difference between the area board's demand during "potential peak warning" (PPW) periods and its basic demand level.

During the winter months the CEGB issues PPWs on days of anticipated peak demands on the system. In this manner, it reduces the need for additional capacity and lowers operating costs. As of 1977/78, the CEGB broadened the use of PPWs to include periods when there is likely shortage of capacity relative to demand, due, for example, to severe weather or plant breakdown. This broadened application is now termed load management and serves to identify the hours of greatest expected demand. The PPW tariff encourages the area boards and their large industrial customers to reduce their loads when short-run marginal costs are especially high.[12]

High-Voltage Tariffs

The area boards convert the Bulk Supply Tariff into published industrial and residential tariffs that include demand and energy charges for specified time periods. Because the peak rates in the Bulk Supply Tariff apply to the period of the *actual* system peak, the area boards must forecast both their own and the CEGB load curves for the winter in order to establish retail tariffs that will minimize their own costs. Not surprisingly, despite a general structural uniformity the industrial tariffs of the various area boards differ in some of their details. These tariffs tend to have winter (November through February) maximum half-hour demand (kilowatt) charges, sometimes varying by month to reflect the increased probability of capacity shortages in the dead of winter.

Time-of-Day Rates. Most area boards offer an *optional* time-of-day rate for industrial consumers. Typically a customer may choose a tariff with a single, long peak period from about 8 a.m. until 10 p.m. or midnight. The difference in the rate per kilowatt-hour is about 1¢ between peak and off-peak periods. For some large consumers, the published tariffs are unsuitable because these consumers have quite different load characteristics; in such cases (some 18 percent of all high-voltage consumers) special arrangements are made. Although the terms of these special tariffs are not published, they often contain a provision reflecting the area board's costs during PPW periods. Examples of rates from typical published British industrial tariffs are shown in Tables 17 and 18.

The Residential Tariffs

The typical residential tariff in England and Wales (see Table 19) has a simple flat rate per kilowatt-hour plus a fixed quarterly charge, which is designed to cover consumer costs such as the meter, billing, and consumer service. In two areas, these fixed costs are recovered by charging higher rates for the first few kilowatt-hours of consumption. Households also have the option of purchasing electricity under the White Meter Tariff, which bills all nighttime usage at slightly more than half the price per kilowatt-hour of daytime usage. Customers pay an additional fixed charge to cover the cost of a dual-register meter for this time-of-day tariff.

Since 1961 the area boards have promoted the use of storage radiators for residential heating. The first units drew power during two periods: an 8-hour overnight period and a 3-hour booster period in mid-afternoon that coincided

---

12. The full terms of the Bulk Supply Tariff are found in the Appendix.

Table 17. Midlands Electricity Board Maximum Demand Tariff (over 650 volt supply), 1976

Annual maximum demand charge:[a]	
First 250 kw	$0.72/kw/yr.
Second 250 kw	.53/kw/yr.
Next 2500 kw	.48/kw/yr.
Remaining kw	.44/kw/yr.
Monthly maximum demand charge:[b]	
April to October	.00/kw/mo.
November and March	1.11/kw/mo.
December to February	4.17/kw/mo.
Energy charge:	
All day	2.11¢/kwh
or	
7 a.m. to 1 a.m. daily[c]	2.11¢/kwh
1 a.m. to 7 a.m. daily	1.02¢/kwh

Source: Midlands Electricity Board. Calculated at rates of exchange prevailing January 3, 1977.

[a] Maximum demand for months in question or preceding 11 months, whichever is greater.

[b] If consumer pays the cost of additional demand-metering equipment, the peak rates apply to 8 a.m. to 8 p.m., Monday through Friday only.

[c] Time-of-day rate available only if customer pays for additional metering.

Table 18. Energy Charges under Optional Time-of-Day Tariff for Industrial Customers in England and Wales (> 650 volt supply), 1976

Area Board	Peak Price (¢/kwh)	Off-Peak Price (¢/kwh)	Off-Peak Period Begins	Off-Peak Period Ends	Length of Off-Peak Period (hr)
Eastern	2.03	1.14	1 a.m.	7 a.m.	6
East Midlands	2.21	1.34	11 p.m.	7 a.m.	8
London	2.44[c]	1.59	11 p.m.	7 a.m.	8
Midlands	2.11	1.02	1 a.m.	7 a.m.	6
North East	2.22	1.11	1 a.m.	7 a.m.	6
North West	2.08	1.02	2 a.m.	8 a.m.	6
South Eastern	2.03	1.02	1:30 a.m.	7:30 a.m.	6
Southern	2.05	1.11	midnight	8 a.m.	8
South Wales	2.70	1.15	midnight	8 a.m.	8
South Western	2.11[c]	1.18	11 p.m.[a]	9 a.m.	8[a]
Yorkshire[b]	2.18[c]	1.02	1 a.m.	7 a.m.	8

Source: Published 1976 tariffs of the area boards. Calculated at rates of exchange prevailing January 3, 1977.

[a] The hours that the customer pays off-peak rates are at the board's discretion.

[b] Also has various seasonal, time-of-week, and time-of-day combinations.

[c] Tail block of a declining-block tariff.

Table 19. South Eastern Electricity Board Domestic Tariffs, 1976

Tariff	Fixed Charge (per quarter)	Energy Rates			
		Day		Night	
		Hours	¢/kwh	Hours	¢/kwh
Domestic Two Part	$3.71	–	3.69	–	3.69
Domestic White Meter	5.83	7:30 a.m.–10:30 p.m.	3.86	10:30 p.m.–7:30 a.m.	1.61
Domestic White Meter (Economy Six)[a]	5.83	7:30 a.m.–1:30 a.m.	3.86	1:30 a.m.–7:30 a.m.	1.26

[a] For newer, fast-charging storage devices.

with an afternoon trough in the system load curve. These radiators were supplied and metered on a separate, restricted-hour circuit that was switched on at those hours by clock control. By the late 1960s the first storage-heating radiators were so successful that the midday trough was rapidly filling up. To remedy this situation, new radiators were designed that would not require a midday charge. Beginning in 1969 the new radiators were offered under the unrestricted White Meter Tariff, which has a nighttime discount on electricity used for any purpose during an 8-hour nighttime period. Customers with older restricted-hour equipment were permitted to continue to be billed under the original tariff (although rate levels were adjusted through time). Today, about 14 percent of the 17 million residential customers in England and Wales have some form of storage heating, and they pay a time-of-day or restricted-hour rate for their electricity.

Interruptible Rates. The optional time-of-day tariffs, despite their long peak periods, provide significant incentives for industrial customers to shift loads into off-peak hours on a regular basis. However, the CEGB and the area boards in England and Wales are still exposed to substantial variations in loads that can impose very high marginal costs in an all-thermal system. To achieve additional control over peak loads, the area boards supplement the optional time-of-day tariffs with special tariffs for interruptible power. These tariffs are available only to selected large customers and are based on the Bulk Supply Tariff rates prevailing during potential peak warning (PPW) periods.

Under the PPW procedure, the operating division of the CEGB routinely forecasts system demand and on-line generating capacity a day in advance. When a possible shortage is expected, then (prior to 5 p.m.) the CEGB issues a PPW to the area boards covering specified hours during the following day.[13] The area boards in turn notify by telex each customer supplied under the PPW tariff. Each customer must either shed the amount of load agreed upon for the specified warning hours or pay a very high rate per kilowatt of actual demand. PPW warn-

13. By terms of the procedure, a warning may remain in effect for up to two hours, and more than one warning period is permitted in a single day.

ings can be issued in November through February, but cannot total more than 60 weekday hours during the four winter months. These tariffs for interruptible power currently cover some 120 large industrial customers.

PPW retail customers have a strong financial incentive to shed loads during the warning period. In most cases, customers pay the normal kilowatt charge for the actual maximum load during the warning period and are charged nothing for higher loads in nonwarning hours. Since the interruption is *voluntary,* the customer does have the option of deciding how much load to shed. However, the PPW tariff is sufficiently attractive that failures to comply amount to less than 1 percent of the load under PPW contracts.

WEST GERMANY

In West Germany, electricity is produced and distributed by monopoly supply companies organized as municipal companies or as private firms in which government bodies hold minority ownership. Industrial generation of power, primarily in conjunction with process heat, accounts for about 19 percent of West Germany's total production of electricity. In the main, public price regulation plays the limited role of reviewing and approving tariffs for lower-voltage customers.

The West German electricity network is predominantly thermal, although the high degree of interconnection between regional supply companies and the exchange of power with systems in bordering countries enables utilities to somewhat reduce the variation in short-run marginal costs that would otherwise dominate a thermal system. Utilities rely on special contracts with selected high-voltage customers and active control of storage space- and water-heating for load control.

Companies sell electricity in the following ways:

1. Under published tariffs, available to all customers. This is the normal form of supply for residential, agricultural, and small commercial firms.
2. Under pro forma contracts with standard terms, available at the discretion of the utility. This approach is widely used at medium voltages and for special applications, such as residential storage heating.
3. By special contracts that are privately negotiated with individual high-voltage consumers. The term of these contracts are private and not subject to regulatory review except in cases of alleged discrimination.

High-Voltage Tariffs

Although the exact terms of pro forma contracts for medium-voltage consumers vary from one West German utility to another, those shown in Table 20 for the Westphalian utility (VEW) are representative. Rates are based on both the customer's maximum quarter-hour demand and the energy consumed. Two versions of the basic contract are available, each of which includes a declining-

Table 20. Medium-Voltage Tariffs in Westphalia, West Germany

Zone price tariff (for low utilization customers, up to about 2000–2500 hours per year)[a]

First 60,000 kwh	7.3¢/kwh
Next 240,000 kwh	6.8¢/kwh
Next 720,000 kwh	6.4¢/kwh
Further kwh	5.8¢/kwh

Demand price tariff (for high utilization customers)[b]

Demand charge		$71.69/kw
Energy charge	Day	Night
Oct.–March	6 a.m.–9 p.m.	9 p.m.–6 a.m.
April–Sept.	6 a.m.–7 p.m.	7 p.m.–6 a.m.
First 240,000 kwh	$3.63/kwh	2.35¢/kwh
Next 720,000 kwh	3.16/kwh	1.96¢/kwh
Next 3,840,000 kwh	2.64/kwh	1.62¢/kwh
Next 4,800,000 kwh	2.60/kwh	1.58¢/kwh
Further kwh	2.56/kwh	1.58¢/kwh

Source: Vereinigte Elektrizitätswerke Westfalen.
Note: Both schedules are subject to inflation adjustments based on: (1) the coal price index: and (2) the borrowing rate for utilities in the region.
[a] The consumer is entitled to a percentage rebate, based on annual hours of utilization (i.e., annual kwh/peak kw) in excess of 1000 hours:

Rebate = (hours − 1000)/200, not to exceed 10 percent.

The minimum bill is 1000 hours × 4.27¢/kwh × contracted power.

[b] The minimum bill is 70 percent of the contracted power plus 1500 hours × 1.28¢/kwh × contracted power.

block schedule. In the version that is generally appropriate for low-utilization customers, the rate per kilowatt-hour declines from 7.3¢ to 5.8¢ in four steps, with a percentage rebate for customers with high utilization. Under the alternative "demand price" contract that is appropriate for high load-factor customers, there is a demand charge plus two declining-block energy price schedules—one for daytime and one for nighttime consumption. During the winter the peak (daytime) tariff hours are from 6 a.m. to 9 p.m., and the price per kilowatt-hour is 50 to 60 percent higher than that charged for nighttime hours.

For many of the largest high-voltage industrial consumers, the terms of supply are specified in private contractual agreements that are not generally made public. Prices, hours, and conditions of supply are tailored by the utility to the customer's particular circumstances and reflect both the opportunities for selected customers to modulate their loads and the supply conditions of the utility itself. Several examples of the types of special contracts in use illustrate the ways in which peak-load tariffs can be tailored to specific circumstances. In the case of a cement plant that consumes more than 55 percent of its total energy during the off-peak hours, the terms of a special contract (shown in Table 21) divides the day into peak, shoulder, and off-peak periods. The demand charges are set to encourage successively higher use during the shoulder and off-peak hours.

Steel plants, which account for 15 percent or more of total system load for utilities in the heavily industrialized regions of West Germany, have special contracts that specify a separate peak-hour period for each month of the year, which ranges from a continuous weekday peak period in November-December (8 a.m. to 6:30 p.m.) to the short peak periods in August (10 a.m. to 12 noon, and 8 p.m. to 9 p.m.). Again, the price incentives facing these customers are designed to promote higher off-peak demands (see Table 22). In nonpeak hours, customers can take up to 130 percent of the subscribed power at no kilowatt demand charge.

One large plant that produces acetylene operates under a special contract that specifies peak, shoulder, and off-peak tariff periods (Table 23). During peak hours, power can be interrupted by the utility on 30-minutes' notice; during shoulder hours, supply is guaranteed 50 percent of the time; and during off-peak hours it is fully guaranteed. Because of the interruptible feature of the contract, the firm pays no demand charge. The energy price varies roughly according to the marginal running costs during the three periods.

Table 21. Terms of a Special Contract for a West German Cement Plant

Period	Demand Price $/kw/yr	Energy Price ¢/kwh
Peak[a]	71.69	1.3[f]
Shoulder[b]	0[d]	1.3[f]
Off-peak[c]	0[e]	1.3[f]

Source: Vereinigte Elektrizitätswerke Westfalen.

[a] Effective Monday through Friday, 6 a.m.-8 p.m. during January, February, November and December; 6 a.m.-1 p.m. during March and October; 7 a.m.-1 p.m. during April through September; Saturdays, 6 a.m.-1 p.m. during January, February, March, October, November and December.

[b] Effective Monday through Friday, 1 p.m.-5 p.m. during March and October; 1 p.m.-7 p.m. during April through September; Saturdays, 7 a.m.-1 p.m. during April through September.

[c] All other hours.

[d] $4.05/kw/mo if demand in excess of 130% of contractual amount.

[e] $2.99/kw/mo if demand in excess of 200% of contractual amount.

[f] For utilization rates of at least 2500 hours/year if utilization rates in excess of 4500 hours there is a percentage rebate equal to

$$40 \times \frac{\text{hours} - 4500}{\text{hours} + 4500}$$

or 12.85%, whichever is less.

Table 22. Peak Periods of Special Electricity Contracts for West German Steel Firms

Month	Monday-Friday (except holidays)	Saturday
January	7 a.m.–noon 5:30 p.m.–8:30 p.m.	8 a.m.–noon
February–March	8 a.m.–noon 6 p.m.–8:30 p.m.	8 a.m.–noon
April	10 a.m.–noon 7 p.m.–8 p.m.	10 a.m.–noon
May	10 a.m.–noon 8 p.m.–9 p.m.	–
June–July	10 a.m.–noon	–
August	10 a.m.–noon 8 p.m.–9 p.m.	–
September	10 a.m.–noon 7 p.m.–8 p.m.	10 a.m.–noon
October	10 a.m.–noon 5 p.m.–8 p.m.	10 a.m.–noon
November–December	8 a.m.–6:30 p.m.	8 a.m.–noon

Table 23. Special Contract for Interruptible Power Supplied to a West German Acetylene Firm

Period	Relative Price per kw	Supply Conditions
peak hours	100%	Interruptible on 30-minutes' notice
shoulder hours	60%	Power guaranteed 50% of time
off-peak hours	45%	Power guaranteed 100% of time

The periods are defined as:

Month	Peak	Shoulder	Off-Peak
May–August	9:30 a.m.–Noon	6 a.m.–9:30 a.m. Noon–10 p.m.	10 p.m.–6 a.m.
September–April	7:30 a.m.–Noon 6 p.m.–7:30 p.m.	6 a.m.–7:30 a.m. Noon–6 p.m. 7:30 p.m.–10 p.m.	10 p.m.–6 a.m.

Source: Vereinigte Electrizitätswerke Westfalen.
Note: Times are for Monday through Saturday. Sundays and holidays are off-peak.

Low-Voltage Tariffs

West German households can typically choose one of two general two-part tariffs consisting of a fixed monthly charge plus a price per kwh (Table 24). The monthly price increases with the number of rooms in the dwelling (bathrooms and kitchens are not counted) to reflect the capacity costs of service at low-voltage.

Table 24. West German Residential Tariffs, 1976

	Tariff I	Tariff II
Fixed monthly charge, five-room dwelling	$5.29	$8.79
Energy price	5.3¢/kwh	4.1¢/kwh

For agriculture and business customers using power at low voltage (220 to 330 volts), the fixed charges are similarly scaled according to acreage or installed lighting and power capacity. For low-voltage customers, surcharges can be added for especially electricity-intensive appliances, such as saunas.

Residential time-of-day tariffs in West Germany are limited to pro forma special agreements that are used for power supplied for off-peak storage heating. Such agreements apply only to the electricity delivered to separate storage-heating circuits. Table 25 illustrates the terms for storage units taking up to 8 hours of nighttime and 2 hours of daytime charging.

FINLAND

Electricity in Finland is produced and distributed by the State Power Board, by municipal utilities, by supply companies with a mixture of local-government and private ownership, and by a few privately owned utilities. In addition, a nuclear power company is owned and operated by a large industrial group for its own members. Through the efforts of the Finnish Power Association there has been some standardization of rate structures. Finland has a winter-peaking system and relies on thermal units for about two-thirds of its generating capacity. In

Table 25. Terms of Special Agreement for Storage Heating, Westphalia, 1975

Fixed charge
$2.13 per month for the first storage unit.
Plus $1.71 per month for each additional unit.

Added Charges
$0.77 per month for the first two rooms.
$0.21 per month for each additional room.

Energy charge
2.1¢ per kwh, subject to the fuel-adjustment clause.

Source: Vereinigte Elektrizitätswerke Westfalen.

Table 26. Finnish State Power Board High-Voltage Tariffs, 1973 (110 kv)[a]

Flat-Rate Tariffs

Tariff[b]	Fixed charge ($/yr)	Maximum Demand Charge ($/kw/yr)	Energy Charge[c] (¢kwh)
T0	–	$8.37	2.22¢
T1	$ 4098	6.66	2.03
T2	20,522	6.66	1.66
T3	40,979	4.92	1.66

Time-of-Day Tariffs

Energy Charges[c] (¢/kwh)

Tariff[b]	Fixed charge ($/yr)	Maximum Demand Charge ($/kw/yr)	Day (7 a.m.-10 p.m.)	Night (10 p.m.-7 a.m.)
T0	–	$3.57	4.31¢	2.22¢
T1	$ 4098	3.57	4.31	2.22
T2	20,522	2.22	4.31	2.22
T3	40,979	2.22	4.31	2.22

[a] At rates of exchanges prevailing January 3, 1977.
[b] Customers are assigned to the tariff (T0, T1, T2 or T3) that produces the lowest bill, according to their load duration. Customers may choose either a flat rate or a time-of-day rate.
[c] The kwh charges are multiplied by h_i/h_b, where h_i is an index of fuel prices at time i, and b is the base period. Fixed and maximum-demand charges are multiplied by $1 + 0.5(P_i/P_b - 1)$, where P is a cost-of-living index. Peak rates apply seven days a week.

Helsinki, municipal district heating plants are used for cogeneration of power and make lower-cost electricity available at night.

The tariffs for the State Power Board and the municipally owned Helsinki Electricity Works typify Finnish tariffs. Under the high-voltage tariffs of the State Power Board (Table 26), customers choose either a flat rate or a time-of-day tariff with charges for maximum winter demand. Until 1977, industrial and commercial customers of the Helsinki municipal utility faced uniform kilowatt and kilowatt-hour rates at all hours, with the exception of several firms that shifted significant loads and received about a 50 percent discount on energy consumed during the nighttime hours (Table 27). Starting in 1977 the utility switched to a time-of-day tariff for all large consumers. At the residential level, customers in Helsinki pay a fixed annual charge and a constant rate per kilowatt-hour of energy consumed.

Table 27. Helsinki Electricity Works Tariffs, 1977

For residential customers	
Domestic tariff	
Fixed charge	$9.58/yr
Running charge	5.32¢/kwh
For commercial and industrial customers	
Energy tariff	
Fixed charge	$9.58/yr
Running charge	6.79¢/kwh
Double tariff[a]	
Fixed charge	$41.51/yr
Running charges	
Winter (November–February)	7.37¢/kwh
Summer	5.32c//kwh
Low-voltage demand tariff[b]	
Fixed charge	$242.68/yr
Active demand charge	41.51/kw/yr
Running charge	3.86¢/kwh
High-voltage demand tariff	
Fixed charge	$1692.40/yr
Active demand charge	25.55/kw/yr
Running charges[c]	
Day (7 a.m. to 10 p.m.)	4.04¢/kwh
Night (10 p.m. to 7 a.m.)	3.01¢/kwh

[a] Used largely by small commercial establishments and craftsmen.
[b] Because of the high fixed charge, only the largest low-voltage customers are on this tariff. Demand (kw) is measured in 15-minute periods. The customer is billed for the mean of the two highest values during the restricted time (November–February). If reactive demand exceeds 50 percent of active demand, an additional charge is levied.
[c] Running charges in the high-voltage tariff include taxes of approximately 0.3¢/kwh.

SUMMARY

In many European utilities tariffs are designed to reflect the marginal costs of generating and supplying electricity. The rate structures for customers supplied at high voltage contain detailed terms that approximate the costs of meeting peak-load conditions in both generation and transmission.

The specific forms of electricity rate structures vary from one European utility to another. These differences are due primarily to differences in generating resources and demand patterns. The contrast in the peak-load nature of the cost and rate structures is most extreme in a comparison of all-thermal and all-hydroelectric utilities. Most systems either have a mixture of thermal and hydroelectric generating plants or are interconnected with other utilities, and are characterized by both seasonal and daily variations in peak loads.

At high voltages, European tariffs frequently differentiate the charges for both energy and capacity in the peak and off-peak hours. The relative importance of each charge reflects the cost characteristics of the individual utility. Provision is often made to reduce or even eliminate maximum-demand charges during periods of excess capacity and low running costs (off-peak seasons in hydroelectric systems and off-peak hours and months in thermal systems). Many utilities offer optional tariffs or negotiate special contracts in order to better meet the particular load characteristics of selected customers.

For residential and other low-voltage consumers, European utilities simplify the detailed structure of the high-voltage tariffs into a single energy charge and very often include a charge based on the size of the residential fuse or circuit breaker. In the thermal and mixed systems, residential customers have the option of selecting a peak-load tariff with a reduced overnight energy price.

These peak-load rate structures produce an improved allocation of economic resources and greater energy efficiency only if they cause consumers to modify their uses of electricity. Chapter 5 examines the nature and extent to which industrial customers served by European utilities have in fact responded to peak-load rates, and Chapter 6 is devoted to appraising the effectiveness of European load management efforts in the residential sector.

Chapter 5

The Response of European Industries to Peak-Load Tariffs

Industrial customers account for a large portion of the total electricity consumed in an industrial economy. In Europe such customers are typically supplied at medium (5 to 60 kv) or high (60 to 250 kv) voltage. Frequently the load of a single customer is sufficiently large that it is worthwhile for the utility to supply power under rather elaborate pricing and metering techniques that encourage the individual customer to reduce usage at peak hours.

Evidence on the nature and extent to which industrial customers in several countries can modify their use of electricity in response to tariff provisions will be reviewed in this chapter.[1] As discussed in Chapter 4, very diverse circumstances governing the cost of supply prevail in various utilities and can give rise to quite different price signals. Thus, one utility will emphasize maximum-demand charges in its industrial tariffs, while another will rely on time-of-day energy rates. As a result, actual load patterns in a single industry will vary from country to country.

The nature of the load modulation that occurs in different industries will depend importantly on the characteristics of the firms' production processes and on the markets for their products. Firms whose electricity costs represent a high percentage of their total fabrication cost (that is, value-added), or that generate some of their own power, or that operate in multiple shifts, may be especially sensitive to tariff incentives. In some processes the output is relatively easily stored; in others it must be supplied continuously to the final customer; in still others there are opportunities for storing intermediate products.

As a result of these factors there is no simple pattern of industrial load re-

---

1. In the case of West German utilities, load-curve data were not available for inclusion in this study.

90 The European Experience

sponse to electricity tariffs. The common element that does exist is that when the appropriate economic incentives are present, a significant portion of the total amount of electricity consumed by industrial customers is susceptible to decentralized adjustment.

In the discussion that follows, the principal features of each country's industrial tariffs will be reviewed to establish the incentives they provide for load shifting, and then several types of evidence of industrial load response to these incentives will be examined. Whenever possible, data from detailed load studies of specific firms and industries will be utilized, since these data most directly reveal the magnitude of responsiveness to peak and off-peak rates. Much of the analysis is devoted to French and British industry, where peak-load pricing incentives have been pronounced and where load research has generated a data base on customer response that is unmatched in U.S. experience.

FRANCE

Figure 16(a) reproduces the fundamental structure of the wintertime French Green Tariff, which was described in detail in Chapter 4. The triple level of peak/shoulder/off-peak rates is in effect Monday through Saturday, while on Sunday the off-peak rates apply for all 24 hours. In addition to the variations in energy prices, as shown in the figure, the charges for subscribed demand follow the same three tariff periods and vary by even greater ratios from peak to shoulder to off-peak period.

Idealized Load Response

For a firm that has the flexibility to schedule its production activities or the possibility of adjusting its productive capacity to take advantage of off-peak rates, the structure of the Green Tariff provides the opportunity to significantly reduce electricity costs. Conceptually, one can envision an idealized firm responding to the Green Tariff by modulating its load in the fashion shown in Figure 16(b). Such a firm would produce at a maximum rate during the off-peak hours. For six days a week during the shoulder hours it would curtail marginal activities to reduce load, and during the mid-morning and late-afternoon peak periods it would eliminate all but essential activities. On Sundays the firm would maintain production at the maximum rate, day and night. This stylized load curve of Figure 16(b) is, in effect, the mirror image of the rate structure depicted above it in Figure 16(a). Although few if any firms are likely to respond so precisely to the incentives of the tariff, this hypothetical example provides a useful standard against which to compare the patterns of actual loads.

Examples of Response in Specific Industries

Actual load measurements from selected industrial plants provide the strongest available evidence of the response of industrial consumers to peak-load pricing

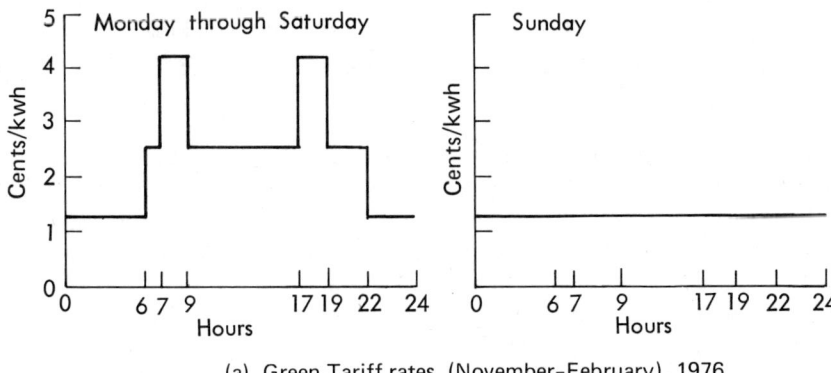

(a) Green Tariff rates (November–February), 1976

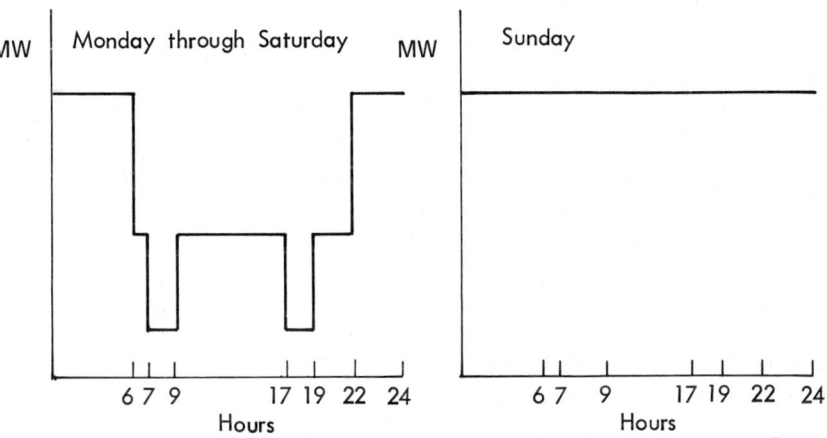

(b) Hypothetical load curve

Figure 16. The Potential Effect of the French Green Tariff on Industrial Loads

and of the ability of certain firms to modulate their loads. To illustrate this responsiveness, examples of daily load curves measured by Electricité de France (EdF) during a recent winter have been selected for examination. These data are drawn from two recent EdF statistical investigations; together they constitute the most extensive body of data available on industrial uses of electricity under peak-load tariffs.

The first EdF study (Pioger 1977a) investigated all industrial customers served at high voltage in two regions of France; these customers account for approximately one-half of all French industrial users served at high voltage. Data were collected for loads measured on Wednesday, Saturday, and Sunday of the third week in December 1974.[2] Nearly all of these customers require substantial

2. Historically, this is the week most likely to include the system annual peak demand.

amounts of power 24 hours a day, 7 days a week. The second load study (Pelletier 1977) was conducted in the Lyons region in 1973 using a sample of 190 medium-voltage customers.

The Cement Industry. Figure 17 shows typical winter load curves of a large French cement manufacturing plant. On weekdays and Saturday the three-period tariff is in effect. The response in the peak hours (7 a.m. to 9 a.m. and 5 p.m. to 7 p.m.) is dramatic; about 50 percent of the peak load is shed during each of the daily peak periods. In addition, average load is reduced somewhat on workdays during the remaining daytime (shoulder) hours. However, on Sunday, when only the off-peak price applies, the load is essentially constant for the entire 24-hour period at the maximum level observed on weekdays. The empirically observed behavior of this plant bears a striking resemblance to the hypothesized response of the ideal firm in Figure 16(b).

Figure 18 shows the weekday load curves for the same plant in each of the four seasons. The pronounced 7 a.m. to 9 a.m. and 5 p.m. to 7 p.m. dips during the peak hours in December are not present in March, June, and September, the months in which only shoulder (6 a.m. to 10 p.m.) and off-peak (10 p.m. to 6 a.m.) prices apply. Instead, there is a consistent daytime-nighttime load differential of 40 to 50 percent. This seasonal differentiation in hourly load confirms the incentive effect of both the peak-period rate itself and the overall effect of the three-period rate structure.

Because electricity costs are a significant proportion of value-added in the French cement industry, cement plants have strong incentives to make the most economical use of power. These plants are normally staffed in three shifts. Although the quarry, kiln, and packing processes run continuously (the kiln is typically fueled by coal or natural gas, with electrical accessories), load can be modulated by shutting off some or all of the cement mills and the raw mills that

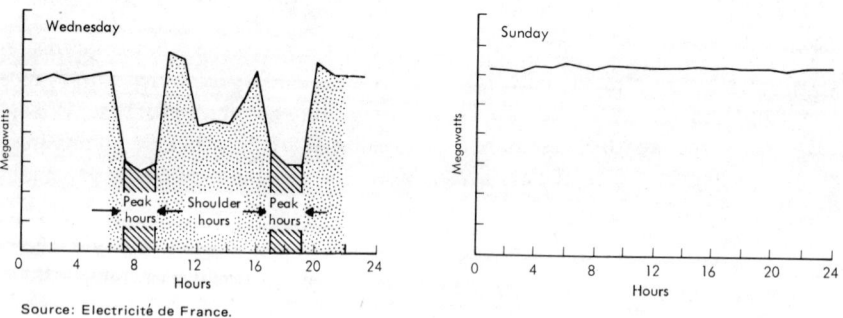

Source: Electricité de France.

Figure 17. Winter Load Curves for a French Cement Plant

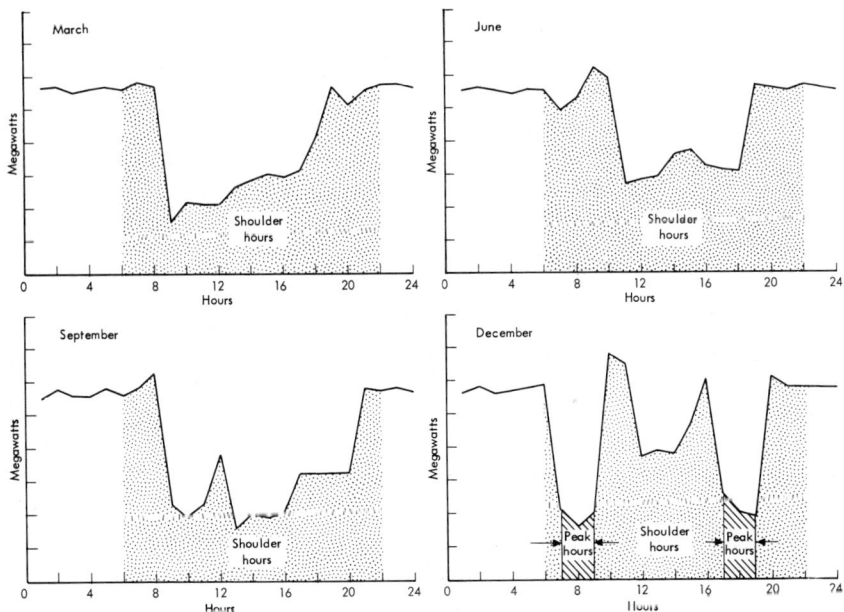

Source: Electricité de France.

Figure 18. Midweek Load Curves for a French Cement Plant in Four Seasons of the Year

are used to grind and crush stone.[3] Milling machinery requires frequent regular maintenance in order to keep equipment in good condition and to ensure a gradation of sizes of the crushed stone that will economize on operating costs. Maintenance is routinely scheduled during the peak and shoulder tariff hours.

Cement plants exhibit the greatest load modulation when the demand for their product is less than their production capacity. Plants are typically constructed in anticipation of growing demand so that during the initial years of operation they can operate predominantly at night and yet produce sufficient product.

Cement plants have only limited ability to modulate load by season. To some extent, however, they are run at maximum rates in the summer, and the more extensive maintenance is done during the winter; this practice coincides with seasonality of product demand. Clinker (an intermediate product) is accumulated in the spring, and even stored in the open when silo capacity is fully used.

3. Control is automatic in a few plants. In most installations, however, a production engineer monitors the kilowatt meter and manually turns off mills when demand exceeds the subscribed level.

94 The European Experience

The load curves of individual customers, such as those of the cement plant just described, provide clear evidence of the responsiveness of these customers to the structure of the electricity tariff. The extent to which such load modulation can be practiced throughout the industry is illustrated by the aggregate daily load curves for the cement plants located in the two major industrial areas of France for which data are available. As shown in Figure 19, the combined weekday loads of several plants in these regions are closely parallel to the weekday pattern of the individual plant just discussed.

Ferro-Alloys, Iron and Steel, and Electrometallurgy. In this industrial group a variety of processes lend themselves to some degree of electricity load management. Electrical smelting furnaces can be slowed down, or—where there are several furnaces in one plant—the smelting periods can be staggered. Because

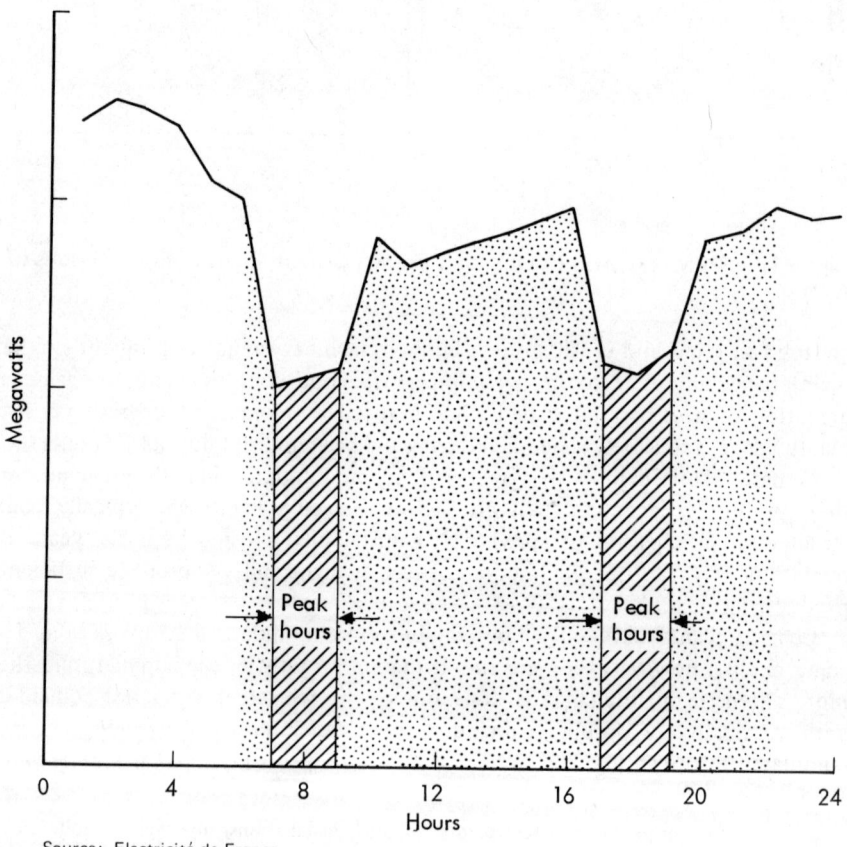

Source: Electricité de France.

Figure 19. Winter Weekday Load Curve for a Sample from the French Cement Industry

ovens retain heat well over short intervals, load modulation during short tariff periods need not disrupt production, and furnaces used to heat ingots prior to running them into rolling mills can be shut off during peak hours. Similarly, the maintenance for rolling mills can be scheduled during peak hours.

A number of plants in this industry generate some of their own power by using waste heat, steam, or gases from a primary production process, such as the operation of a blast furnace. In these instances there are opportunities to modulate the amount of electricity purchased from the electric utility by increasing the quantity of self-generated power during peak hours. Self-generation can be increased by using industrial gases produced at other hours and held in storage or by adjusting the rate of production. Finally, certain types of equipment, notably electric arc furnaces, are capable of rapid shutdown without detrimental effect on the process of production.

Figure 20 shows representative winter (December) daily load curves for a large ferro-alloy plant. During peak hours the plant sheds some 80 percent of the load it draws from the utility in both morning and afternoon periods. Outside of peak hours, however, there is no discernible modulation between daytime and nighttime operation for this plant. On Sunday, when only off-peak rates apply, the plant operates uniformly at the maximum weekday level.

In the case of another ferro-alloy plant shown in Figure 21, load is completely shut off during peak hours. The process itself is visibly more irregular from hour to hour, even on Sunday when the price of electricity is constant at all hours. Little difference between daytime and nighttime operation is apparent. The aggregate weekday load curve for the electrometallurgy industry is shown in Figure 22. Significant load reductions—on the order of 200 MW in these regions of France—can occur at peak hours.

Electrochemical Processes. The opportunities to modulate load in the electrochemical industry depend on the nature of the production processes being

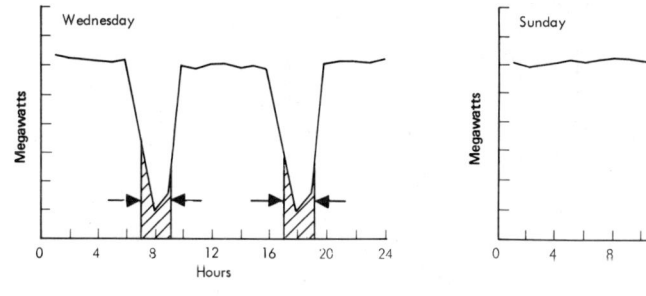

Source: Electricité de France

Figure 20. Winter Load Curves for a French Ferro-alloy Plant

96 The European Experience

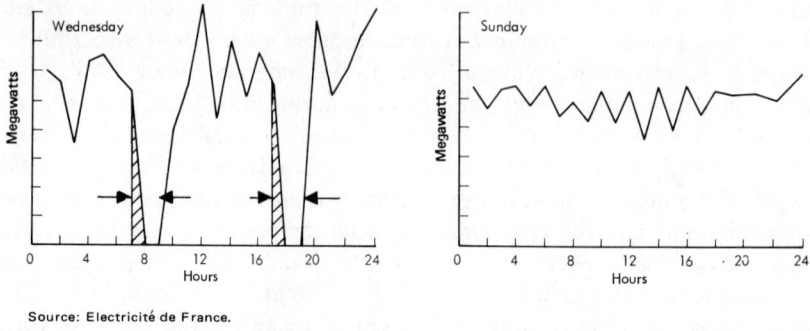

Source: Electricité de France.

Figure 21. Winter Load Curves for a French Ferro-alloy Plant

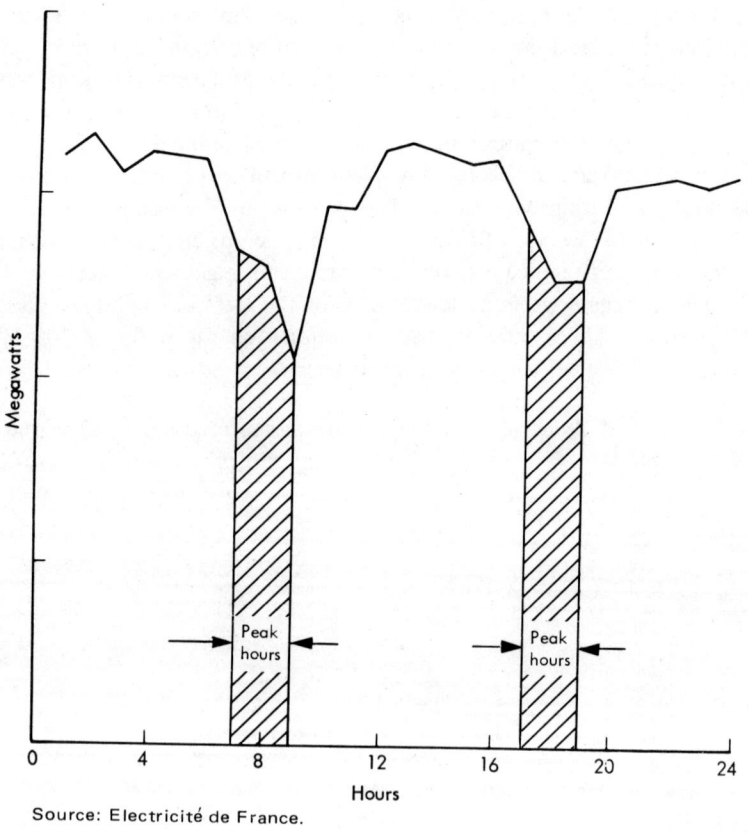

Source: Electricité de France.

Figure 22. Winter Weekday Load Curve for a Sample from the French Electrometallurgy Industry

used. For example, in the production of chlorine by electrolysis, the mercury cell process can be readily adjusted, whereas the diaphragm process must be run continuously. Because steam is required for some electrochemical processes, plants frequently install generators to provide some of their own electricity. To a certain extent the amount of self-generated power can be regulated so as to reduce the load on the utility at peak hours. Since the production of liquified industrial gases can be totally stopped on short notice, liquefaction plants are amenable to special contracts for interruptible power.

The aggregate load response of electrochemical plants in two regions of France is shown in Figure 23. Here, in contrast to the industries already discussed, the response is far smaller at the peak hours, reflecting the more limited degree of modulation that can be achieved. The relative smoothness of the aggregate curve is indicative of the averaging effect of measuring total response when individual plants have load patterns that do not coincide.

Transportation of Liquids and Gases. Customers in the business of transporting and distributing liquids or gases by pipeline show a moderate to total ability to curtail load during peak hours. The load curves of two water-pumping plants are shown in Figure 24(a) and (b). The first plant is regularly able to

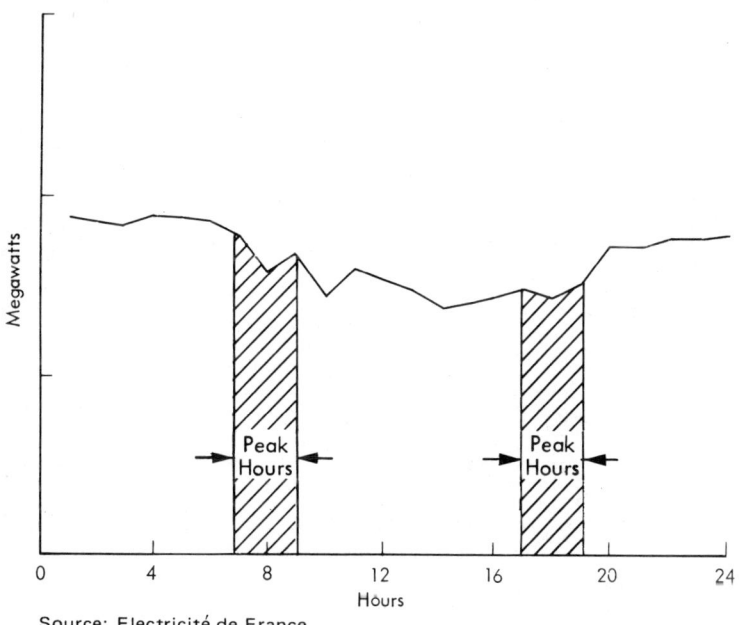

Source: Electricité de France.

Figure 23. Winter Weekday Load Curve for a Sample from the French Electrochemical Industry

Figure 24. Winter Load Curves for Liquid and Gas Transportation

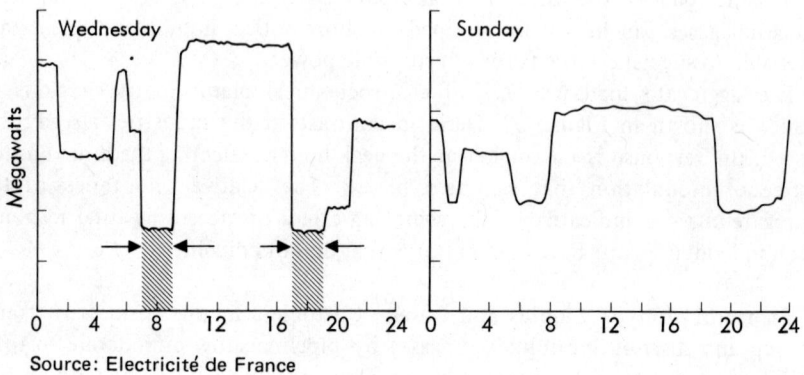

Source: Electricité de France

Figure 24a. French Water-Pumping Plant

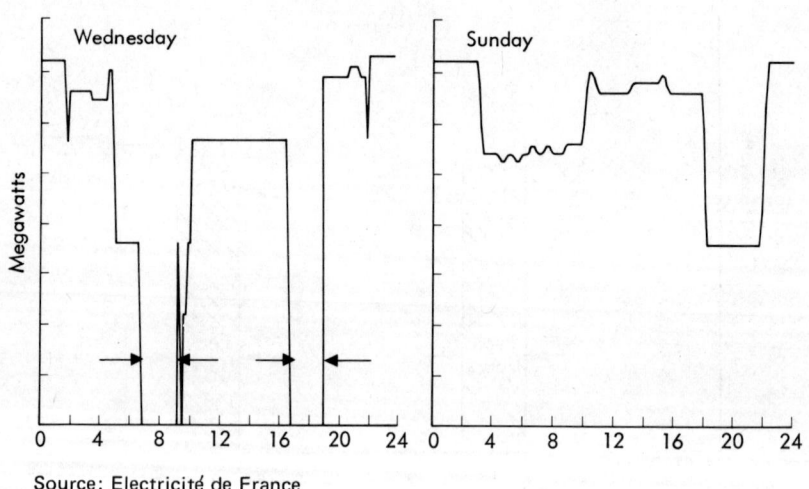

Source: Electricité de France

Figure 24b. French Water-Pumping Plant

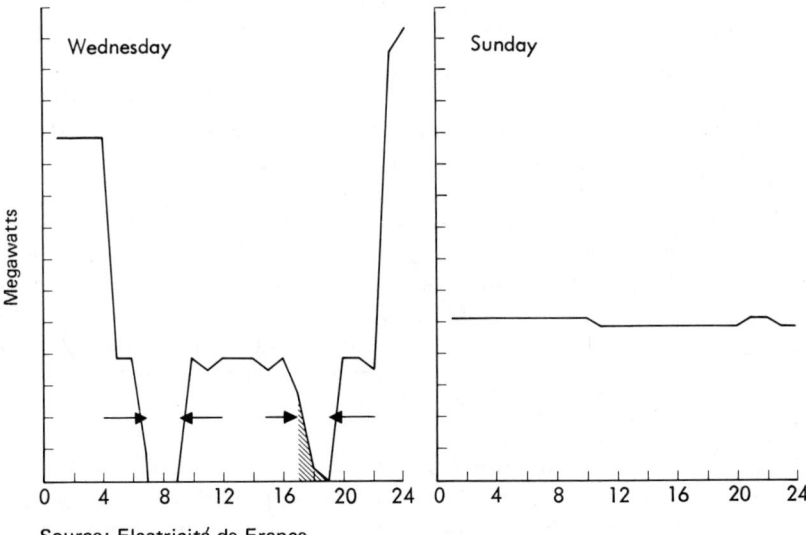

Figure 24c. French Petroleum Pipeline

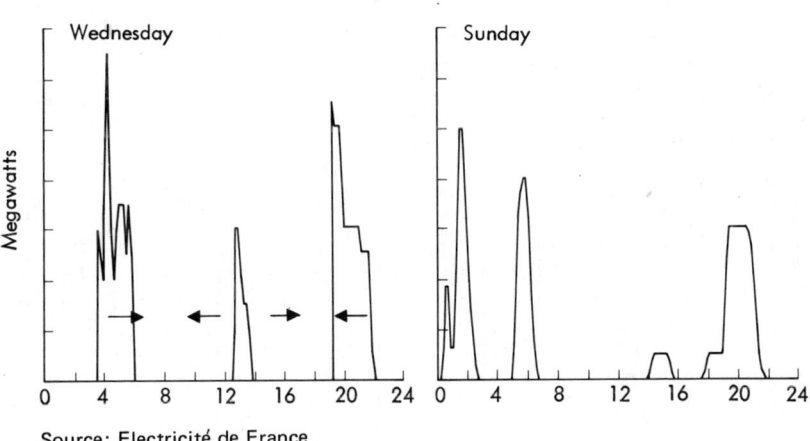

Figure 24d. French Natural Gas Transportation Plant

reduce peak-hour loads by about 65 percent, while the second one effectively interrupts pumping operations altogether. The load of the petroleum pipeline in Figure 24(c) can be similarly adjusted.[4] In Figure 24(d) one can observe the intermittent nature of the power demands for transportation of natural gas, which lend themselves to scheduling outside of peak hours.

Cold Storage. Firms that supply cold-storage and freezing services can take advantage of the insulation characteristics of their warehouses and lockers to chill storage spaces during off-peak hours and then to maintain cold temperatures during peak periods with relatively little power. Figure 25 illustrates load reductions of up to 88 percent at peak hours in one plant. In a less extreme fashion, a commercial firm in the trade sector that supplies meat and fish reduces peak loads on weekdays (see Figure 26).

Other Commercial and Industrial Customers. Some additional examples are found in the load curves of the water purification plant in Figure 27 and the raw materials and fuels supply firms in Figure 28. Finally, the important possibility of modulating loads in the service sector is illustrated by the load curves (Figure 29) of a financial institution.

Self-Generation

A wide variety of large firms in France have facilities for generating electricity to meet at least some of their own requirements for power. The bulk of self-generating capacity is concentrated in the coal, railroad, and steel industries. Some self-generation is also practiced by firms engaged in refining of petroleum

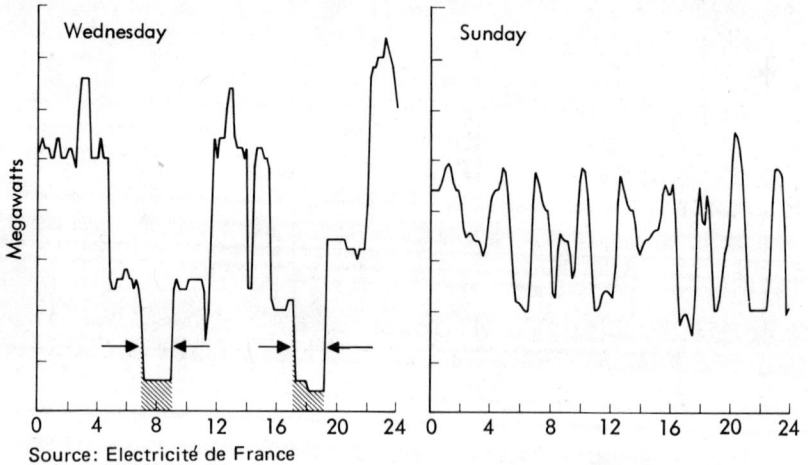

Source: Electricité de France

Figure 25. Winter Load Curves for a French Cold Storage Plant

[4]. The petroleum pipeline is the one example in this section of a plant served at high, rather than medium, voltage.

The Response of European Industries to Peak-Load Tariffs 101

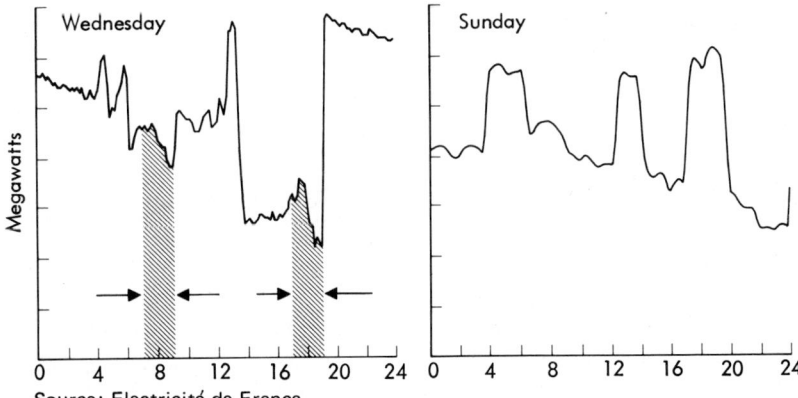

Source: Electricité de France

Figure 26. Winter Load Curves for a French Commercial Meat and Fish Supplier

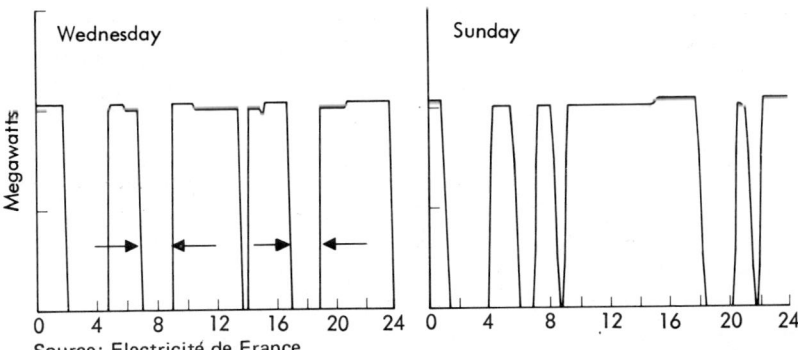

Source: Electricité de France

Figure 27. Winter Load Curves for a French Water Purification Plant

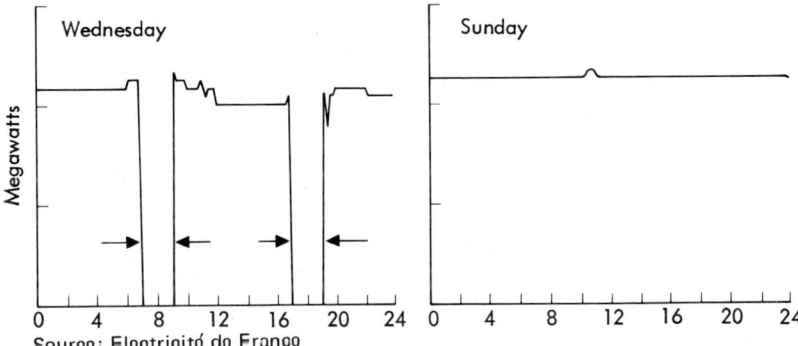

Source: Electricité de France

Figure 28. Winter Load Curves for a French Raw Materials and Fuel Supply Firm

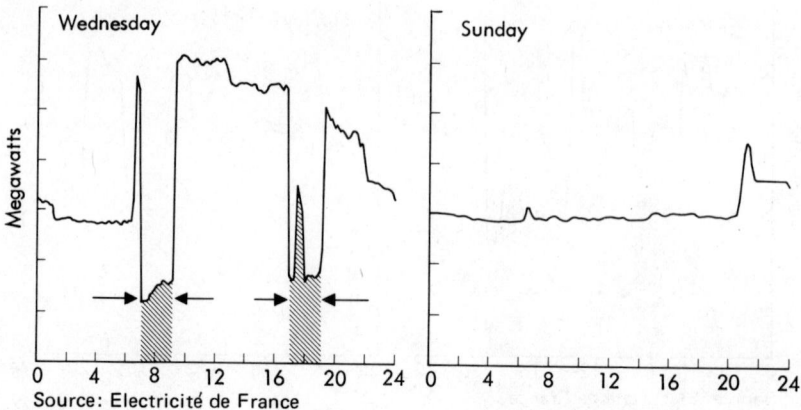

Figure 29. Winter Load Curves for a French Financial Institution

products, aluminum production, paper and pulp production, manufacturing of synthetic fibers, and in numerous branches of the chemical industry—particularly in the production of chlorine, acids, compressed and liquefied gases, and plastics.

Nearly all of this capacity consists of thermal generation of electricity. In some instances firms use self-standing oil-fired generating units, but more often they are able to use either by-product gases or waste heat contained in industrial steam to generate electricity. In industries that require large amounts of water for their production processes, firms occasionally have their own hydroelectric generating facilities; examples are found in plants that produce paper and pulp, powder and explosives, and carborundum.

At high voltage, a number of French firms have a sizable amount of self-generation capacity available to augment EdF's capacity. In 1975 EdF's total annual maximum demand from the high-voltage sample of some 250 French plants was about 3300 MW. These customers had in addition nearly 1000 MW of self-generating capacity, about 30 percent of the effective maximum EdF high-voltage demand in these regions of France. Customers with self-generation units purchase standby capacity from EdF to protect themselves against forced outages of their own units. The EdF emergency tariff for this purpose is similar to the short-utilization verision of the Green Tariff, except that it imposes a higher charge for subscribed power (see Table 15).

Where firms have sufficient self-generating capacity available, they have the possibility of modulating their EdF load and economizing on power drawn in peak and shoulder hours. This response to the Green Tariff is illustrated in the following two examples.

Petroleum Refining. The load curves in Figure 30(a) and (b) are those of a modern French refinery that requires a nearly constant amount of electricity for its continuous production processes. However, during the peak and shoulder

The Response of European Industries to Peak-Load Tariffs 103

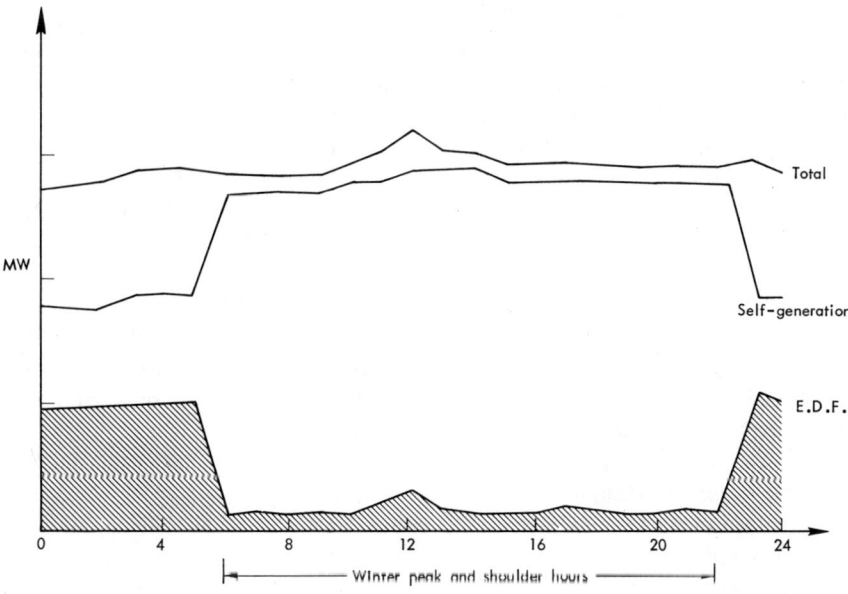

Figure 30a. December

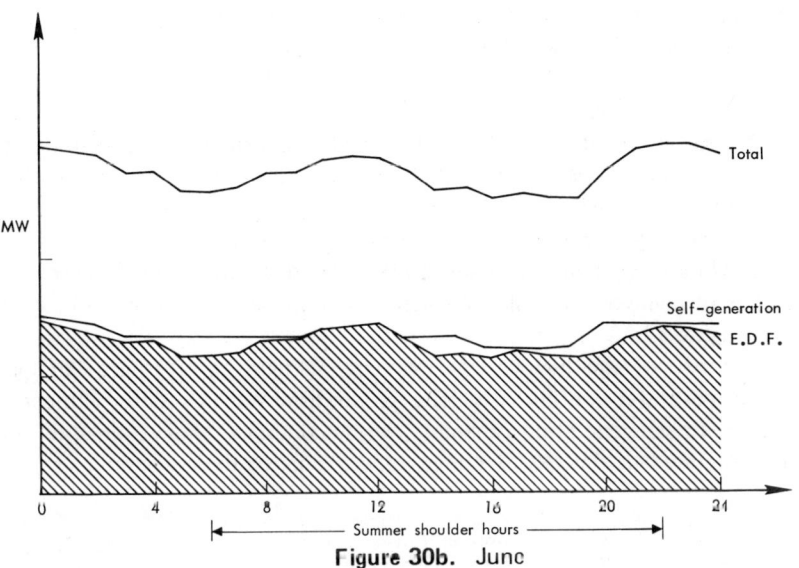

Figure 30b. June

Source: Electricité de France
Figure 30. Winter and Summer Load Curves for a French Petroleum Refinery with Self-Generation

hours on winter weekdays (Figure 30[b]), it increases production from its own generators and is able to reduce its EdF load by about 90 percent, thereby economizing on the high peak- and shoulder-hour energy charges.[5] In the summer season (Figure 30[b]), when there is no peak rate and the shoulder rate is lower, a contrasting load pattern is found. In this season the firm runs its own generators at a nearly constant level equal to about one-half of its power requirements, and uses electricity from EdF to accommodate variations in total quality of electricity required for production.

Electrochemicals. Figure 31 shows the winter weekday load curves of an electrochemical plant with a relatively small amount of self-generating capacity. In this instance, the plant is able to operate at reduced total power during peak hours and chooses to modulate its EdF load while keeping its own generation at an approximately constant level.

Interruptible Customers

In addition to the regular versions of the Green Tariff, EdF has an optional tariff for interruptible service to industrial customers. This tariff has the same structure as the Green Tariff but provides for discounts on the charge for subscribed power based on the number of kilowatts that can be interrupted.

Under terms of this service, EdF notifies customers of an impending break in service that will occur either immediately or from 2 to 24 hours later, depending on the specific contract. Some 300 MW of demand in steel mills and chemical plants can be shut off with short notice.

Other Industries

The strong pattern of reduced demand at peak and shoulder hours in the industries reviewed above is evidence of the potency of the time-of-day incentives in the Green Tariff. Despite these financial inducements to shift uses of electricity, the majority of French industrial firms have loads during peak hours that are equal to or greater than their loads in off-peak hours. Pioger's (1977a) statistical analysis of high-voltage customers identifies four basic types of load curves, shown in Figure 32.[6]

The majority of the high-voltage customers (Figure 32[a]) have flat load curves and use power continuously. This group, however, includes a number of customers with self-generation capability whose *combined* load—from EdF plus that self-generated—is flat. As described above, some of these customers reduce

---

5. This firm subscribes to a uniform level of demand in all five tariff periods. The fact that it nevertheless modulates its load during peak and shoulder periods is compelling evidence of the incentive effects of the kilowatt-hour charges alone.

6. In this study the 258 customers were consolidated into 147 entities by combining all substations serving the national railway, deleting a small number of firms with zero consumption or anomalous data, and using the total load of firms with self-generating facilities.

The Response of European Industries to Peak-Load Tariffs 105

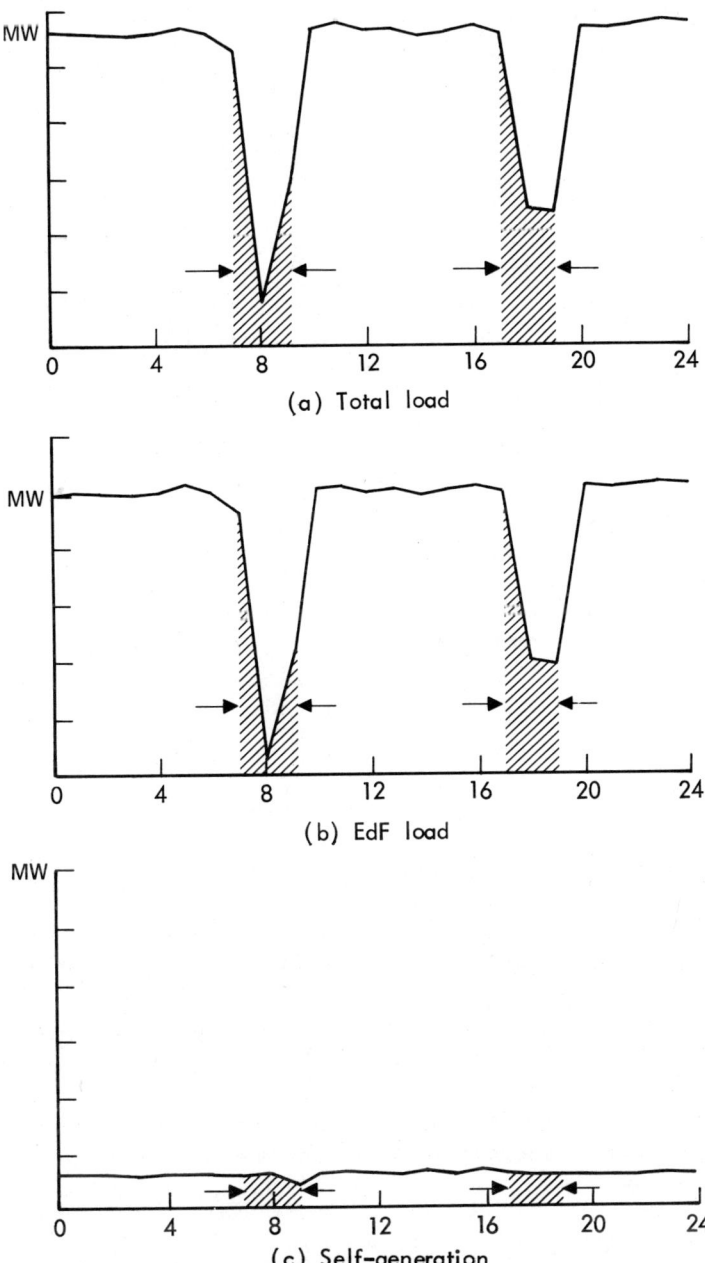

Source: Electricité de France

Figure 31. Winter Load Curves for a French Electrochemical Firm with Self-Generation

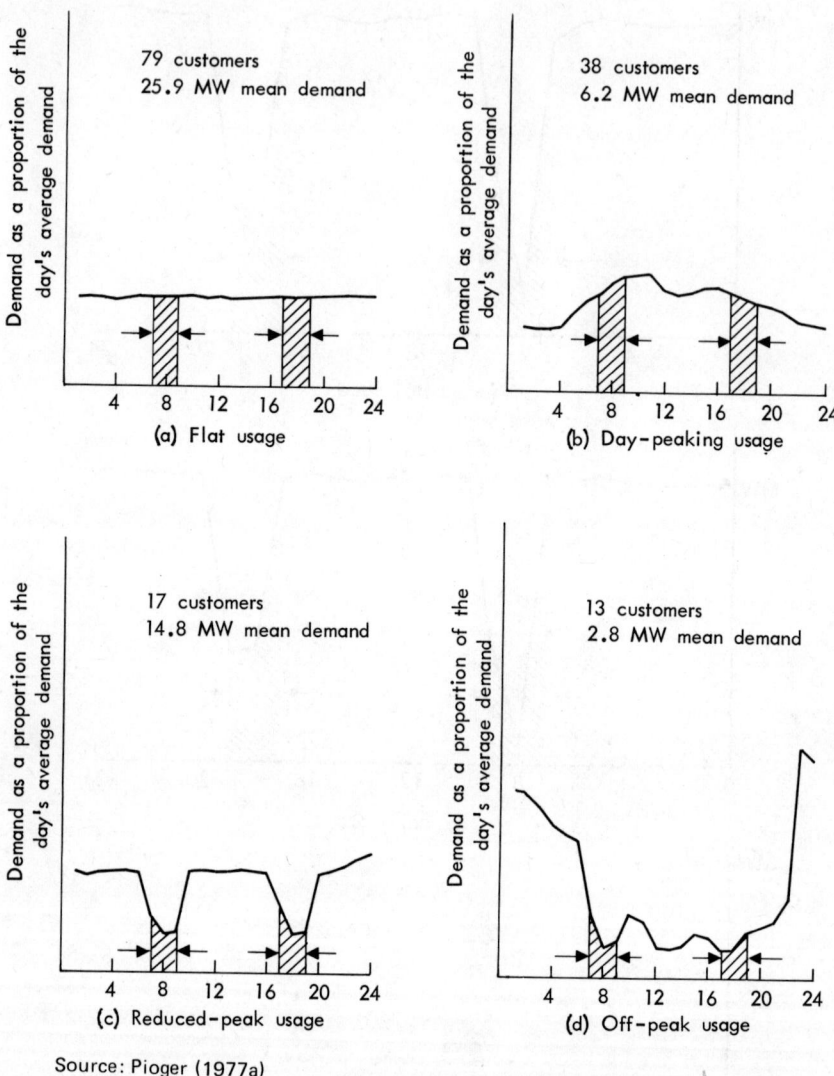

Source: Pioger (1977a)

Figure 32. Classification of Load Curves of French High-Voltage Industrial Customers—December Weekday, 1974 (hours of peak prices are shaded)

their EdF load during peak and shoulder hours. The load curves of a second group (Figure 32[b]) follow a regular daily pattern that corresponds closely to the pattern of business activities, reaching a peak in the late morning and a second, somewhat lower, peak in the early afternoon. Two smaller groups of customers correspond to the detailed examples of load reductions described above. These industrial firms modulate their power usage in order to economize on charges during either the morning and afternoon peak hours (Figure 32[c]), or during the entire 6 a.m.–10 p.m. period of peak and shoulder hours (Figure 32[d]).

The fact that many industrial customers have their greatest loads during peak hours does not necessarily mean that the Green Tariff has had no effect on their electricity consumption through the years. The present day load curves of individual industries—such as aluminum refining, automobiles, and aircraft, as well as subways and railways, show maximum usage of electricity during peak or shoulder hours. However, without load-curve data for the same firms supplied under a tariff with uniform pricing at all hours, it is not possible to infer that such industries have made no reductions in peak-period demands. All one can say is that the changes, if any, have not been large enough to reduce their loads below those occurring in off-peak hours. In some operations, perhaps subways and aluminum refining, the tariff is unlikely to have had any effect at all on the total use of electricity. In others, high prices during hours of greatest usage may have encouraged industries to use processes with greater electrical efficiencies and thus reduce loads at all hours of the day. In Chapter 8, where the potential for load-shifting in the United States is assessed, the inferential problems associated with use of data from contemporary load patterns in France to measure the quantitative effects of introducing peak-load tariffs will be considered in some detail.

ENGLAND AND WALES

As described in Chapter 4, electricity in England and Wales is distributed by twelve publicly-owned area boards that set their own tariffs on the basis of their costs of local distribution and the cost of power purchased at wholesale under the Bulk Supply Tariff. The industrial customers in most regions in England and Wales have a choice between tariffs with and without time-of-day rates, and firms that are able to modulate their loads will select a peak-load rate. Furthermore, a customer who uses a significant quantity of electricity at night or who has a fairly flat load curve will usually find that the time-of-day rate is cheaper, even if he cannot alter his pattern of consumption.

British and French pricing practices differ in several important respects. While all French industrial customers face a rate structure with the mandatory time-of-day provisions of the Green Tariff, British customers may voluntarily select to be billed under time-of-day rates. Moreover, French plants face two short, 2-hour peak periods, a long shoulder period, and an overnight off-peak period with differences between periods of several cents in the effective price per kilowatt-hour. In contrast, British plants that choose time-of-day rates are offered only a single, very long peak period of some 10 or more hours with a much smaller difference—about 1¢ per kilowatt hour (about one-half the peak-period price)—between peak and off-peak periods.

Load Response in Specific Industries

Despite the important differences in the specific price incentives in the tariffs on both sides of the English Channel, the degree of the load response to peak-load tariffs of firms that operate similar processes is much the same in England and Wales as in France.

Cement. As Figure 33(a) indicates, an English cement plant that selects service under a time-of-day tariff is able to reduce more than 50 percent of its load during the winter weekday peak period from 8:00 a.m. to 6:00 p.m. This plant is billed for maximum demand in other hours at a reduced rate if its off-peak demand exceeds its on-peak demand. Figure 33(b) shows how the same

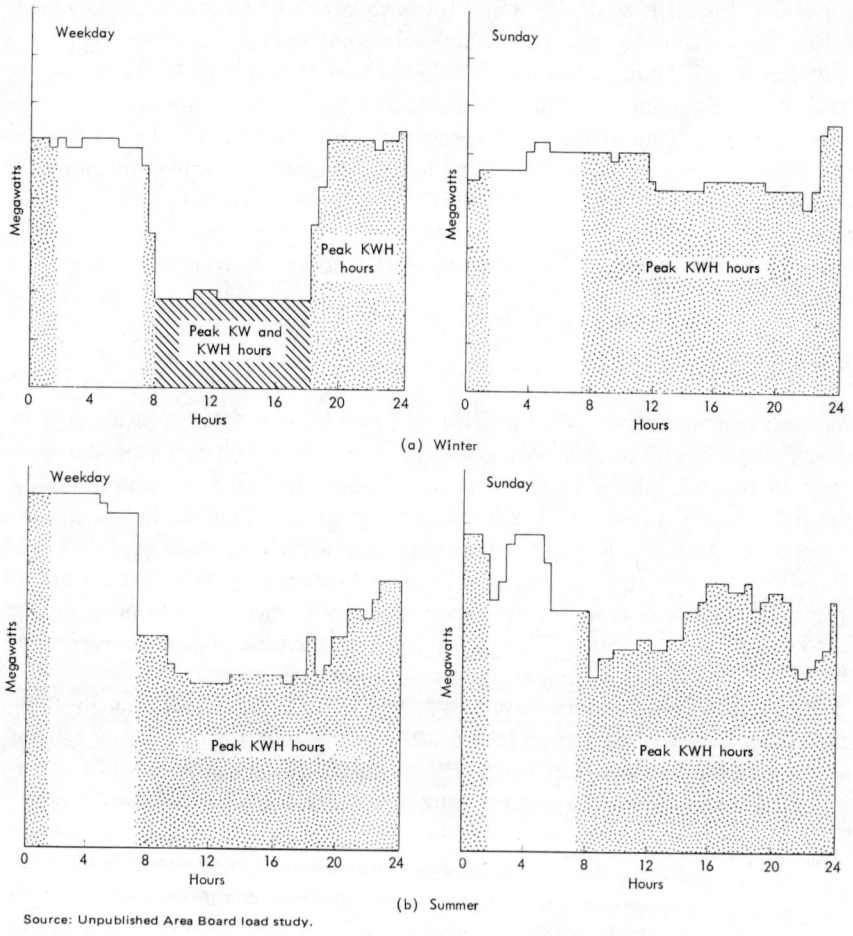

Source: Unpublished Area Board load study.

Figure 33. Load Curves for an English Cement Plant

plant responds to the time-of-day energy rates by reducing its peak demand during the summer, when it faces only peak-load energy charges from 7:30 a.m. until 1:30 a.m. the next day.

These reductions are comparable to those in the French cement industry (see Figure 19), which sheds about 40 percent of its load in response to the 4-hour peak-load periods of the Green Tariff. The British load curves indicate that a 1¢ summertime differential between peak and off-peak rates is sufficient to induce a marked response in the cement industry even when the peak period is as long as 18 hours.[7]

Petroleum Refining. One English petroleum firm is able to lower its peak-period consumption of electricity by using about 20 MW of power generated from back-pressure steam available from its refining process. Because of its self-generation capacity, this firm has a special arrangement under which it pays a higher energy charge from 7:30 a.m. until 1:30 a.m. the following day, and a higher maximum demand charge on winter weekdays from 7:30 a.m. to 7:30 p.m. As Figure 34 indicates, the weekday demand is lower during the daytime, and on Sunday follows the same pattern of lower demand when the higher rates for energy—but not demand—also prevail. The greater reductions during the weekday peak period are accounted for by the combined effects of kilowatt-hour and kilowatt charges on weekdays.

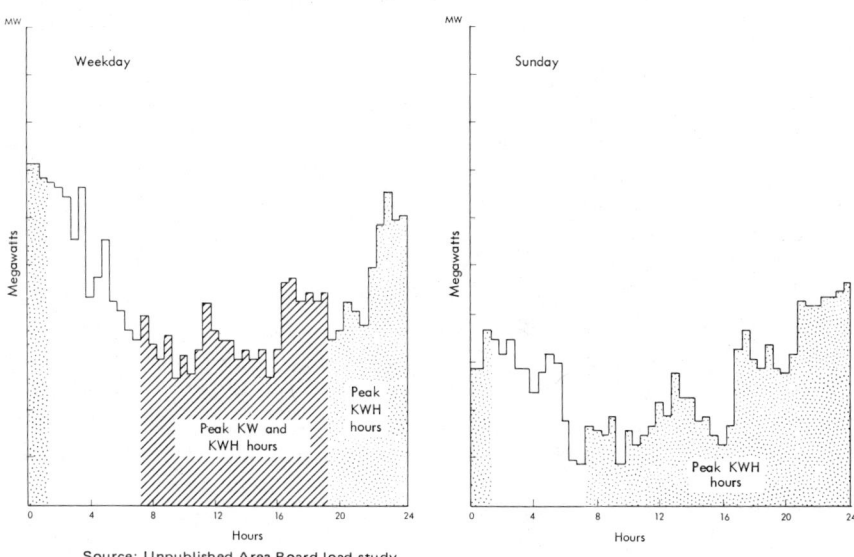

Figure 34. Winter Load Curves for an English Petroleum Refinery

7. The energy rates are 2.03¢/kwh during peak periods and 1.02¢/kwh during off-peak periods. Maximum-demand charges are levied only during the winter months.

Industrial Gases. A firm producing industrial gases in several plants throughout the country responds differently to the various tariffs offered by the area boards serving the regions in which the firm's plants are located. The nature of the response varies with the terms of the tariff and the demand for the firm's product. Where one board has a charge for maximum demand during the peak hours on winter weekdays, the firm routinely operates its liquifying process only during the off-peak (weeknight and weekend) hours. The same plant does not respond to the differential time-of-day energy rates during the summer. When its customers require continuous gaseous feed, little of the industrial gas firm's load can be shifted or dropped. In other plants having tariffs with smaller daytime/nighttime rate differentials, the operations are run at a uniform level 24 hours a day.

Foundries. At least one area board supplies several medium-sized foundries under time-of-day tariffs. A plant producing pig iron operates with additional overnight and weekend capacity in the winter and achieves a saving of about 2 percent in total cost, net of additional labor costs for shift differentials. Another foundry, which produces large steel castings, is able to meet all of its winter mold shop requirements by using its arc furnaces for melting during off-peak periods. In doing so it has shifted nearly 9 million kwh—out of a total demand of 10.6 million kwh—from peak periods to off-peak periods.[8]

Other Industries. Load curves for broadly defined industries confirm the French experience that some industries can respond significantly to published time-of-day rates, while other industries do not make a change that results in lower peak than off-peak consumption. Figures 35 and 36, from a recent Electricity Council load study of 350 large industrial consumers, show that two industrial groups—the chemical and allied trades and the bricks/pottery/glass/cement works—have lower demands from 8 a.m. to 10 p.m. than during the rest of the day; the other industrial groups studied had flat or day-peaking load curves. These data establish that these two industrial groups are responsive to voluntary time-of-day pricing and can achieve about a 25 percent reduction in demand during peak hours. From all but one of the area boards, firms can obtain about a 50 percent discount on energy used during nighttime production, roughly between midnight and 8 a.m., which provides the principal incentive to use more electricity during the night.[9]

The load reductions in Figures 35 and 36 do not show the sharply defined responses observed for similar French industries. The English and Welsh tariffs tend to rely on kilowatt-hour charges for time-of-day pricing rather than on the

---

8. See Harmsworth (1975).
9. Some area boards reinforce this incentive by exempting nighttime consumption from demand charges.

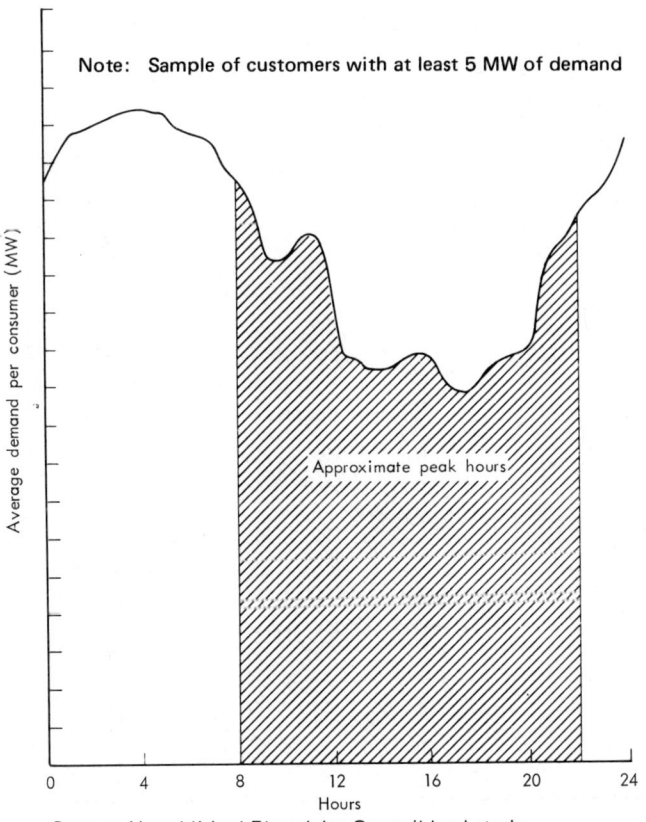

Source: Unpublished Electricity Council load study.

Figure 35. Average Winter Weekday Load Curve for the Chemical and Allied Industries in England and Wales

mix of both kilowatt-hour and kilowatt charges used in France. As a result the response patterns in the load curves of a sample of firms in Figures 35 and 36 should be smoother than those observed for the same industries in France, where the kilowatt charges for different periods of the day heavily penalize failure to reduce load sharply at the beginning of the tariff period. This discrepancy in industrial behavior is also partly due to a statistical artifact. In the case of the French data, all firms faced precisely the same hours for the peak, shoulder, and off-peak tariff periods. In England and Wales, however, the hours vary from one area board to another.[10] In fact, some area boards stagger the hours from customer to customer in order to smooth out the distributional load. As a result, in Figures 35 and 36 a few customers are starting their off-peak period as early as

10. See Table 18.

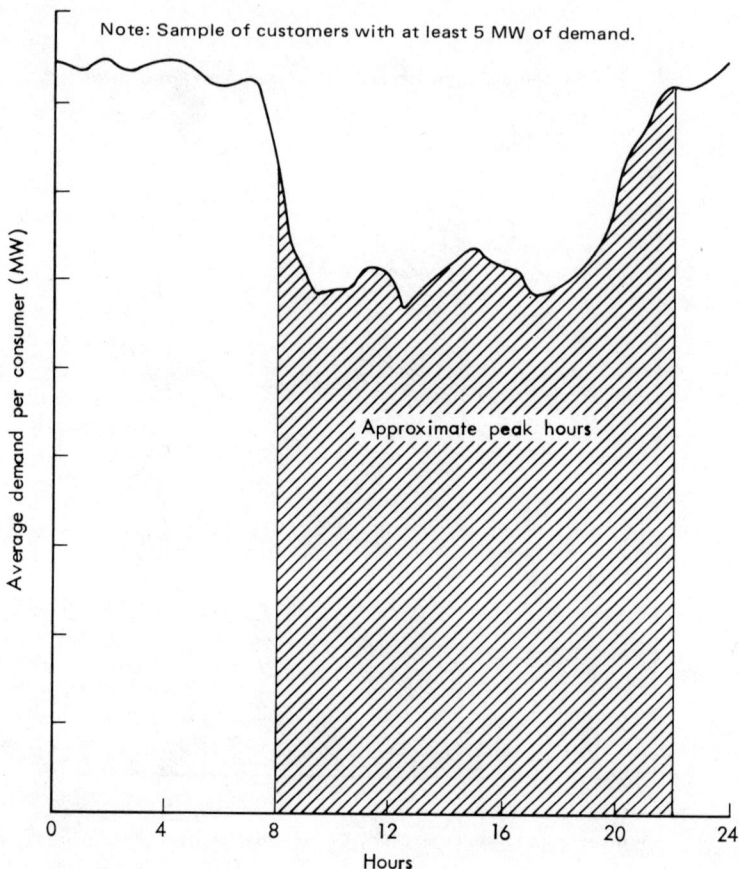

Figure 36. Average Winter Weekday Load Curve for the Brick, Pottery, Glass, and Cement Industries in England and Wales

11 p.m. and ending at 7 a.m., while others start as late as 1 a.m. and run to 9 a.m.

Area boards stand ready to negotiate the purchase of electricity generated by industrial firms, typically as a by-product of the production of industrial heat. Although these transactions accounted for only 0.2 percent of the total kilowatt-hours consumed in 1974/75, the existence of a market for privately generated power will provide some encouragement to firms with sources of waste heat to install generators when the board's purchase terms are sufficiently attractive.

Potential Peak Warnings (PPWs)

A particularly striking feature of the English and Welsh tariff system for higher-voltage consumers is the rather extensive use by some large industrial customers of a tariff for the voluntary interruption of power. As noted in Chapter 4, during the peak season (November-February) the operating division of the Central Electricity Generating Board (CEGB) prepares a daily forecast of the generating capacity available for the next day. When a shortage is predicted the CEGB issues a PPW to the area boards covering specified hours for the following day. In their turn, the area boards notify each of their customers supplied under the PPW tariff by telex. Each customer is responsible for shedding the amount of load agreed upon for the warning hours specified.

For a PPW contract to be implemented, it must be mutually advantageous for the area board and for the customer. Before the board will offer a PPW tariff, the customer must have a telex terminal (to ensure prompt and reliable communications), a staff ready to implement load-shedding procedures (to ensure compliance), and a sheddable load large enough to cover the administrative and metering costs incurred. For the PPW clause to be to the customer's advantage, he must have processes that can be quickly turned off for short periods of time or the ability to store intermediate products at a cost less than the savings in electricity charges.

The nature of the potential peak warning responses is illustrated by the behavior of two firms. As Figure 37 indicates, a steel company operating arc furnaces is able to shed about 60 MW (over 95 percent) of its load in order to save the $7.16 per kilowatt charge it faces for demand during warning periods. A producer of industrial gases has PPW clauses in contracts for two different plants. One plant that produces only liquefied gases reduces its demand almost 80 percent by turning off its liquefiers. Another plant, producing both liquefied gas and a direct gaseous feed, sheds about 53 percent of its load by turning off liquefiers and throttling back other processes to the level demanded by the customers to whom it supplies direct gaseous feed. This plant does not have PPW clauses covering its gaseous production, because the customers for its direct gaseous feed require a continuous input to their own processes.

Although data on PPW contracts and responses are not generally available, we do know that a sample of PPW customers was able to shed nearly 40 percent of its load during a recent PPW day; the response during the PPW periods is seen in the shaded hours in Figure 38. In total, the load shed by the nearly 125 PPW customers in England and Wales is between 1100 MW and 1200 MW during a typical warning period.[11] This amount represents nearly 11 percent of the entire industrial load in all of England and Wales and 3 percent of the system's wintertime peak load.

SWEDEN

In reviewing the tariffs of the Swedish State Power Board in Chapter 4, we observed the use of an unusual 6-hour maximum demand rate to reflect peak

---

11. These data are from an internal Electricity Council load forecast paper.

114 The European Experience

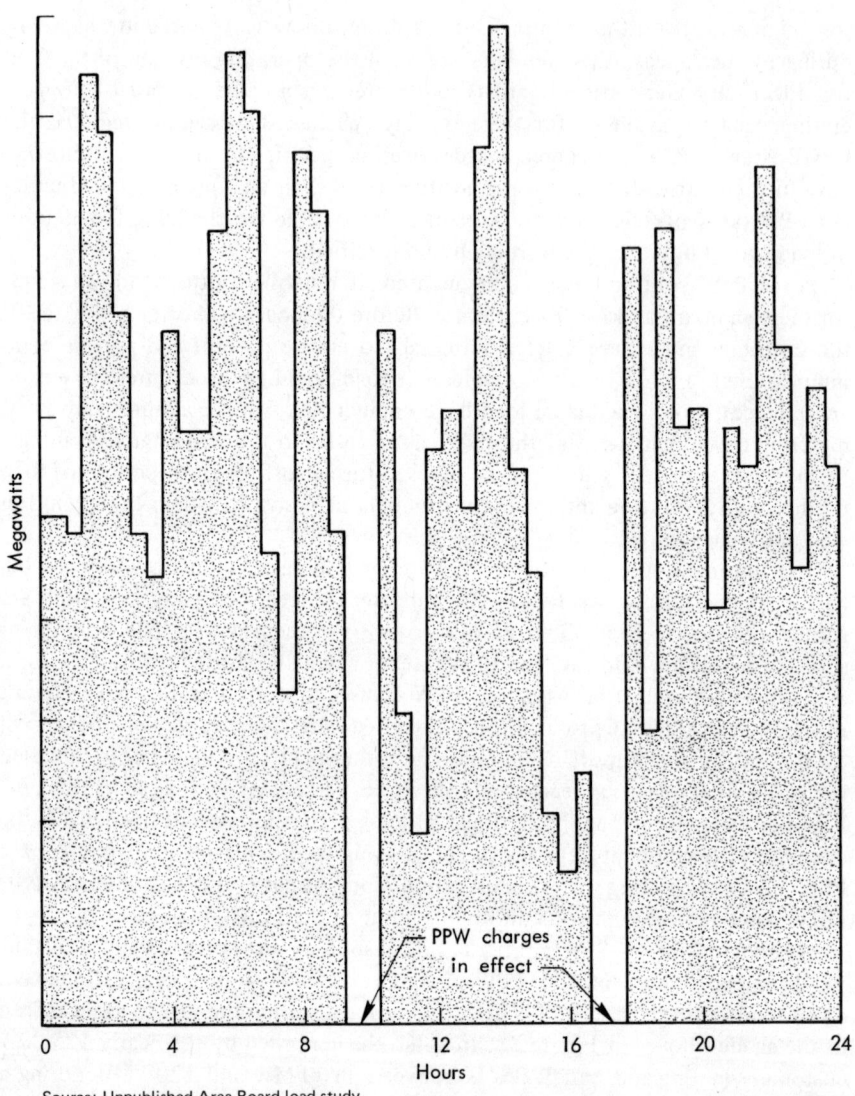

Source: Unpublished Area Board load study.

Figure 37. Load Curve for an English Steel Company during a Potential Peak Warning (PPW): 9 to 10 a.m. and 4:30 to 5:30 p.m.

capacity costs of generating and distributing electricity to high-voltage consumers in the predominantly hydroelectric national system. In this northern climate, the 6-hour peak demand of most industrial customers is nearly coincident with the system peak on winter days, and it is therefore difficult to detect directly a time-of-day response. Load-curve data for industrial users that select

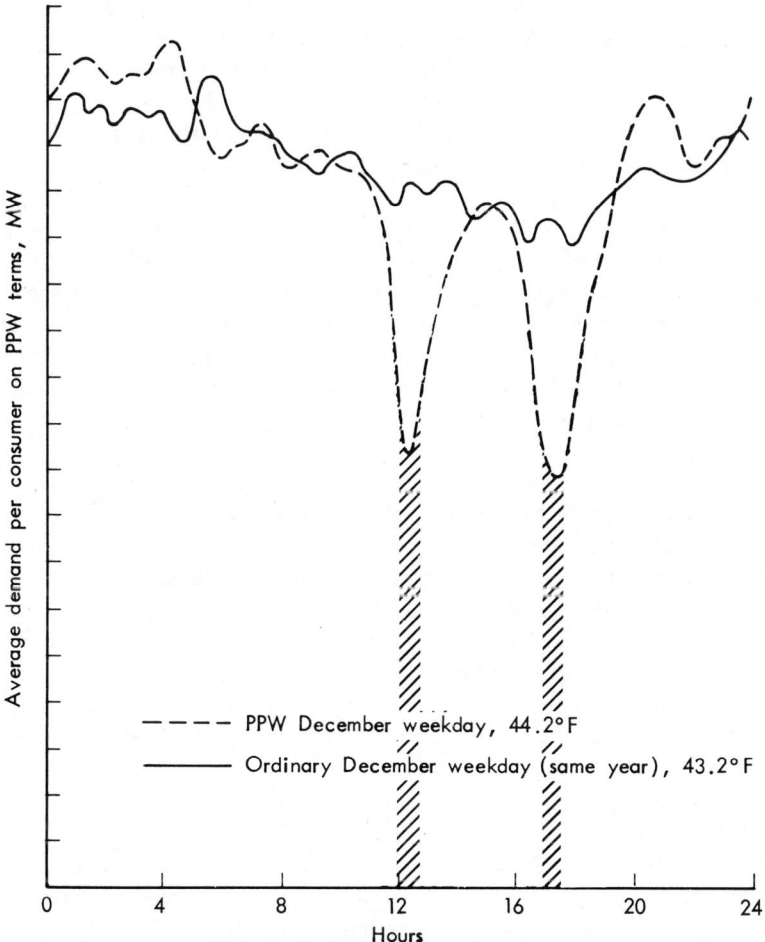

Source: Unpublished Electricity Council load study.

Figure 38. Response to Potential Peak Warnings (PPWs) by a Sample of British Industrial Customers

the optional tariff that provides for disconnection of the demand meter during nighttime hours were not readily available.

Time-of-Day Rates. Several of the larger municipal utilities generate much of their own power for distribution to retail customers, and take advantage of steam used for district heating to drive back-pressure turbines. This type of generation achieves quite high fuel efficiencies for the combined heating/generating processes. In such circumstances the low opportunity cost of nighttime steam justifies a time-of-day tariff.

Although it has such a time-of-day rate, the Stockholm municipal utility has observed little industrial response to its peak-load tariff, since most of the industry near Stockholm is supplied directly by the State Power Board. Nevertheless, there has been some commercial response. One large office building uses off-peak power to charge its storage heating system. Its daytime demand is 1400 kw, compared with a nighttime demand of 2800 kw.

Self-Generation. The Swedish State Power Board has an important provision in its high-voltage tariffs that encourages self-generation of electricity by large customers. The board permits private firms that generate some of their own power, as well as municipal and private utilities, to transmit energy by "wheeling" electricity from one area to another over the national grid. This practice arose because hydroelectric facilities for many companies and utilities are located in the north of Sweden, while most of the population and industry is located in the southern and central areas.

A firm that has its own generating units has both a regular contract for power produced and delivered by the State Power Board, and a reserve-supply contract covering purchases in the event that its own units fail. The reserve-supply contract contains two important provisions. First, the self-generating firm must subscribe to reserve supplies equal to 100 percent of the capacity of its first generator, plus 50 percent of the capacity of its second generator, plus 33 percent of its third, and so on, in order to cover the possibility of failure. Second, the customer must agree to join the national pool and place its generating units under economic dispatch by the State Power Board, so that only the most efficient generators are in use at any time.

NORWAY

Because the national Norwegian power system relies entirely on hydroelectric generation, its rate structures have no time-of-day pricing. In such systems, as we noted in Chapter 2, storage capacity and the amount of rainfall constrain the quantity of electricity that can be delivered during the dry season.

Interruptible Tariffs. To provide for major uncertainties in annual water supplies, the State Power Board offers special tariffs to selected large consumers—such as aluminum and hydrogen producers—who may have their power interrupted for several months. For example, up to 20 percent of the load consumed in aluminum production can be dropped by shutting off a portion of the electrolysis cells. In return, interruptible power is priced at 75 percent of the secure-power price.

Time-of-Day Rates. The Oslo municipal utility produces almost all of its own power and is a net exporter of electricity to other utilities. It offers a special time-of-day and seasonal tariff to some of its large industrial customers who use electricity for water heating and other thermal purposes. During the summer runoff period (mid-April to mid-October), surplus electricity is sold on a when-available basis at night (7 p.m. to 7 a.m.) at a price of 0.70¢/kwh, with no maximum-demand (kilowatt) charge. In order to benefit from this special contract, the customer must have equipment, such as boilers and water heaters, that can be quickly switched from electricity to another fuel. Although the Oslo utility does not guarantee delivery, in a typical year it supplies electricity for about 2000 hours for such uses.

Since electricity is priced slightly below the equivalent cost of oil under these contracts, the Oslo utility has been able to add 130 MW to its summer nighttime demand. The 2400 water heaters and 50 boilers covered by the special tariff represent 15 percent of the Oslo system's capacity. This is a very sizable response in view of the fact that the uncertainty of delivery is borne completely by the customer, who must maintain a supply of alternate fuel.

FINLAND

Time-of-Day Rates. Both the State Power Board and some of the municipal utilities in Finland have tariffs for industrial customers with peak-load rates. The normal high-voltage tariffs have maximum-demand charges and include the option of time-of-day kilowatt-hour rates, which are applicable to a single peak period of some 15 hours. In response to time-of-day pricing, some Finnish industries have shifted their peak demands to off-peak hours. The chemical and chlorine products industries are reported to have nighttime peaks, and deep-freezing processes in the food industry have shifted loads in response to off-peak rates. In addition, some agricultural crops are now dried during the fall harvest in the off-peak period.

An Industrial Experiment. An interesting experiment in pricing industrial electricity was conducted in Helsinki during the winter of 1971/72. The electric utility informed a random sample of 80 industrial customers that for a 1-month period they would be charged the normal rate per kilowatt-hour, but that their bills would be unaffected by the level of their individual maximum demand during that month.

Figure 39 compares the aggregate load curve for the experimental customers during the month that no maximum demand charge was in effect with the corresponding curve during a normally billed winter month. There is a discernible difference in behavior, and the changes are in the expected direction: daytime demands were higher and nighttime demands were lower. If one considers 7 a.m. to 4 p.m. to be the daytime period, then the daytime energy consumed increased by 4 percent and the nighttime energy consumption fell by about 7 percent. The responses of individual firms were presumably larger, because less-then-perfect coincidence of demands reduces the response reflected in an average load curve.

118 The European Experience

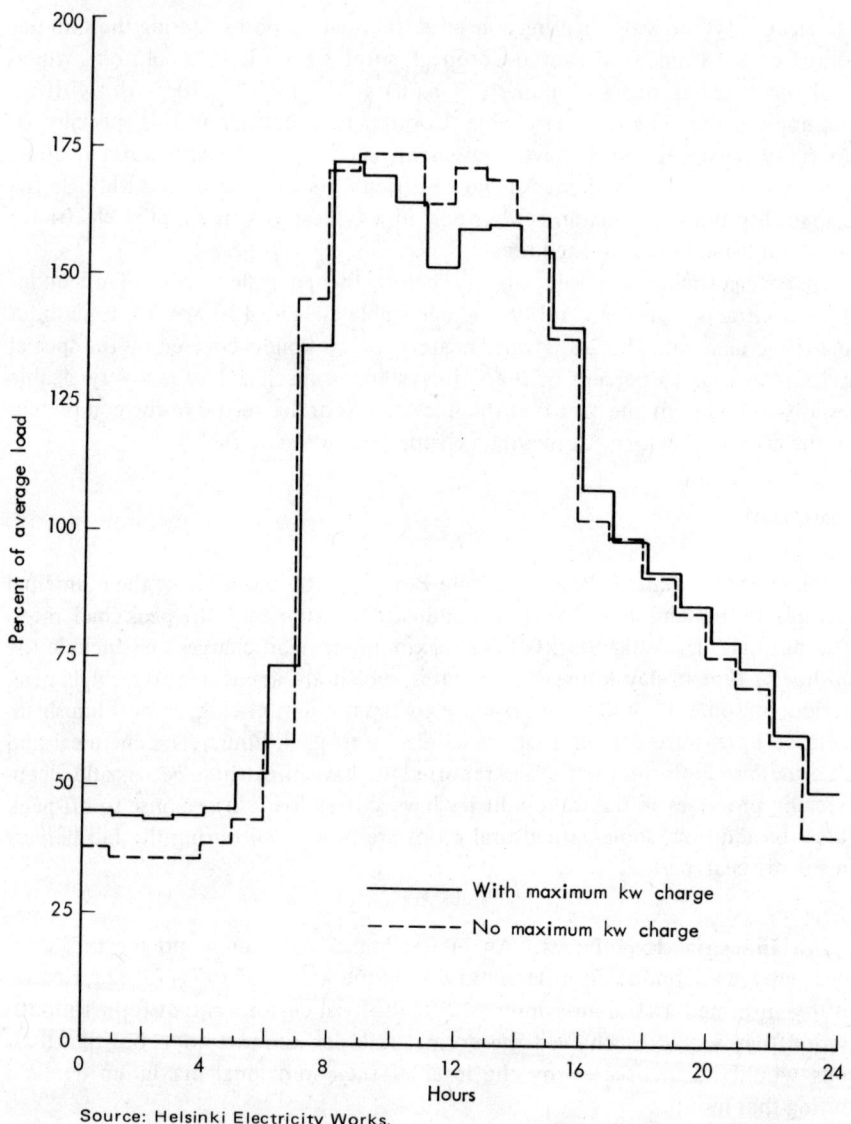

Source: Helsinki Electricity Works.

Figure 39. Winter Load Curves for a Sample of Finnish Industrial Customers

The short duration of the experimental period suggests that the size of the observed load shifts is significant.

SUMMARY

Industrial customers use a large fraction of the electricity generated in economically developed countries. The terms of electricity tariffs influence their use of electricity, and a relatively small number of firms account for much of the observed load response to peak-load pricing.

The load curves of individual firms and major industries both in France and in England and Wales show that significant quantities of industrial load are shifted to off-peak hours. Measured load reductions in cement, brick, glass, iron and steel, electrometallurgical, and petroleum refining industries establish that some individual firms can reduce their peak-hour consumption of electricity by 25 to nearly 100 percent in response to peak-load tariffs. The quantitative response of firms with comparable industrial processes is similar under both short-period peak-load tariffs with wide price differentials and time-of-day rates that apply for 10 to 18 hours at a time. Moreover, in return for special terms, some firms are willing to curtail their operations sharply during peak hours, and to have their supply of power interrupted in response to announced warnings of impending excess peak demands during the season of greatest consumption.

Industrial firms undertake a variety of activities to reduce peak loads. Some of the most important activities are recapitulated in Table 28. Depending on the processes involved, customers can adjust their scheduling of full-scale production and maintenance activities, increase their levels of productive capacity and operate at that level only in off-peak hours, and generate their own power from industrial by-products.

Table 28. Summary of Industrial Responses to Peak-Load Tariffs

Industry	Responses to Time-of-Day Tariffs
Cement	Schedule regular maintenance of milling machinery. Shut off crushers, grinders, and cement mills.
Foundries, Iron and Steel, and Electrometallurgy	Throttle-back smelting furnaces. Schedule maintenance for rolling mills. Shut down arc furnaces. Self-generate, using waste heat and natural gases.
Electrochemical	Reduce mercury cell production of chlorine.
Air Reduction	Interrupt liquefaction of gases.
Liquid and Gas Transportation	Interrupt pipeline pumping.
Cold-storage	Freeze and chill at off-peak hours.
Paper and Pulp	Self-generate, using waste products or process water.
Petroleum Refining	Self-generate, using by-product fuels.
Agriculture	Pump water in off-peak hours. Dry crops at off-peak periods.
Commercial Buildings	Heat or chill water at off-peak hours. Use storage-space heating devices.

Data from load studies of individual industrial customers in European utilities that have practiced peak-load pricing for many years establish the effectiveness of using electricity rate structures to reduce industrial loads at peak hours. The role of peak-load rates in managing residential loads is taken up in Chapter 6.

Chapter 6

Residential Tariffs and Load Management in Europe

Residential users constitute the most numerous group of customers supplied by any utility distributing retail electricity. Although each individual household's load is quite small, when these loads are aggregated they can account for one-third or more of a typical utility's total sales and present a significant opportunity for pricing and load-shifting efforts. In this chapter the extent to which European utilities have affected the pattern of residential loads will be examined.

MODULATING THE SYSTEM LOAD CURVE

The utility can influence its customers' loads, and thus the total system load curve, in two fundamental and interrelated ways. First, by providing financial inducements—most importantly through the rates charged for power at different periods of use—it can encourage its customers to alter what would be their habitual pattern of using electricity. Second, it can undertake more direct methods of altering some consumers' loads, including actual control of consumer equipment as well as the promotion of types of appliances that produce a systematic shift of load to off-peak periods.

In Europe, many electric utilities have adopted a direct approach to the management of residential loads. The detailed tariffs that signal levels of system marginal costs to large industrial consumers are generally not employed at the residential level. They would be too costly to administer for the hundreds of thousands of small residential customers and too likely to be ignored because their complexity would exceed the potential saving to be realized by most households.

Yet a more favorable load pattern for even a single end-use of electricity, such as water heating, can offer significant system savings if adopted by a sizable fraction of households. To realize such savings, some foreign utilities actively promote the purchase and replacement of specific appliances—by advertising, financing customers' capital investments, assisting manufacturers to design new appliances, and selling appliances directly to consumers. These efforts are accompanied by special tariffs or supply contracts that make it financially worthwhile for the customers to modify their loads. Thus, load management in the European residential sector is characterized by centrally made decisions to encourage development of more favorable patterns of household electricity use.

Load-Management Considerations

Residential load management requires an analysis of the system load pattern in order to determine what broad changes in residential loads can achieve the greatest savings in system costs. Generally speaking there are two load-management approaches. The first is designed to shift the load to the off-peak periods of the *system* daily load curve. The second is designed to achieve more nearly flat *residential* load curves on a household-by-household basis over the 24-hour day. The marginal costs of generating and distributing electricity, the investment costs of different appliances, and the acceptability of load-management procedures by consumers affect the load-management approach that is adopted.

Three important factors are involved in the management of residential loads. The first factor concerns the relationship of peak and off-peak marginal costs to the investment costs of load-shifting appliances. In largely thermal systems, such as those in West Germany and in England and Wales, the differences in peak and off-peak generating costs dominate the costs of amortizing investment in residential storage-heating systems, including the expense of reinforcing the local distribution networks to handle the additional storage load. In contrast, in systems in which there are only small differences in marginal costs over the daily load cycle, as in Norway, in much of Sweden, and in climates where extreme temperatures would require large investments in storage-heating units, it becomes relatively more important to minimize the capacity of the low-voltage distribution network by encouraging high-utilization appliances, such as resistance heating and continuous water heating.

A second factor in the management of residential loads is the choice of a method of controlling appliances. Signals, propagated over the electrical network itself (ripple control) or by means of radio (telecontrol), enable the utility's dispatcher to directly control a large number of the water heaters and space heaters in homes throughout a service area. Such direct control systems are costly, because they require a series of transmitters located throughout the distribution networks, a receiving unit in each home that can switch the controlled loads through separate circuits, and—in some cases—additional metering that can record the time of electricity consumption.

Direct control systems do offer numerous opportunities to modulate residential loads. Residential storage devices can have their starting times staggered in order to level out the load on local distribution equipment. Direct-resistance heating systems can be cycled on and off several times an hour to reduce system load during the peak hours of those days when capacity is actually in short supply. Water heaters can be shut off in the case of an outage or the threat of a system overload.[1]

A less costly but also less flexible control method is the use of a time clock at each residence to regulate the controlled loads and the metering at pre-set hours. Within a neighborhood, clock settings can be staggered to avoid local distribution network peaks.[2] But loads under time-clock control cannot be interrupted or modulated to deal with system peak conditions due to unusual weather or to outages.

A third factor in the management of residential loads is that of offering price incentives to consumers to encourage them to purchase or modify appliances. Storage applications, for both space and water heating, are invariably offered with a time-of-day rate that provides for reduced charges in the off-peak hours. There are two basic approaches. The first, exemplified by the White Meter tariff in England and Wales, is simply to impose a time-of-day tariff for all electricity consumed by the household. Typically, a clock controls both the meter and storage loads, switching them on at the predetermined off-peak hours; during the off-peak period all electricity is billed at the lower rate. The second is to install two separate circuits with different meters, one for the storage appliances and one for the rest of the house. The restricted circuit for the storage appliances is powered only during off-peak hours and is controlled either by a clock or by radio signal; other uses of electricity are billed at a uniform price at all hours. The restricted-circuit approach was the first used in England and Wales, but has now been supplanted by the White Meter option.

In contrast, in Hamburg, Germany, the utility initially offered an unrestricted time-of-day tariff, but now limits the amount of additional load-shifting by supplying off-peak power to new customers for storage heaters only. This change became necessary because the promotion of storage heating was so successful that the system's evening peak had threatened to become as large as the morning peak. In the discussion below the residential load-management techniques used in several countries will be reviewed.

---

1. Similar load-management controls for residential air conditioning are being introduced on an experimental basis by some utilities in the United States. Residential water heaters have been under remote control for several years in a few U.S. utilities.
2. Area boards in England and Wales have been able to reset residential clocks in substantial numbers to better modulate their loads in order to reduce their payments under the Bulk Supply Tariff to the Central Electricity Generating Board. In one recent case, an area board adjusted 800 MW of installed storage space- and water-heating load.

ENGLAND AND WALES

Storage Heating

In 1961 the area boards of England and Wales began an active campaign to promote the residential use of storage units for space heating. The first units were initially one-room radiators that drew power during two periods—an 8-hour overnight period and a 3-hour booster period in midafternoon. Radiators were supplied and metered on a separate circuit that was switched on by a clock control during hours of low system loads. The area boards used direct advertising to promote conversion from coal and gas heating to electric storage heat, and sold new units to the public in their own appliance stores located throughout the country.

Sales of the first storage radiators were so successful that by the late 1960s the midday trough in the system load curve was rapidly filling up. To remedy this situation, new radiators were designed that would not require a midday charge. Because area boards, in fact, sell the vast majority of all storage radiators through their retail outlets, they can ensure that new appliances meet certain performance standards. The new radiators were first offered to the public in 1969 under the White Meter Tariff, with its 8-hour overnight discount on kilowatt-hours.[3]

Today, about 14 percent of the 17 million domestic customers have some form of storage heating, 1.7 million of whom are served under restricted-hour tariffs and 600,000 under the White Meter tariff. In all, storage heating has an installed capacity of some 15,000 MW. In addition, these tariffs have encouraged widespread use of storage water heating. In recent years, however, the use of electric storage heating has been increasing more slowly as natural gas has become the market leader for central heating.

The restricted-hour and White Meter tariffs were initially promoted under the slogan "half-price electricity." Until the mid-1970s, this phrase accurately described the off-peak rates of 0.30 to 0.36 pence/kwh compared to the normal rate of 0.66 pence/kwh (Table 29). However, in the wake of the 1974 oil embargo the marked increase in the price of fuel oil led to a uniform increase in running costs at all hours, causing the area boards to increase the off-peak rate by a disproportionate percentage amount, thus invalidating the marketing slogan. Widespread consumer complaints, that the utility was reneging on its implicit promise of low-cost energy for storage appliances, forced the government to return the off-peak rate temporarily to a half-price level. This subsidy was reduced in 1975 and discontinued in April 1976.[4]

---

3. The restricted-hour tariff has been continued for those households with the older equipment. A typical White Meter tariff is shown in Table 19.
4. See Boley (1976).

Table 29. Comparative Energy Charges in England and Wales, 1965

Tariff	Pence per Kilowatt-hour
Normal domestic rate	0.66
15-hour off-peak rate	0.36
11-hour off-peak rate	0.32
8-hour off-peak rate	0.30

Source: D.L. Walker, "Design of Electricity Tariffs in England and Wales and Experience in Their Application," in C.J. Cicchetti and W.K. Foell, eds., *Energy System Forecasting, Planning and Pricing* (Madison: University of Wisconsin Press, 1975), p. 333.

Shifted Load

The Electricity Council has analyzed the effect of storage space-heating on the pattern of residential electric loads.[5] Data from this study enable one to compare similar homes heated by direct-resistance devices with those using storage heating.[6] The differences in electricity use by time of day are the differences that would result from converting a home heated by a direct-resistance system to storage heating. They are also the differences in an area board's additional electrical load that would result from converting a house heated by coal to storage heating rather than to direct-resistance heating.

These data are summarized in Table 30 and Figure 40. When homes with normal insulation are compared, those using direct-resistance heating consume 22 percent of their energy during off-peak hours, whereas those with high-capacity storage radiators consume 72 percent at off-peak times. Similar figures for homes with electricaire heating[7] suggest that some 50 percent of annual electricity consumption would be shifted from daytime to nighttime use by converting a home from direct-resistance heating to storage heating and placing it on a time-of-day tariff. For homes with high-quality insulation, the magnitude of the shift is approximately the same.

The difference in household energy consumption in response to the time-of-day tariff is composed of two elements, one type attributable to the space heating, and the second type attributable to differences in uses of electricity such as dishwashing, clothes washing, and water heating. By comparing, in Table 30, the high-insulation homes using direct-resistance heating with homes using two types of storage heating, most of which are on the White Meter tariff, we calculate that the storage heater is responsible for shifting 37 to 46 percent of the annual electricity consumption to the off-peak period.

5. Unpublished load study of domestic customers.
6. A valid comparison is possible because homes with storage heating had only slightly higher total electricity consumption than homes with direct-resistance heating.
7. A central heating system using a storage heater and forced-air distribution.

Table 30. Percent of Annual Electricity Consumption During Off-Peak Hours in English and Welsh Households[a] (year ending March 31, 1975)

	Percent of Consumption	
Type of Heating System	High Insulation	Normal Insulation
Direct-resistance heating (other than ceiling)	34	22
High-capacity storage radiators	71	72
Central-storage heating	80	74

Source: Electricity Council, unpublished load study of domestic customers.
[a] Sample from throughout England and Wales. All storage radiator and central storage (electricaire) homes were on White Meter tariffs. Of the homes using direct-resistance heating, 31 percent of the high-insulation homes and 95 percent of the normally insulated homes were on conventional, rather than time-of-day, tariffs.

The second element of the shift in consumption—one that is not associated with space heating—can be calculated from Table 30 by comparing the off-peak consumption by homes with direct resistance heating but which face different tariffs. For this group of customers the difference between high-insulation homes, two-thirds of which have White Meter tariffs, and normally insulated homes, almost all of which are on conventional tariffs, is a shift of as much as 12 percent of annual kilowatt-hour consumption. This is a sizable difference in view of the fact that the off-peak price prevails only during the relatively inconvenient period of 11 p.m. to 7 a.m.[8]

Since we do not know the degree to which homes vary in quality of insulation, the national impact of storage heating is difficult to measure precisely. However, the British Electricity Council study of household load curves suggests that the installation of storage heating has typically resulted in shifts of 0.8 to 1.4 kw in a household's morning and early afternoon demand on an average day during December and January. On cold days the shifts are larger, ranging up to 5 kw per home. Ignoring the midday charging period for older heaters purchased under the restricted-hour tariff, these data imply that on an average winter day the use of storage heating, rather than direct-resistance heating, shifts a total of 2000 to 3000 MW out of the daytime system load curve and a smaller amount

---

8. Some of this 12 percent shift may be due to differences in heat losses between high-insulation homes and normally insulated homes. Homes with high insulation will be able to retain some of the heat that is produced at night into the daytime hours. Homes with normal insulation will lose enough heat during the day to require higher daytime loads. Comparing high-insulation homes with normally insulated homes that have high-capacity storage radiators and electricaire heating suggests that heat-loss differences may account for up to half of the difference in the percentage of annual electricity consumption that occurs off-peak between high-insulation and normally insulated homes with direct heating.

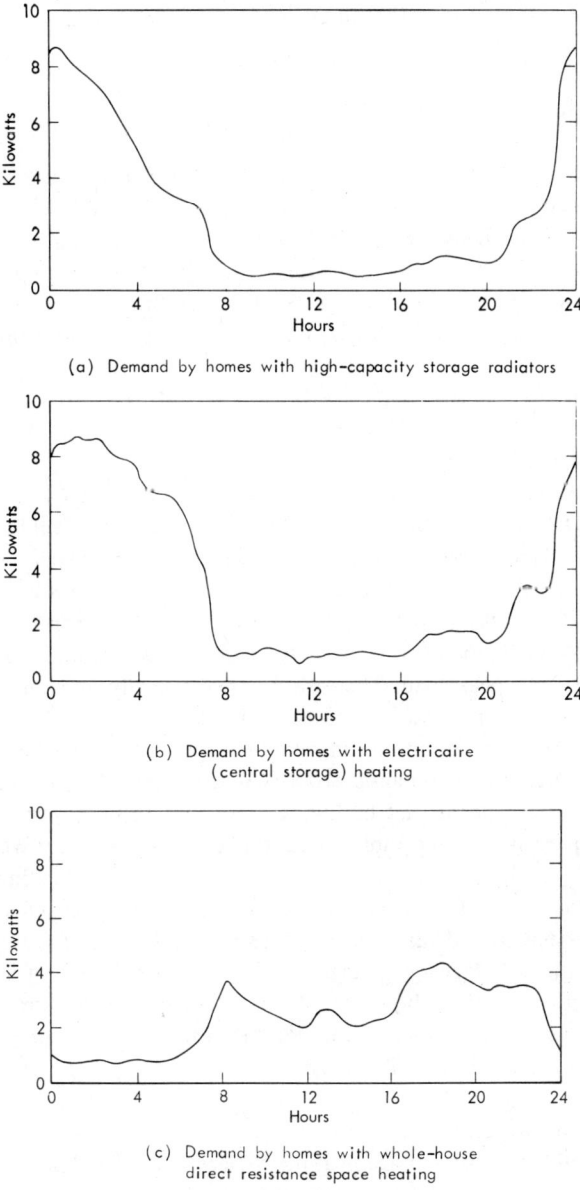

(a) Demand by homes with high-capacity storage radiators

(b) Demand by homes with electricaire (central storage) heating

(c) Demand by homes with whole-house direct resistance space heating

Source: Unpublished Electricity Council load study.

Figure 40. Daily Pattern of Electricity Consumption in English Homes with Different Methods of Space Heating (at a winter weekday temperature of 32°F, normal insulation)

out of the evening load into the nighttime load. On a cold day the shift can be 9000 to 10,000 MW.

WEST GERMANY

In the predominantly thermal West German utilities, residential load management has concentrated on the control of space-heating loads. Several metropolitan areas in West Germany have large district heating plants that supply steam to heat multifamily and commercial buildings. Such plants are equipped with back-pressure turbines and constitute a significant generating resource for the utility to use in managing peak loads. In Hamburg, for example, the utility can interrupt the flow of steam for heating on 15 minutes' notice and use it to supplement other sources of generation for a 1- to 2-hour period.

Storage Heating

Over the last 10 years, residential storage heating has been widely promoted by several West German utilities and has had a pronounced effect in shifting system loads. For the 1964-1974 period, total electrical energy used in West Germany increased 109 percent, but the peak load increased only 84 percent; as a result the mid-December load factor improved from 77 percent to 88 percent. The average overnight load (10 p.m. to 6 a.m.) increased from 54 percent to 75 percent of the daily peak load. These shifts are especially apparent in the comparison of the relative national load curves in Figure 41.

During this 10-year period the installed capacity of storage-heating units in West Germany increased from about 1000 MW to 20,000 MW; 89 percent of this load is used to heat residential buildings, 6 percent to heat business establishments, and 5 percent to heat public office buildings. Throughout West Germany about 7 percent of the 22 million households now use storage heating.

The importance of domestic storage heating in the total load curve of a single utility can be seen in the mid-December curve (Figure 42) for Hamburg. The storage heaters are charged on a staggered schedule, beginning at about 8 p.m. The bottom curve, which shows the load of residential consumers, peaks at about 7 p.m. and stays at roughly that level into the early morning hours, when most storage units have been fully charged.

Avoiding Distribution Peaks

The rapid adoption of storage-heating devices has shifted such a significant fraction of load in several West German systems that if the trend continues, the system peak will occur during the evening at the time the storage units are first switched on. To cope with these difficulties, several load-management techniques have been employed: controlling the installation, design, and timing of use of storage appliances.

Installation of new capacity has been controlled to keep pace with the in-

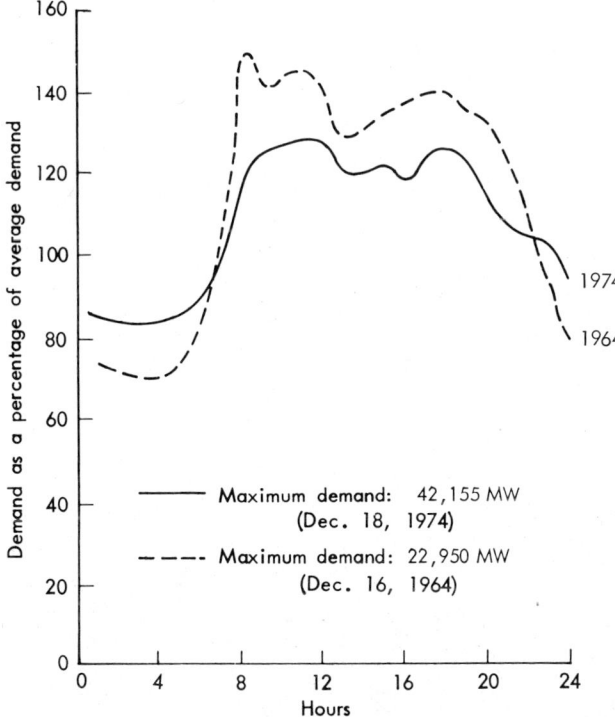

Source: "Die Öffentliche Elektrizitätsversorgung, 1974."

Figure 41. West German Network Load Curves on Days of Peak Demand, 1964 and 1974

crease in system load. Because West German utilities have supplied electricity for storage heating under special contracts rather than by tariff, they are allowed to determine which customers will receive service.[9] This selectivity enables the utility to balance the growth of the aggregate load curve and to avoid creating sharp peaks in the local distribution network.

Increasingly sophisticated regulation devices have been built into the storage-heating units. When first introduced, these units were predominantly of the "forward-charging" variety; that is, they would charge at the greatest rate when

---

9. When storage heating was first introduced, it was available under an optional tariff at off-peak rates that applied to all electricity consumed during the nighttime hours. However, by 1974 the nighttime load had increased significantly. Thus, to avoid additional load-shifting of discretionary household activities, the utilities decided to offer service to new storage heating customers under special contracts in which nighttime rates applied only to heating. ("Old" customers continued to take all of their nighttime energy at the off-peak rates specified in the optional tariff.) A comparison of the load curves of the two groups would be an interesting way to identify discretionary load shifting, but such a study has not been made.

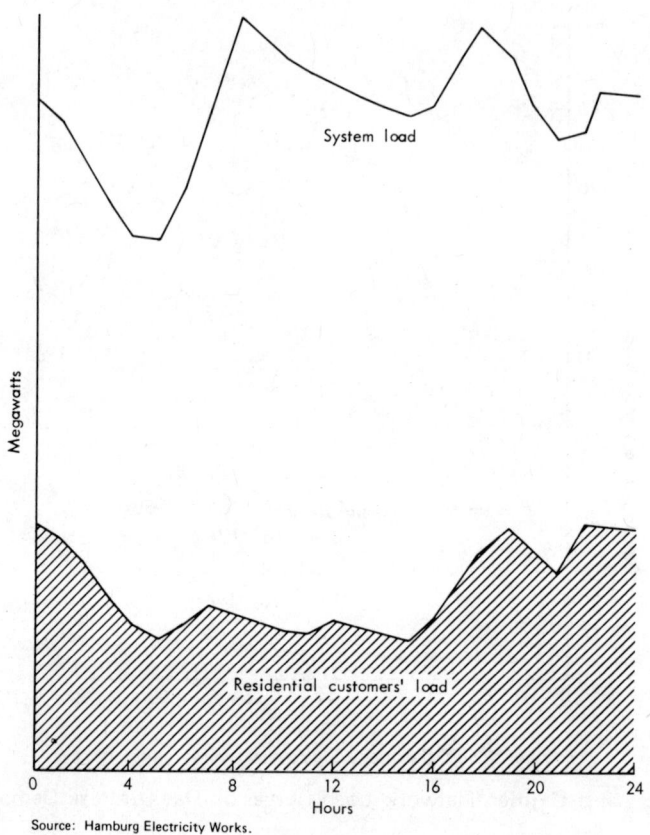

Figure 42. System and Residential Load Curves for Hamburg: Mid-December Weekday, 1975

initially switched on and gradually draw a reduced amount of current, as shown in Figure 43(a). By about 1971 the demand between the start-up times of 10 p.m. and 11 p.m. had increased to the point that the system peak threatened to shift into that period. As a result the utilities have introduced "backward-charging" units, which begin with a low initial charge rate that builds up to a maximum at the time that they shut off, as shown in Figure 43(b).[10] By adjusting the mix of these types of units, the utility can influence the aggregate load on any node of the distribution system, as well as the system load curve.

The starting, stopping, and charging times of storage units can be staggered

---

10. The newer units also contain logic for sensing both the outside temperature and the residual charge in the storage unit, data that are then used to compute the total charge needed.

to avoid local needle peaks. Control is accomplished by a mixture of clock control and low-frequency ripple-control signals superimposed on the power system. The staggered charging hours shown in Table 31 illustrate the flexibility of control that is possible. In some cases the schedule also provides for a 2-hour afternoon charge period.

Terms for storage-heating installation typically include a fixed charge for the restricted circuit and an energy price that is roughly one-half of the normal domestic rate for unrestricted service. In 1975, for example, a representative storage-heating customer in Hamburg paid an additional annual charge of $20.58, plus an energy charge of 2.13¢ per kwh instead of 4.05¢ per kwh.

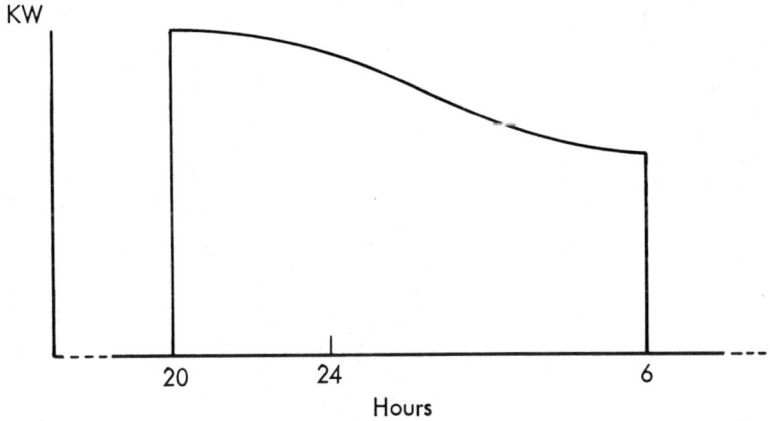

(a) Forward-charging storage heating

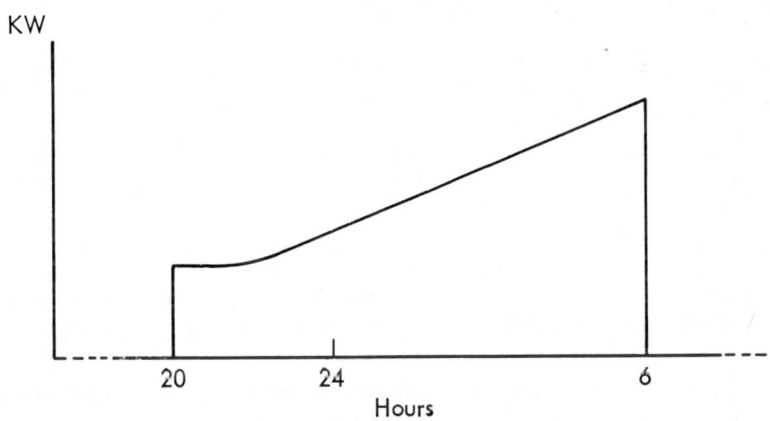

(b) Backward-charging storage heating

Figure 43. Load Patterns in West German Storage Heating Systems

Table 31. Examples of Staggered Charging Periods for Storage Heating in Hamburg (winter 1974)

Type of Control	Installed Capacity (MW)	Charging Times			
		Night		Afternoon	
		From (p.m. and a.m.)	To (a.m.)	From (p.m.)	To (p.m.)
Forward	20	8:00	4:00	–	
Forward	35	8:10	4:10	–	
Early Charge	23	8:20	4:20	1:25	3:25
Forward	31	8:30	4:30	–	
Forward	14	8:40	4:40	–	
Forward	39	8:50	4:50	–	
Forward	33	9:00	5:00	–	
Early Charge	29	9:10	5:10	1:05	3:05
Forward	31	9:20	5:20	–	
Forward	38	10:20	6:20	–	
Backward	28	10:20	6:20	–	
Early Charge	18	10:30	6:30	1:25	3:25
Forward	35	10:50	6:50	–	
Backward	22	10:50	6:50	–	
Forward	39	11:00	7:00	–	
Backward	10	11:00	7:00	–	
Forward	37	11:10	7:10	–	
Backward	6	11:10	7:10	–	
Late Charge	13	11:20	7:10	3:30	5:30
Backward	21	11:20	7:20	–	
Forward	34	11:30	7:30	–	
Late Charge	18	11:40	7:40	3:30	5:30
Forward	46	11:50	7:50	–	
Backward	17	11:50	7:50	–	
Forward	45	0:10	8:10	–	
Backward	23	0:10	8:10	–	
Late Charge	21	2:00	8:20	3:10	5:40
Late Charge	42	4:00	8:40	4:20	6:20
Backward	39	5:00	8:50	–	
Forward	49	1:40	9:40	–	
Forward	35	1:30	9:30	–	
Floor Heating	1	11:35	6:35	5:00	– 7:00

Source: Hamburgische Elektrizitäts-Werke.

The West German utilities expect to install storage heating on a controlled basis until the mid-1980s, when the valleys in system load curves will be filled up. In planning for that condition, residential load management is turning to newer types of heating systems. For example, many new buildings are being heated by floor (radiant) heating, with an 8-hour nighttime charge plus a 2-hour daytime boost. Still in the demonstration phase, bivalent residential heating systems that operate on both electricity and another fuel are being tested. During mild periods these units use electricity to operate the heat pump; but at low temperatures (below 32°F), the second fuel (such as oil or gas) is used for direct heating, thus mitigating the weather-generated peaking of the electrical supply systems.

FRANCE

The load curves of the majority of French residential customers, who obtain their electricity under a simple kilowatt-hour tariff with a fuse change for subscribed capacity (see Chapter 4), have the day-peaking features characteristic of many countries. The weekday average load curves of a sample of 450 consumers measured in January 1973 are shown in Figure 44. These consumers all pay a uniform rate for electricity at all hours, and their patterns of response are classified into four groups according to their level of annual consumption.[11] In each group substantially higher loads occur during the daytime.

As described in Chapter 4, French residential and small business customers have the option of buying electricity on a double-tariff under which they obtain energy at about one-half the regular price per kilowatt-hour during the 10 p.m.–6 a.m. period. The double tariff is advantageous for two groups of households— those with storage space and water heating and those that use a substantial quantity of electricity for direct heating. The average weekday load curves for two such groups, taken from the related load study of 227 double-tariff subscribers,[12] are shown in Figure 45. This form of peak-load pricing has clearly encouraged the development of off-peak loads. As storage devices have become more widespread, the increase in residential nighttime loads has caused local peaks to begin to appear in segments of the distribution system. Both clock control and remote telecontrol methods are increasingly being used to stagger the switch-on times of storage-heating devices.

FINLAND, NORWAY, AND SWEDEN

Residential load management plays only a limited role for most utilities in these Scandinavian countries. Since hydroelectric plants are the predominant source of power, there is at most a small daytime/nighttime differential in short-run marginal costs. As described in Chapter 4, the industrial tariffs that emphasize maximum-demand charges reflect the constancy of marginal running costs over the day and the importance attached to avoiding peak loads in the distribution system. This attention to smoothing individual consumers' loads is also seen at the residential level, where the traditional load-rate tariff imposes a surcharge for consumption in excess of the subscribed kilowatt load.

Significant off-peak differences in marginal costs do occur in some Scandinavian utilities, such as the Stockholm and Helsinki municipal supply companies,

11. See Canal and Fourati (1977).
12. See Canal (1976).

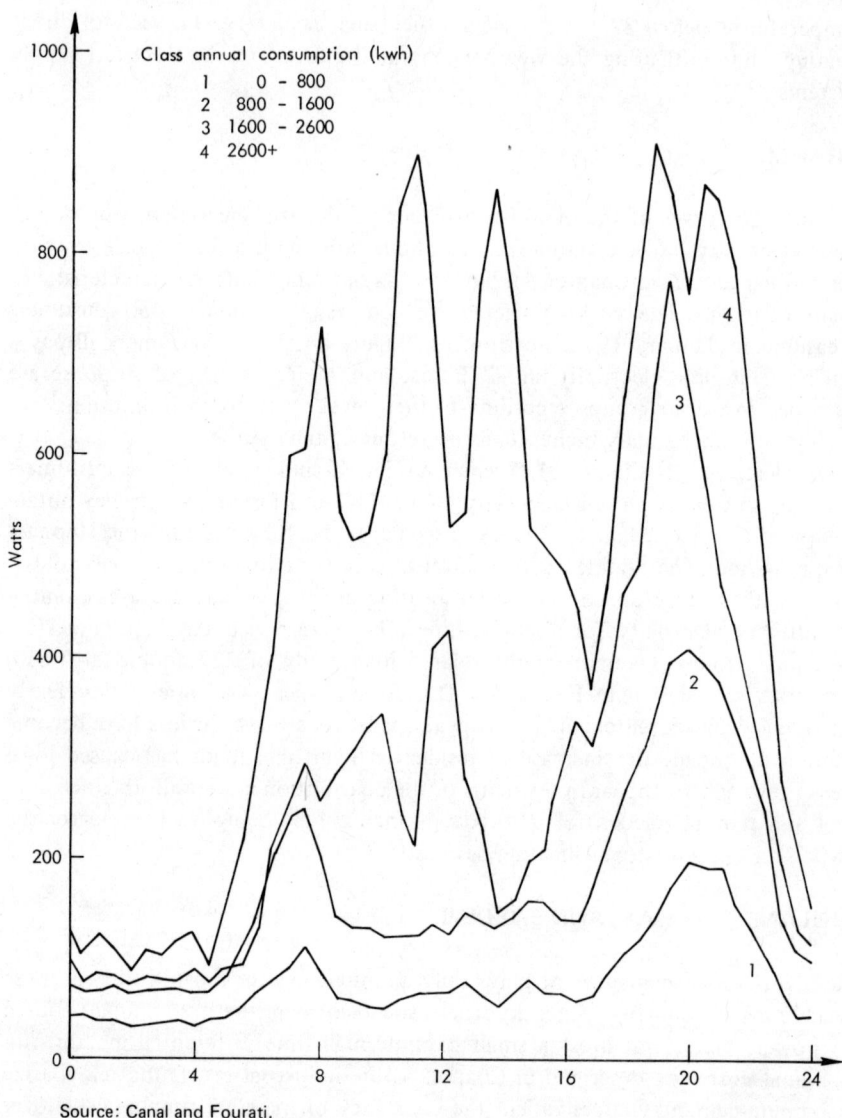

Source: Canal and Fourati.

Figure 44. Load Curves for French Residential Customers on the Single Tariff

which obtain a portion of their power from thermal district heating plants. However, these cost differences are considered insufficient to justify the roughly $2500 investment needed for a residential storage space-heating unit adequate for severe winter temperatures. Furthermore, any widespread adoption of storage space-heating units would require reinforcement of the distribution system to handle local peaking and thus offset at least some of the savings in generating costs.

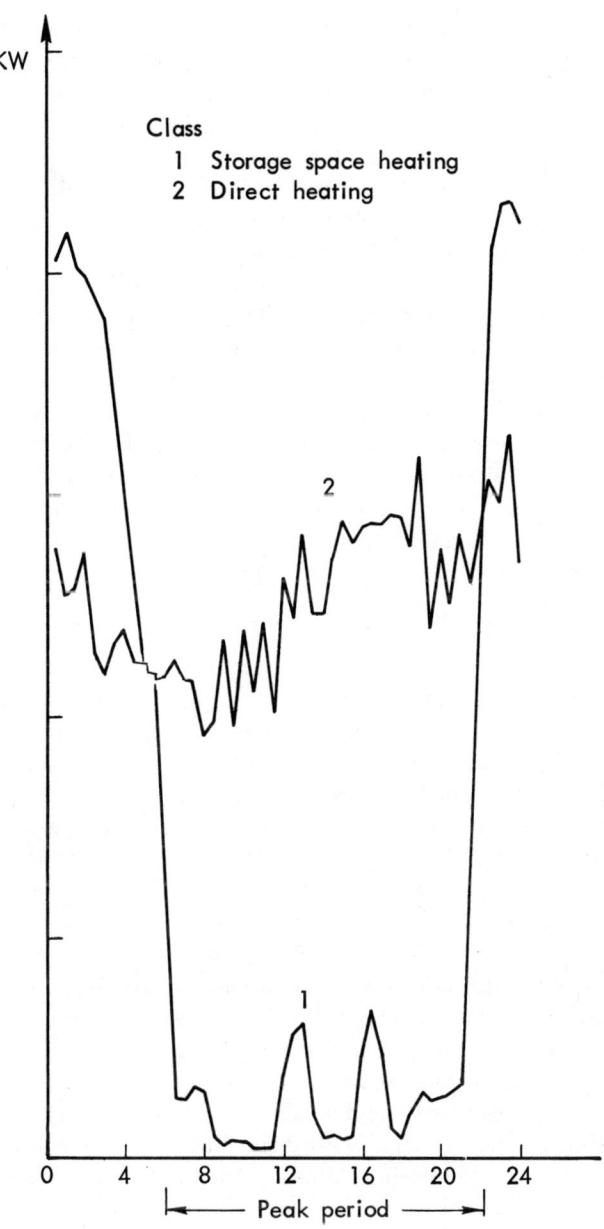

Figure 16. Load Curves for French Residential Customers on the Double Tariff

Although storage space-heating is not widely used in Scandinavia, storage water-heating can be cost-effective. In the Stockholm system, only a small fraction of the dwellings—that is, semidetached and detached homes—are eligible for the time-of-day tariff. The observable annual shift in load from daytime to nighttime is about 3000 kwh per home for storage water-heating, plus an estimated 1000 kwh for other uses such as clothes washing and dishwashing. In aggregate, this amounts to a shift of 25 million to 30 million kwh/year or about 3 percent of the Stockholm system's residential load.

In Norway, Sweden, and Finland, several utilities use ripple-control systems. In most instances these systems were initially installed to control street lighting, and with the advent of solid-state receiver units, control is being extended to residential loads. Although there is a limited amount of ripple-controlled storage space-heating, remote load-control techniques are increasingly being used with direct heating. In advanced systems, computer control permits the utility to turn down or turn off residential heating and rotate the reductions among houses. These techniques are effective in meeting emergencies of short duration. Longer interruptions can be tolerated, for example, in newer Swedish houses that are constructed to high insulation standards.

SUMMARY

European utilities take a direct approach to modifying the electrical loads of their residential customers. They promote the use of specific appliances that can improve the shape of the system load curve and offer optional time-of-day tariff to customers who install such devices. A variety of possible methods of modulating residential loads is available. The differences between peak and off-peak marginal costs, the importance of having some residential loads under central control, and the magnitude of the price incentive offered to consumers are important determinants of the load-management approach used in a particular utility.

Storage space-heating have proved effective in the predominantly thermal systems and moderate winter climates found in England and Wales and in West Germany. Storage water-heating is cost effective in most systems that have a significant daily variation in marginal costs.

Unless suitably regulated, residential storage loads can cause undesirable peaks in the distribution system. These difficulties can be minimized by staggering the charging times preset into clocks on the customers' premises, by computer control of individual storage appliances, or by remote control of selected customer loads.

The major benefits to a utility of using peak-load rate structures for both industrial and residential customers are the potential leveling of system load curves and consequent savings of capacity costs. Chapter 7 assesses the magnitude of the benefits achieved in European systems.

 *Chapter 7*

Assessing the European Experience

European utilities have accumulated as much as 20 years of experience supplying electricity under peak-load tariffs. In this chapter both the successes and the shortcomings they have enjoyed with such rate structures will be assessed in terms of the effects on capacity requirements and shifts in system peak loads. The relevance of this experience, much of which has been accumulated in nationalized utilities, will then be examined for the predominantly private electric utility sector in the United States.

EFFECT OF PEAK-LOAD PRICING ON CAPACITY REQUIREMENTS

In Chapter 5 selected load curves for individual plants and industry groups were examined, and strong evidence was found showing that peak-load rate structures motivate a wide variety of industries to modulate their loads in a significant and even striking fashion. And in Chapter 6 the use of residential time-of-day rate structures in conjunction with load management to encourage investments in storage technologies and shifts of discretionary loads to off-peak hours was reviewed.

The importance of such customer responses for the total load curve of the utility system might, in principle, be determined by systematically measuring the loads of a representative cross-section sample of all industrial and residential customers and aggregating the demands measured in each tariff period. Unfortunately such data are not available. Moreover, examination of present-day load curves would not necessarily reveal the full change in loads that have occurred over the course of several years. Here, therefore, the quantitative effect of peak-load pricing will be assessed by examining the evolution of system load curves

138 The European Experience

since time-of-day rate structures were introduced and by reviewing other aggregate indicators of changes in system loads. Most of the discussion will be focused on the systems in England and Wales, France, and West Germany where peak-load tariffs have been used most extensively.

France

There are several ways to assess the aggregate effectiveness of the French Green Tariff. These will be examined separately below.

Evolution of the System Load Curve. Figure 46 illustrates the shapes of the Electricité de France (EdF) system load curves in 1952, before the peak-load tariff was introduced, and in 1975. During this period EdF's load curve became substantially flatter, with pronounced relative reductions of load during the peak hours. Moreover, the peak load no longer occured during the 7-9 a.m. peak

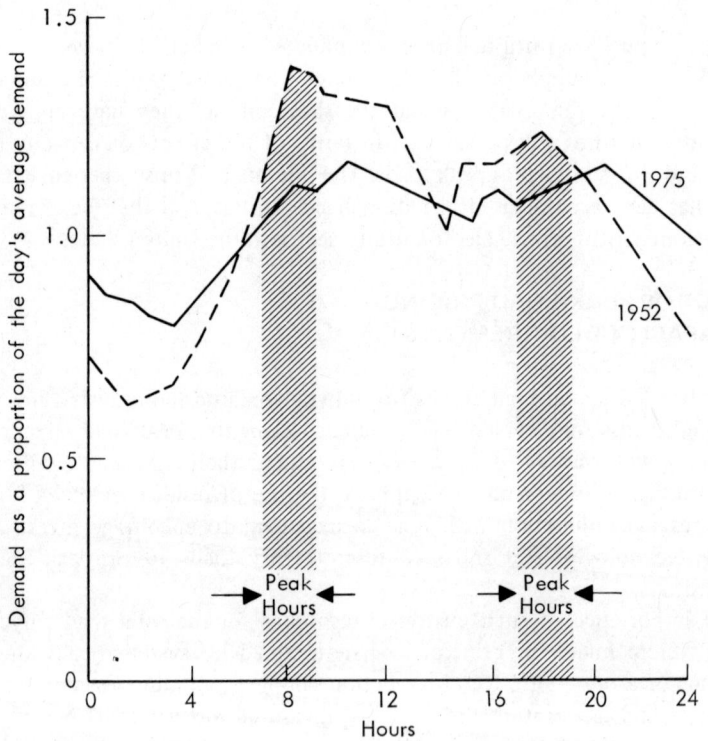

Source: Y. Pioger, in Cicchetti and Foell (1975).

Figure 46. French Daily Load Curves for Representative January Workdays, 1952 and 1975

hours of the tariff. Instead, the absolute growth in load during peak hours had declined to the point that the system peak had shifted to about 10 a.m.

Since the hours of the Green Tariff's peak period were not changed, by the 1970s energy consumed at the time of the actual system peak was priced at less than its marginal cost. This situation caused some loss of economic efficiency for the EdF system. At the same time, this movement of the system peak to a period of lower rates provided additional evidence that the terms of the Green Tariff and the Universal Tariff had influenced the shape of the system load curve.

The evolution of the French medium- and high-voltage loads provides further evidence of the long-term effect of the Green Tariff. The load duration curves in Figure 47 allow a comparison of changes in the average demands in each of the five pricing periods of the Green Tariff over a 20-year period (1952-1972). These curves show that in relative terms the peak- and shoulder-hour system loads have decreased significantly, and that off-peak demands have grown in both winter and summer months.

Balasko (1976) has considered the hypothetical situation that would exist in 1980 if EdF were required to supply the quantity of energy now projected for that year, but in the shape of the 1956 load curve rather than the load curve that is projected under the Green Tariff. He reports that an increase of 6500 MW of capacity would be necessary—some 14 percent of EdF's projected capacity in 1980.

It is, of course, possible that in addition to the favorable incentives established by the Green Tariff, a variety of secular trends in industrial production practices, changes in work habits, and various other factors have also contributed to the flattening of EdF's load curve. However, the dominant role of the Green Tariff's price incentives is clearly established in the firm-by-firm evidence of industrial load responses presented in Chapter 5.

November Load Changes. The second method of assessing the Green Tariff's effect on the EdF system load—one that is largely independent of other long-term effects—is based on measuring the weekday system load when the winter peak prices go into effect on November 1. Any change in load over the space of a few days before and after this date may be termed a daily effect that results from tariff-induced adjustment in the operating and production schedule of electricity consumers, rather than from structural changes in the economy, weather condition, and other factors.[1] This daily effect will also largely exclude reduction in peak-period electricity consumption due to longer-run changes in plant capacity and labor force employment patterns that may have resulted from the tariffs. However, a direct comparison of system load level in October and November will still be confounded by seasonal trends in economic activity, temperature, and daylight.

1. See Balasko (1976).

140 *The European Experience*

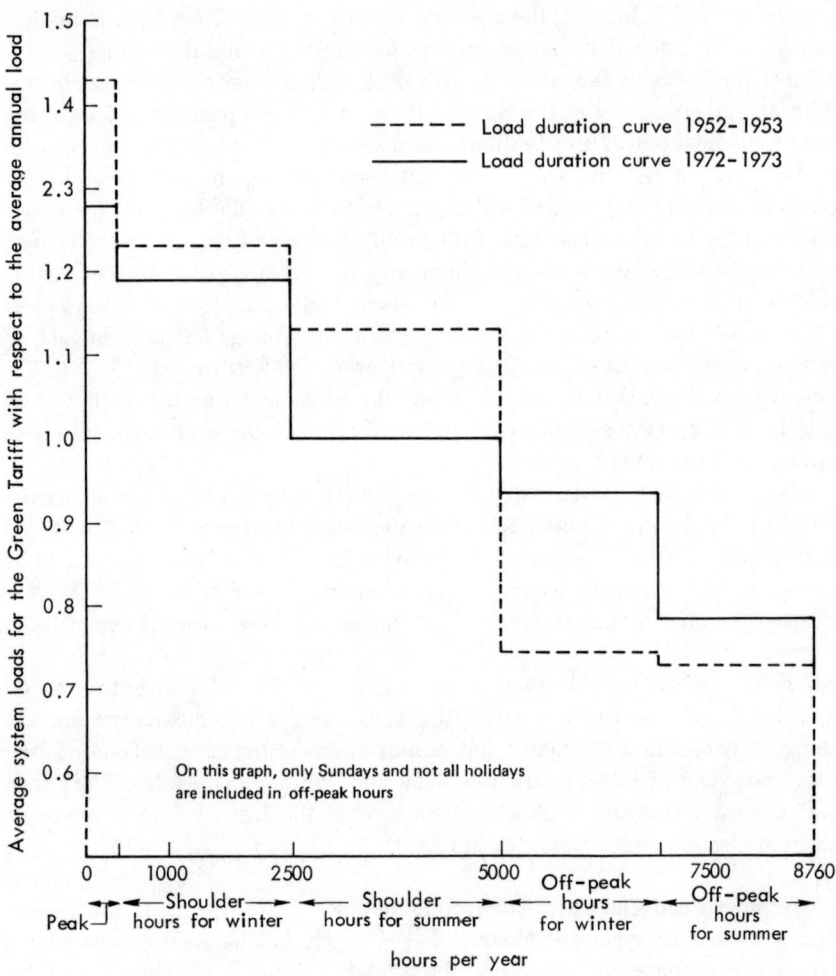

Source: Y. Pioger, in Cicchetti and Foell (1975).

Figure 47. Change in French Load Duration Curves over 20 years: 1952-1972

To remove the influence of these extraneous factors, one author has carried out the detailed statistical analysis of the evolution of the EdF load over 25 years.[2] For each week of the year the average workday load is calculated for each hour of the day. These observations are then used to estimate the annual trend in the hourly load relative to the average daily load.

The trend line for the third week of October and the first full week of November during the first 10 years of the Green Tariff (1957-1966) show that

2. Pioger (1977b).

relative to the average daily load, the demand at both 8 a.m. and 10 a.m. in October and at 10 a.m. in November declined at nearly identical rates. Each of these loads is subject to the same wintertime shoulder period price. But when the peak-period price takes effect in November, the 8 a.m. load fell twice as rapidly. Moreover, the differences grew larger week by week until at least early December.

To estimate the magnitude of the daily effect of the Green Tariff, Pioger (1977b) has averaged the slope of the 8 a.m. weekday trend lines during the peak-period weeks (November-February) and the shoulder-period weeks (October and March). By taking the difference between these slopes and then subtracting the trend observed on Sunday to remove the effect of other factors—principally variations in daylight—Pioger estimates that the Green Tariff has resulted in a net reduction in the 8 a.m. system load of 700 MW in 1965 and 1400 MW by 1975.

Subscribed Demand. A third method of assessing the effect of the Green Tariff is based on the fact that in the long run firms are able to take the pattern of electricity prices into account in the design of production facilities. By comparing the levels of subscribed demand during different tariff periods we may partially measure this structural effect. Since the tariff itself provides strong price incentives for not subscribing for power that is not needed, and also imposes significant surcharges for exceeding subscribed levels, subscribed-demand levels should provide an accurate indication of the long-term pattern of industrial consumers' usage: firms are committed to those power levels for a 5-year period.[3]

At the end of 1974 the total subscribed power for all Green Tariff (medium- and high-voltage) consumers was 22,741 MW during winter peak hours, 25,478 MW during winter shoulder hours, and 26,560 MW during summer off-peak hours (Table 32). These figures imply a contractual reduction of 2737 MW, or 11 percent, between shoulder and peak hours in the winter season. Data for the 600 largest high-voltage industrial consumers show a comparable 13 percent reduction during winter between the power subscribed in shoulder hours and that subscribed during peak hours.

3. However, for several reasons a comparison of the total amount of power subscribed in each period can provide only an approximate measure of the effect on system maximum demands that results from the tariff. (1) When several customers actually use power, the peaks in their individual loads during each tariff period will not exactly coincide, so that the sum of their subscribed demands will be an overestimate of their coincident demands at the time of the system peak. (2) To the extent that firms have not merely reduced loads during the high-cost hours but have shifted usage into lower-cost tariff periods, the measured differences will overstate the simple reduction in the system-wide peak-period load. (3) There are unmeasured reductions over the years in peak-period subscribed-demand levels for firms that nevertheless continue to have their maximum demands in the peak period. (4) Finally, customers cannot subscribe to a lower level of demand in lower-priced than in higher-priced periods. For these reasons, calculations based on subscribed power levels should be considered to be rough estimates of the effect of peak-period pricing on the system load.

Table 32. Subscribed Power under the Green Tariff, December 1974

Period	All Green Tariff Consumers		600 Customers Served at High Voltage (60kv and up)	
	Subscribed Power (MW)	Decrement (MW)	Subscribed Power (MW)	Decrement (MW)
Off-peak				
Summer	26,560		7930	
Winter	26,527	33	7921	9
Shoulder				
Summer	26,011	516	7683	238
Winter	25,478	533	7554	129
Peak	22,741	2737	6558	996
Total		3819		1372

Source: Electricité de France.

England and Wales

Figure 48 shows the comparative load shapes in 1960/61 and in 1972/73 for power supplied by the Central Electricity Generating Board (CEGB) in England and Wales. Pricing and load-management policy appear to have considerably leveled off the earlier peaks and have substantially increased the level of the system load in the pre-dawn valley.

The successful use of interruptible tariffs that permit about 3 percent of the total system load to be shed on short notice to some 125 customers was noted in Chapter 5. An undetermined additional amount of load reduction at peak hours is attributable to the effect of the optional time-of-day tariffs and special arrangement contracts for industrial customers. Of at least equal importance has been the significant shift in residential loads achieved by the adoption of storage space and water heating. Peddie (1975) calculates that if the CEGB's 1972/73 energy requirements had been met by deliveries according to 1960/61 load shapes, an additional 4700 MW of demand would have resulted—an increase of 13 percent of the 1972/73 system peak load.[4]

West Germany

Figure 49 shows the changes in the relative load shapes for the West German electricity network over the 1964-1974 period. As in France and England, the relative peak loads in West Germany have been reduced since the widespread introduction of peak-load pricing and residential load management. Because the terms of electricity contracts for large industrial consumers in West Germany

---

4. As noted in the discussion of the French Green Tariff, changes in load shapes over time are not solely the result of the incentive effects of electricity rate structures. The estimate of additional demand should be considered a rough approximation to the system-wide effects on required capacity.

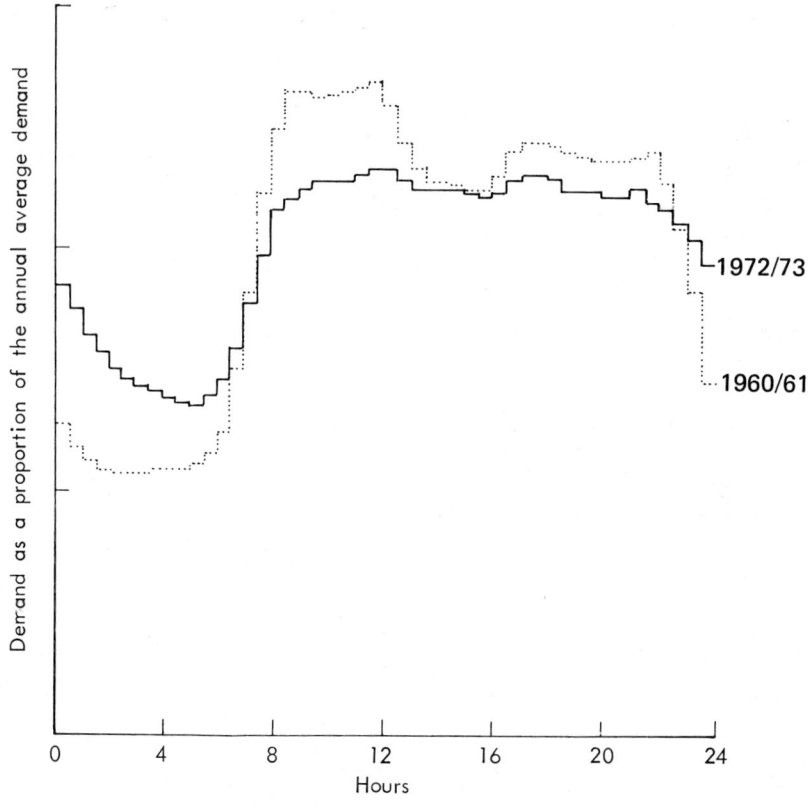

Source: Central Electricity Generating Board, "The Bulk Supply Tariff," abridged version, January 1975.

Figure 48. British Daily Load Curves, Annual Average, 1960/61 and 1972/73

are not publicly available, it is not possible to assess the extent to which peak-load pricing at the industrial level accounts for the reduction in system peak loads. However, the rapid and widespread adoption of residential storage-space heating and water heating indicates the potency of time-of-day rate structures for low-voltage customers.

SHIFTING PEAKS

The economic literature on peak-load pricing has recognized the possibility that charging prices based on marginal costs may cause the location of the peak load to shift to a new peak period. If prices are set on the basis of marginal costs calculated for the load curve observed under a tariff with constant prices throughout the day and year, demand responses to peak-load pricing may indeed be

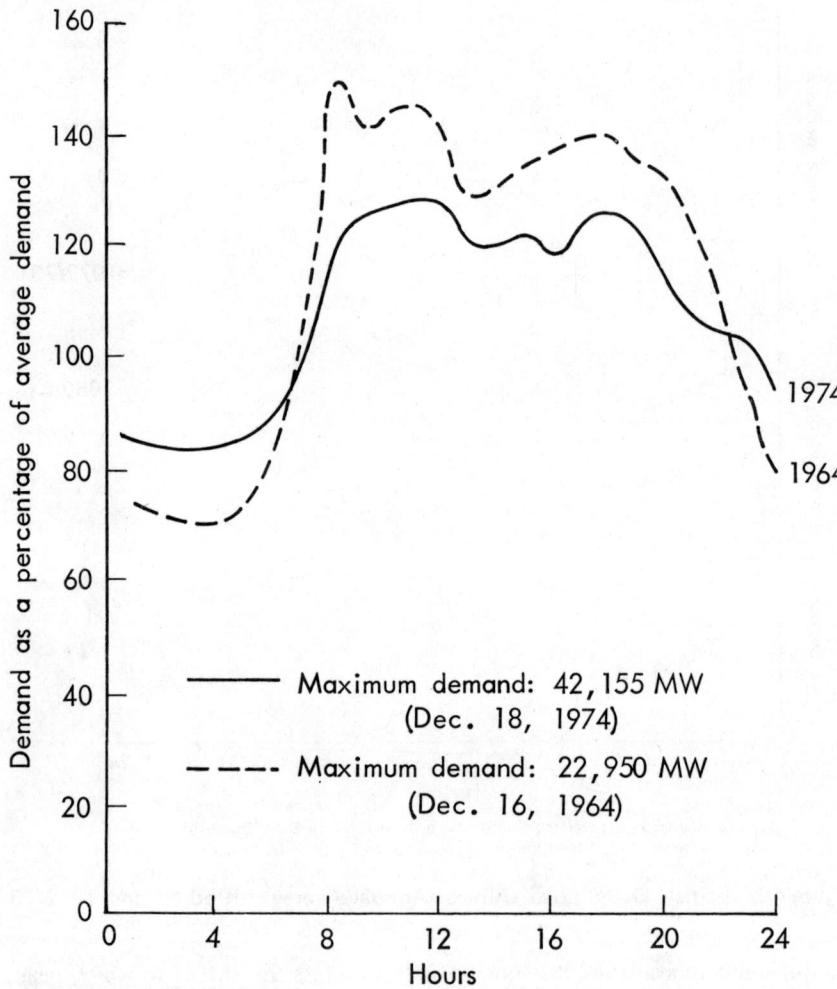

Source: "Die Offentliche Elektrizitätsversorgung, 1974."

Figure 49. West German Network Load Curves on Days of Peak Demand, 1964 and 1974

sufficiently large that, over time, a new peak will appear at different hours. Managers of utilities have understandably expressed reservations about the merits of peak-load pricing if it leads to such effects.

Theoretical Solution

The theoretical solution to a shifting-peak condition requires that if a shift in the peak is anticipated, each potential peak period should be priced so as to reduce demand in those periods to a common level that is equal to available capacity.[5] This rule implies that different prices may be charged in various peak periods for the same quantity of output. Nevertheless, such prices are based on the concept of marginal costs; in this situation marginal costs include—in addition to the running costs of supplying electricity—the opportunity costs that measure consumers' marginal valuations of the foregone output in the peak periods.

European utilities have dealt with the shifting-peak problem with a combination of tariff, load-management, and marketing strategies. In designing peak-load tariffs, some European utilities have attempted to anticipate potential shifts in peak loads and have established rates that include subjective judgments about the degree of shifting that will occur. For example, in the basic Swedish tariff only a portion of the differences in marginal costs between peak and off-peak hours is included in differential energy rates; the remainder of the difference is included in the 6-hour demand charge that automatically follows any shift in the customer's individual peak demand. In French practice the probabilities of outage at different hours are used to define the pricing periods, and part of the expected shortage costs are incorporated into the energy rates and contractual demand charges for each period.

Evidence of Shifting Peaks

That the concern about a shifting peak is a real one may be appreciated from examples in several countries. The French system load now peaks outside of the 2-hour morning peak pricing period as was made clear in Figure 46. This shifted peak constitutes a deficiency in the current peak-load rate structure of the Green Tariff—a more efficient tariff would include weekday hours as late as 10 or 11 a.m. in the peak-pricing period.

In the United Kingdom and West Germany a continuing shift in residential load has accompanied the increasingly widespread adoption of storage heating devices for residential use. The utilities have monitored this shift and modified their load-management programs where necessary. The earliest models of storage heaters used in Britain required a 3-hour midafternoon period for a supplementary charge, in addition to the 8-hour overnight basic charge, in order to deliver satisfactory heating service. By 1967 the growth in afternoon load that was occurring threatened to create a new system peak. This perceived difficulty prompted technological improvements in the design of the storage units that eliminated the need for the supplementary afternoon charge.

In West Germany the promotion of storage heating units has been so successful in several utilities that the system peak has threatened to shift from midday to about 10 p.m. To avoid this problem, West German utilities limit the rate at which new storage units may be installed, and have developed storage units that reach their maximum demand late in the off-peak period.[6]

5. See Boiteux (1949); Steiner (1957); and Panzar (1976).
6. In the case of residential storage heating, the theoretical solution to the shifting-peak problem—that the off-peak price be set at the level necessary to just equate peak loads in

In Sweden, utility system planners have deferred a decision to introduce off-peak rates that would encourage storage heating by domestic customers. As compared with the potentially large growth in the off-peak load that could result, there is, at present, only a limited valley in the system load curve that could be filled before a new system peak would result. Instead, the utilities are examining the effectiveness of constructing a pumped-storage facility.

A secondary complication introduced by time-differentiated rates is the potential for sharp increases in demand to appear just after the off-peak rate goes into effect. Clock-controlled storage and water heaters in the United Kingdom were initially set to begin drawing power within a few minutes after 11 p.m. As these loads have grown, area boards are staggering the clock settings to smooth loads throughout the generation and distribution system. In West Germany and France, similar loads in urban areas are frequently controlled remotely by injecting ripple-control signals into the power circuits, which then switch on customer space heaters and water heaters on a staggered, computer-controlled schedule.

DOES NATIONALIZATION MAKE A DIFFERENCE?

It is occasionally suggested that because a number of foreign electric utilities are operated by a national public authority their experience has little relevance for U.S. energy pricing and policy.[7] A point of particular confusion is the belief that nationalized electric utilities receive regular subsidies from the public treasury and that such financing invalidates data either about consumer behavior in response to price incentives or the potential for increased efficiency that could be achieved by peak-load pricing. In fact, however, the nationalized electric utilities—such as those in France and the United Kingdom—are customarily operated as independent authorities whose revenues must cover their operating and capital costs.[8] Despite the potentially greater efficiency in the use of economic resources that could be obtained from strict marginal-cost pricing, countries with nationalized electricity supply companies have settled for second-best pricing structures in which total revenues are equal to total costs. Since most U.S. electric utilities must operate subject to the constraint that their total revenue equals total cost (including, for private utilities, the allowed rate of return on equity), the financing requirements confronting European and U.S. utilities are similar.

Not surprisingly, European utilities—no less than U.S. utilities—do come

---

both periods (rather than at the marginal supply cost)—is not easily applied. Because of the similarity of demands of thousands of residential customers, the market demand curve for electricity for storage heating is highly elastic over a very narrow price range; below the break-even price differential, few households will invest in the appliance, whereas above that price differential, such heating is rationally preferred by almost everyone.

7. For example, Nissel (1976) expresses this view.

8. In the case of nationalized utilities that finance construction by borrowing from the government treasury, the investments are required to show a competitive rate of return.

under considerable public pressure to limit increases in the overall level of their rates. The 1973/74 oil embargo caused nearly all utilities to incur sharply higher operating costs, and foreign governments were reluctant to permit electricity prices to rise immediately. The nationalized French and English utilities, for example, incurred significant deficits that will only be recouped from higher rates that took effect after 1974. But this experience is not dissimilar to the difficulties that the regulated U.S. utilities faced in obtaining rate relief during the same period, and it is also reminiscent of the low rates of return earned during the period of national price control in the United States after August 1971.

Regardless of whether the level of a utility's tariff was sufficient to cover all of its costs at the time, the focus in assessing the European experience here has been on consumer *responses to the tariff structures* and other load-management techniques that were actually in operation. Consumers' incentives to shift loads from peak periods to off-peak periods depend principally on the *differences* between peak and off-peak prices. Those differences are only slightly affected by a change in the general level of rates, such as the increase that would be required to convert a modest deficit into a balanced budget or even a revenue surplus. For this reason, the nature of the ownership or the financing of European utilities is irrelevant to an analysis of consumer responses to tariff structures and load-management policies.

SUMMARY

Foreign utilities have undoubtedly failed to achieve all of the cost reductions that are possible from shifting the system load curve. In some instances the practical implementation of the marginal-cost principles on which tariffs were originally designed has contained shortcomings. During the last several years the system peak load in France has shifted from the early morning period, when peak prices are in effect, into the later morning hours, yet the hours used for peak pricing have remained unchanged. In England and Wales the Central Electricity Generating Board has constructed facilities for generating capacity at a more rapid rate than the rate at which demand has increased, with the result that substantial excess capacity is now in place. In West Germany, rapid adoption of storage heating has threatened to shift the system peak into the late evening. And in several countries political consideration of potential adverse effects on local employment in particular industries has led to selective price subsidies for electricity.

It is not, however, necessary that a utility be operated perfectly in order to derive valid information about the effectiveness of its tariff structures. In the last several chapters the pricing incentives provided to individual industrial and residential customers by European peak-load tariffs have been analyzed. Data have been assembled that show their specific load responses to these incentives in order to determine how successful peak-load pricing can be in influencing consumers' uses of electricity. Of course the system-wide benefits to be achieved by using peak-load pricing will depend on how consistently the rate structure of each utility is related to the structure of its marginal costs. When considerations other than economic efficiency intervene, some of the gains that could be achieved are sacrificed for other objectives.

The extensive body of load-curve data from both industrial and residential customers in Europe establishes that consumers are responsive in varying degrees to the pricing signals of peak-load rate structures. Many firms operating in a wide variety of industries are able to reduce loads at peak hours and increase off-peak loads to take advantage of lower off-peak rates. Given appropriate price incentives, other plants will interrupt production processes. Still other firms find it advantageous to engage in cogeneration of their own electricity. At the residential level, peak-load tariffs can induce millions of consumers to invest in storage technologies and to permit remote control of selected loads. The aggregate effect of these responses to peak-load pricing has been to reduce the capacity requirements of European utilities, permit increases in the fuel efficiency with which electricity is generated, and achieve significant savings in national resources.

The relevance of this experience for the United States is that peak-load pricing of electricity is a tested and well-established concept in major utilities. If U.S. utilities modify their rate structures to include peak-load rates, significant gains in the efficiency of the electricity sector should be realized. The magnitude of the changes in load and the net benefits that could be achieved do require careful assessment in terms of specific U.S. conditions, and this is the subject of Part III.

❋ *Part III*

Peak-Load Pricing for the United States

Until very recently the rate structures of U.S. electric utilities received the attention of only a small group of engineers in public utilities and staff members of state regulatory commissions. In the decades prior to 1970, electricity prices—when adjusted for inflation—were declining, and the general public had little interest in electricity rates.

In the early 1970s public-interest groups began to express concern for the effects on the environment of continued growth in electricity consumption and the need to construct new generating plants, especially nuclear reactors. Then, in late 1973, the Arab oil embargo dramatized the rapidly changing nature of the energy economy. During the same period rapid inflation in fuel and construction costs was compelling electric utilities to seek increases in their rates. These factors have all created a critical public attitude toward traditional utility practices and a receptivity to new ideas for pricing electricity.[1]

In the final chapters of this volume the potential contributions that peak-load rate structures can make to increasing the efficiency of the electricity sector in the United States are assessed. The analysis is based on the experience accumulated by European utilities and the economic principles discussed in Parts I and II. In Chapter 8 the potential effects of peak-load pricing for industrial customers are examined in quantitative terms. In Chapter 9 the issues raised by peak-load pricing for residential and commercial customers are reviewed. The final chapter contains an analysis of the implications of peak-load pricing for energy policy in the United States.

1. Joskow (1974) discusses the history of public involvement in electricity rate structures; and Joskow (1977) also reviews some of the recent activity in rate reform, including the generic rate structure hearings in a number of states and the initial recommendations for peak-load rates.

❋ *Chapter 8*

Peak-Load Pricing for Industry

Studies of the demand for energy have found that under existing rate structures the level of electricity prices has a substantial long-term effect on the quantity of electricity used in U.S. industries.[1] In Chapter 5 it was shown that in Europe, industrial consumption of electricity is sensitive not merely to the level of electricity prices, but also to the structure of the time-of-day variations in peak-load rates. Since conventional U.S. rate structures do not reflect the variations in costs that exist between different time periods, a change to peak-load tariffs based on marginal-cost principles would alter industrial load patterns and potentially increase economic efficiency in the United States. This potential will be realized unless the adoption and administration of new tariffs imposes large costs.

For a utility's largest customers, the costs of implementing a peak-load tariff are only a tiny fraction of the total costs of the electricity they consume, and therefore a clear gain in efficiency will result from applying peak-load pricing to high-voltage customers. In many instances some of the metering equipment needed to implement time-of-day pricing for these customers is already available for billing under currently used maximum-demand tariffs or for conducting load studies. Furthermore, a large proportion of a utility's total sales are made to a small number of high-voltage customers, so equipment and implementation costs for this group will be quite limited. For these reasons the first state regulatory commission rulings to establish time-of-day tariffs have focused on the largest customers.

In California, Michigan, New York, and Wisconsin the public utilities commissions have ordered that time-of-day pricing be implemented for the largest

---
1. See Anderson (1971); Mount, Chapman, and Tyrell (1973); and the studies summarized in Taylor (1975).

industrial and commercial customers. They have also directed that suitable metering be installed for smaller commercial and industrial users so that they too can face time-of-day rates in the future. Several other states are considering peak-load pricing for industrial customers. By 1977 a total of 22 state public utility commissions had either held generic rate hearings, ordered utilities to submit time-of-day rates before filing again for a rate increase, or had received time-of-day rate proposals from the utilities they regulate.[2] Furthermore, both the administration's energy proposals and the congressional bills for electric utility rate reform would require states to consider time-of-day electricity rates for all customers.

In this chapter measurements of adaptation to peak-load tariffs in French industry and data from load studies of U.S. industrial customers are synthesized in order to estimate the opportunities for increasing efficiency in the electricity sector by establishing peak-load rate structures for industrial customers throughout the United States. The estimates are limited to manufacturing, and do not include all industrial customers because of the lack of detailed information for nonmanufacturing industries in Europe and the United States. However, some of these other industries that use large quantities of electricity—including mining and transportation—can also be expected to shift loads and thus increase the aggregate effect of peak-load electricity rates.[3] The calculations are made at the level of individual manufacturing industrial groups, and indicate that the potential increases in efficiency and savings in generating capacity are substantial.

POTENTIAL INDUSTRIAL RESPONSE TO PEAK-LOAD PRICING

To assess the potential gains from peak-load pricing, estimates of the changes that could be expected to occur in the amount and pattern of industrial use of electricity, if U.S. utilities were to adopt peak-load tariffs similar to those widely used abroad, are presented. In making this assessment, one must be aware that the response of U.S. firms will depend on several factors that may differ from those prevailing in Europe, including: (1) the relative costs of other types of energy; (2) the relative costs of capital and labor; (3) the specific terms of the tariffs that would be offered by U.S. utilities; and (4) the technological processes employed in U.S. industries.

The peak-load and time-of-day tariffs found in France and in the United Kingdom are of the form most likely to be considered for adoption in the United States.[4] Furthermore, industry-by-industry load data are available for

---

2. Joskow (1977).

3. In France, for example, pumping and pipeline plants are able to eliminate almost their entire load during peak hours. See Chapter 5.

4. This observation is based on a review of rate cases before state utility commissions. In England and France the industrial tariffs have time-of-day components similar to those

French industrial customers. For these reasons the quantitative assessment presented here is based on the French experience. To estimate the potential responses of U.S. industries, the load responses of individual French industries are applied to current load curves of industrial firms served by two major California utilities.

Despite the reliance on data from one country and a single state, the estimates are based on comparisons of load curves on an industry-by-industry basis, and should be reliable for a broad variety of peak-load pricing conditions. In Chapter 5 it was shown that where load curves for the same industries are available in both France and Great Britain, the nature (and often the magnitude) of the peak-period response is quite similar. This similarity exists even though French industries are responding to a three-level tariff with two 2-hour peak periods, while British firms are facing a single 12-hour or longer peak period and a relatively small difference between the peak and off-peak prices per kilowatt-hour. Similarly, the patterns of electricity use in California industries are not specific to that state; rather, they reflect a common technological base that is available nationwide.

The estimates presented in this chapter assess the potential for shifting industrial electricity loads away from peak hours in U.S. utilities. They should not be interpreted as forecasts of the changes that will result from time-of-day pricing; rather, they are comparisons of the patterns of use of electricity in the United States with and without the type of response observed in European data. The extent to which this potential will be realized will depend on the extent to which peak-load rate structures that are based on economic principles are adopted.

In order to make clear the basis for the estimates that follow, several technical issues must be considered that arise from the measurement of industrial electricity loads. The analysis is divided into three parts. First, a discussion is presented of how industrial customers abroad may have adapted their use of electricity when peak-load rates were introduced in their utilities. This discussion is necessary both to enable one to interpret the cross-sectional data observed in Europe today and to envision the possible patterns of adjustment by users in the United States. Second, a description is given of the method used to calculate the magnitude of the adjustment that has taken place in the pattern of electricity use by foreign industrial users, and the similar procedure employed to calculate potential changes in U.S. industrial use. Finally, data from a sample of industrial users served by two major utilities in the state of California is utilized to calculate the potential industry-by-industry load changes throughout the nation.

---

proposed for U.S. utilities. Furthermore, the generating mix in those countries more closely resembles that available in the United States. Tariffs based on a predominantly hydroelectric generation base (as in Norway) are less appropriate for most U.S. utilities.

INDUSTRIAL ADAPTATION OVER TIME TO PEAK-LOAD TARIFFS

The load-curve data from the mid-1970s that were presented in Chapter 5 provide strong evidence that a variety of firms can modulate electricity loads in response to the terms of peak-load rates. However, such data are of limited value in establishing the rate at which industrial firms have modified their electricity consuming activities over time. To understand how rapidly U.S. industrial customers might respond to new peak-load tariffs and to establish the basis for projecting the amount of load shifting that could eventually occur, a number of different initial patterns of electricity consumption must be discussed.

The analysis of hypothetical alternative patterns of adjustment to time-of-day tariffs has three purposes. First, it provides a basis for assessing the reliability of the present quantitative estimates as measures of the true adjustment made by foreign industrial customers. Generally, the measures presented here of the changes that have occurred in the use of electricity in foreign countries provide conservative estimates of the long-run potential impact in the United States. Second, this discussion is useful in suggesting how particular U.S. customers might adapt to peak-load tariffs. Third, this analysis illuminates the conservative nature of customer response to the introduction of a peak-load tariff and helps to distinguish which types of adjustments will occur rapidly and which will require a longer period of time.

Factors Affecting Adaptation

The pattern of adaptation by each customer will depend on a complex set of factors. In addition to the general factors discussed above (relative costs of energy, capital, and labor, as well as the technological process involved), a particular firm's response will depend on the ease with which it can reschedule production activities to off-peak hours, the rate of capital replacement, the rate of plant expansion, and the nature of demand for its final product. In some cases the effect of a peak-period price will be to eliminate altogether some marginal uses of electricity that are not easily shifted to nonpeak hours. Correspondingly, the lower off-peak prices will cause an increase in electricity consumption that is partly composed of electricity uses shifted from peak periods and partly composed of new (or increased) use of electricity in response to the reduced price. The relative importance of these own-price and cross-price effects is difficult to determine in advance, and the neutral assumption is made here that total energy use remains constant and only its pattern over the day is shifted.[5]

Some of the most important factors affecting the consumer's pattern of adaptation can be summarized as extreme alternatives: (a) whether the firm operates

---

5. This assumption will be correct in some cases and inappropriate in other circumstances. Its validity will depend, among other things, on whether the average price of electricity changes relative to other forms of energy.

on a single- or three-shift basis; (b) whether capital costs are a small or a large proportion of total production costs; (c) whether labor costs are a small or a large proportion of total production costs; (d) whether or not a significant shift differential must be paid to labor; (e) whether or not there is significant price sensitivity in the demand for the firm's product; and (f) whether or not the firm has excess production capacity in the short run. Rather than attempt to explore in detail the manner in which each of these elements would affect the evolution of energy use by a single firm, five cases have been selected to illustrate the effect of the most important combinations of factors.

Adaptation to a Stylized Tariff

For simplicity, the process of adaptation over time will be illustrated by using a stylized tariff that does not correspond precisely to the terms of either the French or British peak-load tariff. Instead of the more complicated tariffs with peak, shoulder, and off-peak periods offered in France, the hypothetical tariff has a peak rate during a single 6-hour period and an off-peak rate that applies during the other 18 hours of each weekday. Furthermore, simplified load shapes are used that are constant at different levels of consumption, rather than the continuously varying curves observed in practice.

Case 1. In the first case a firm is considered that initially operates a single-shift production process and does not have important labor costs—either because they are a small part of total production costs or because labor-shift differentials would be insignificant. The load curve prior to the introduction of peak-load rates is assumed to have the shape shown in Figure 50(a).[6]

Unless the firm depicted in Figure 50(a) requires a long period of time every day for maintenance of equipment, it has excess production capacity for its current level of output. Therefore, the initial response by this single-shift firm to the peak-load tariff might be to schedule its working hours either earlier or later in the day so that it can entirely avoid the 6-hour peak charge. Depending on the costs and convenience of operating one or two shifts during off-peak hours, the firm may operate on a single shift at nonpeak hours, or it may settle immediately into a pattern of consumption as illustrated in Figure 50(b). Over time, as the demand for the product grows, the firm will increase its level of production in all off-peak hours, up to the level of installed plant capacity. Only as a last resort will the plant use any electricity during peak-charge hours.[7]

---

6. Such single-shift load curves are commonly observed for a number of industrial and commercial customers at medium voltages, but rarely for very large industrial users.

7. As noted in Chapter 5, the French cement industry follows a pattern of production and plant construction similar to that outlined here. Excess capacity is deliberately created in the short run; all crushing and grinding activities are scheduled for off-peak hours, whereas maintenance of the equipment is scheduled daily for the peak-charge period. Only as total production reaches a plant's maximum capacity is any crushing and grinding scheduled for the peak period.

156 Peak-Load Pricing for the United States

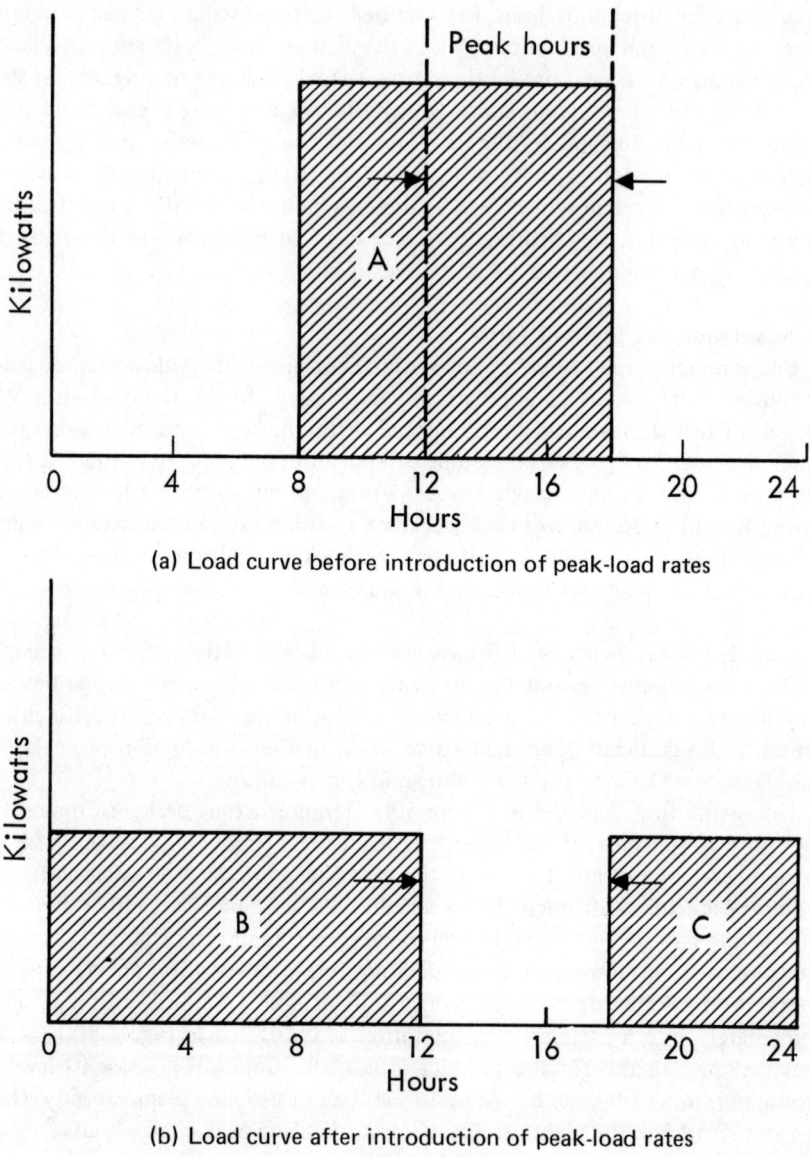

(a) Load curve before introduction of peak-load rates

(b) Load curve after introduction of peak-load rates

Figure 50. Case 1: Initial Single-Shift Operation in which Labor Costs are Small

In general, one will underestimate the reduction in energy used during peak hours for industries in Case 1 if one is only able to observe the load curve shown in Figure 50(b). As long as the total amount of electricity consumed (the area under the load curve) is the same over the course of the day, the difference between the rate of electricity use during peak hours and that used during off-peak hours in Figure 50(b) is smaller than the difference that results from comparing consumption during peak hours in graphs (a) and (b) of Figure 50. Of course, as production during off-peak hours increases to the capacity constraint, the difference between peak and off-peak electricity consumption increases and graph (b) becomes a more accurate measure of the shift that has taken place over time.

Some firms that are initially in the situation of Case 1 will have the additional possibility of changing the energy intensiveness of their production processes. The lower off-peak electricity rate may make it advantageous to substitute electricity for labor, capital, or other inputs. Where such technological possibilities exist, the firm will, over time, shift to a permanent load shape of the form illustrated in graph (b) of Figure 50. Since in this case the amount of energy per unit of output increases, one cannot unambiguously assert that observing only graph (b) will underestimate the amount of energy reduction during peak-charge hours. However, for the same level of plant output, the energy intensiveness of the process would have to increase quite substantially for the lower graph not to be a conservative measure of change.[8]

Case 2. As a second case, a plant is considered that initially uses electricity during three shifts and has a load curve—shown in graph (a) of Figure 51—that peaks during the prime daytime shift. Multishift operation is needed either because the plant capacity is not adequate to meet total production in a single shift or because minimum levels of operation are required at all hours for the technological process involved. Most large high-voltage consumers operate multiple-shift production processes.

As in Case 1, it is assumed that labor-cost differentials are relatively unimportant. If a minimum level of plant operation (at the K' level) is needed, response to the peak-load tariff is shown by the solid line in graph (b) of Figure 51. If there is no reduction in total output of the plant, then area A equals the sum of areas B, C, and D. If it is not necessary to have a minimum level of operation so that all of the load can be shed during peak hours, then the new load curve may be more like the broken line in graph (b), where the sum of areas B, B', C, and C', equals area A.

In Case 2 the firm can minimize cost by rescheduling its operations to concentrate energy use in off-peak hours. Consequently, changes in its load pattern in

---

8. For instance, at the same level of plan output, switching from a one-shift, 8-hour process to an 18-hour off-peak process will yield a conservative measure, unless the amount of electricity per unit of output increases by more than 225 percent.

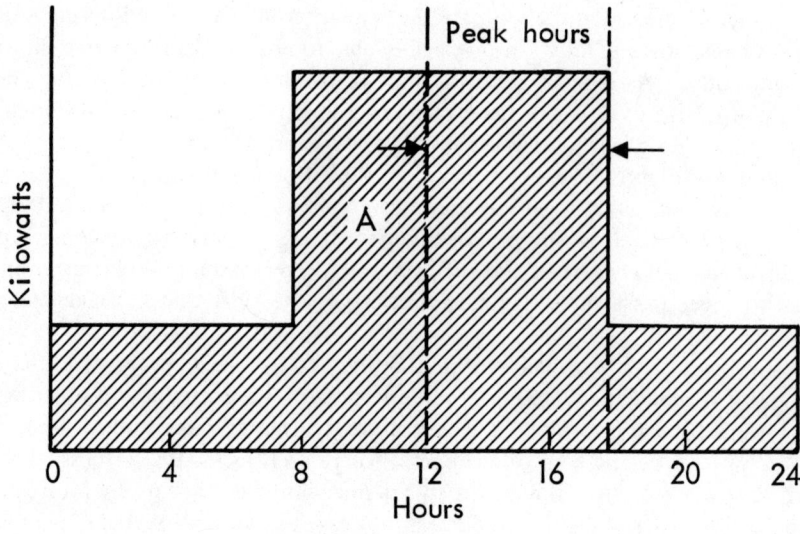

(a) Load curve before introduction of peak-load rates

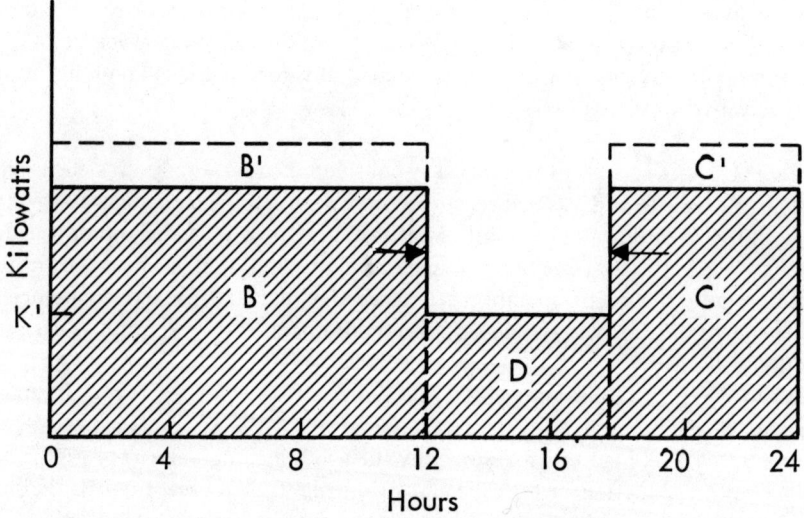

(b) Load curve after introduction of peak-load rates

Figure 51. Case 2: 24-Hour Operation in which Labor Costs Are Small and a Minimum Level of Electricity is Required

response to time-of-day tariffs should be observed relatively rapidly. If the total quantity of electricity used over the day remains the same, then a calculation based solely on graph (b) of Figure 50 will again provide a conservative measure of the amount of energy reduction that occurs in changing from the load curve in graph (a) to that in graph (b).

Case 3. In Case 3 it is assumed that the initial position of the firm is a single-shift operation with significant labor costs. The importance of these costs may be due either to large shift differentials that must be paid to labor or to relatively small pay differentials per worker combined with a large labor cost per unit of product. Under such circumstances, when a time-of-day rate is applied the firm can be expected to shift some, but not all, of its production to off-peak hours. At the same time that electricity costs fall (moving to off-peak production), labor costs rise because shift differentials must be paid to workers. The optimal amount of load shifting will be determined by the way in which the costs of production vary in each period as a result of different combinations of labor, energy, and capital inputs. The form of the new load curve is given in graph (b) of Figure 52. In general, consumption during peak hours will not be reduced to zero. Again because it is possible to observe the load curve only after the tariff has been in effect for some time, a conservative measure of the reduction that occurred in peak-period energy consumption will result.[9]

The conservative estimate of the reduction in peak electricity use is reinforced by the likely adjustment in total plant output. Since in Case 3 labor costs are a significant portion of total costs, the price of the output can be expected to rise and, as long as the demand for the final good is not perfectly inelastic, the overall level of output will fall. Consequently, area A in Figure 52 will generally be greater than area B, and the difference between peak and off-peak electricity consumption observed in graph (b) will understate the reduction that would be calculated from a comparison of peak-period use in graphs (a) and (b).

Case 3 could also be generalized to a situation in which the firm initially has nonzero consumption of electricity in the second and third shifts (as in the initial position shown in graph (a) of Figure 51). After adaptation to the time-of-day tariff, the plant's load shape would resemble that shown in graph (b) of Figure 52.

Case 4. The load curve for the fourth case, starting from a one-shift operation, is shown in Figure 53. In this case it is assumed that labor costs are important and that despite the shifting of some activities to off-peak hours, it is still optimal to use more electricity during peak than off-peak periods. This is an especially important case to note, because if one were to observe only the load curve after the tariff had gone into effect (graph [b] of Figure 53), one

---

9. As noted in Case 1, only a substantial increase in the electricity intensity of the production process would modify this conclusion.

160 Peak-Load Pricing for the United States

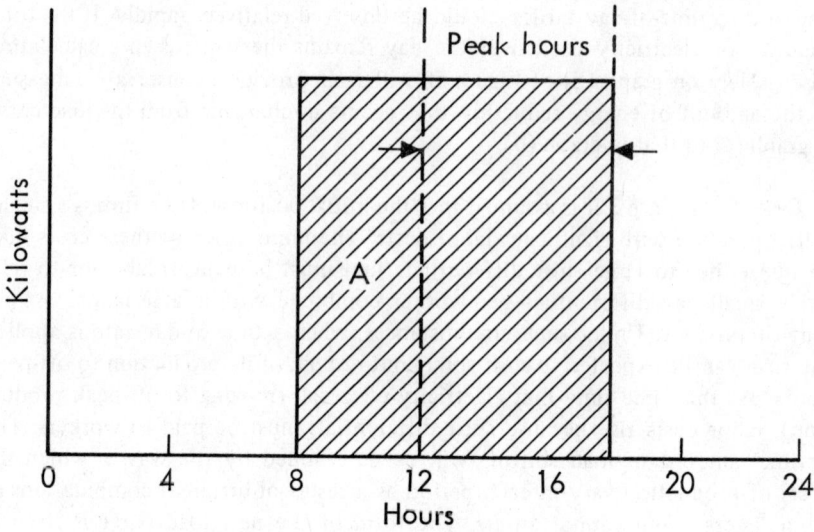

(a) Load curve before introduction of peak-load rates

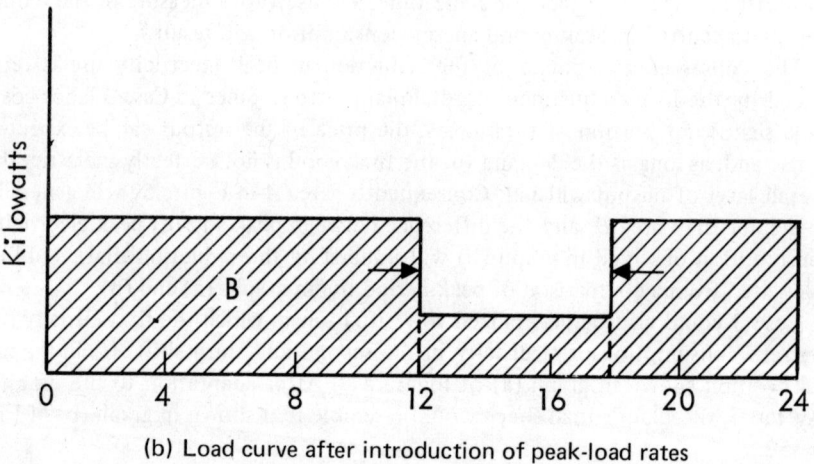

(b) Load curve after introduction of peak-load rates

Figure 52. Case 3: Initial Single-Shift Operation in which Labor Costs are Significant

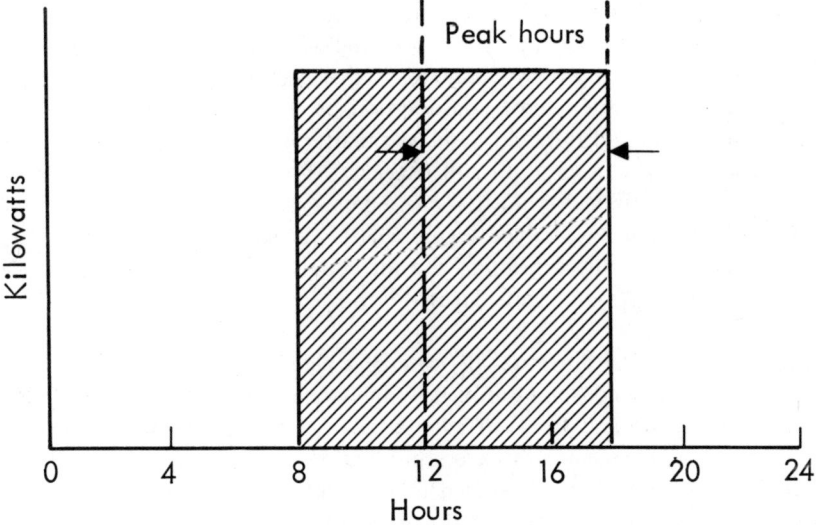

(a) Load curve before introduction of peak-load rates

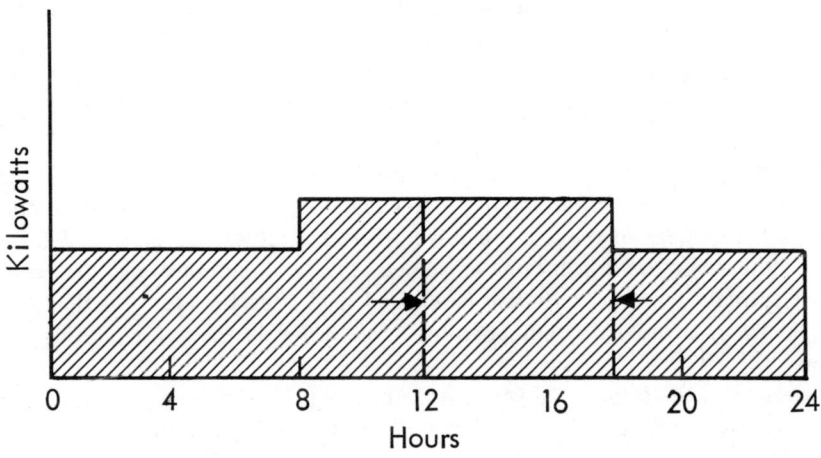

(b) Load curve after introduction of peak-load rates

Figure 53. Case 4: Initial Single-Shift Operation in which Labor Costs are Significant; Optimal Shifting Leaves Peak Use Above Off-Peak Use

might conclude that there had been no response to the time-of-day tariff. But under the postulated conditions, a substantial adjustment has in fact occurred. A similar case, one that may apply to a large proportion of high-voltage customers, will occur when some consumption of electricity initially takes place during the second and third shift and when, after optimal rescheduling of activities, peak energy consumption still exceeds off-peak energy consumption. In Chapter 5 several French industrial customers were pointed out whose current pattern of energy use resembled Figure 53(b). No data are available to indicate whether their load curves prior to the introduction of the Green Tariff were similar to Figure 53(a) or Figure 51(a).

Case 5. Figure 54 illustrates the case of a plant with a three-shift operation in which electricity consumption is reasonably constant throughout the 24-hour period. The nature and speed of adaptation to a time-of-day tariff depend on whether or not the plant has excess production capacity in the short run. In graph (a) of Figure 54, it is assumed that the plant is operating near the maximum of its installed production capacity, and is consuming energy at a rate of K_1 kilowatts, day and night. Under these circumstances, unless there is a decline in the demand for the firm's product, time-of-day pricing will have no effect on the use of electricity in the short run. However, if there is some excess production capacity available, then—as shown in graph (b) of Figure 54—the firm will expand production in off-peak hours up to the maximum available capacity, and consume electricity at a rate of K_2 (greater than K_1) kilowatts during off-peak hours. The plant will reduce its peak-period use of energy as much as possible while still meeting total demand for its product. In the long run the plant may find it advantageous—as in graph (c)—to expand its production capacity in order to take advantage of the less-expensive off-peak electricity rates. Provided that the additional costs of achieving expanded capacity do not outweigh the savings on electricity rates, capacity will be expanded to a level K_3 (greater than both K_1 and K_2) in order to eliminate most or all of the electricity used during peak hours.

Several of the French industries described in Chapter 5 have load curves that are consistent with this hypothetical pattern of evolution. A number of firms—in the petroleum refining, electrochemical, cement, and air products industries—operate continuous processes and are often considered to be unable to modify their daily patterns of electricity use. However, the individual load curves of many of these industries under peak-load tariffs clearly demonstrate that continuous processes frequently have a significant degree of flexibility in the amount of purchased electricity.

Summary. The five cases discussed above illustrate that a variety of initial conditions will underlie the pattern and speed of industrial adaptation to time-of-day electricity rates. Although relatively few differences should occur in the

Peak-Load Pricing for Industry 163

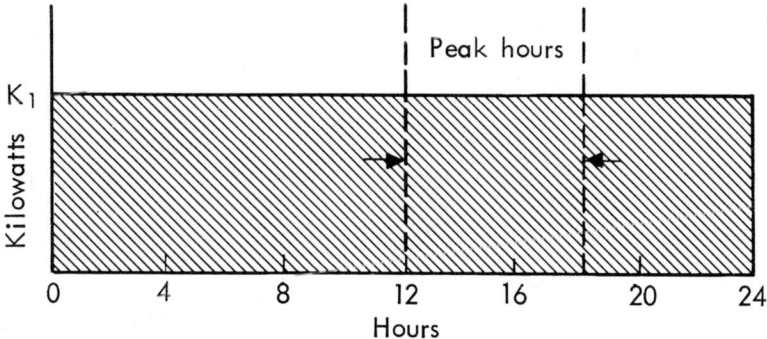

(a) Production capacity constrained in the short run

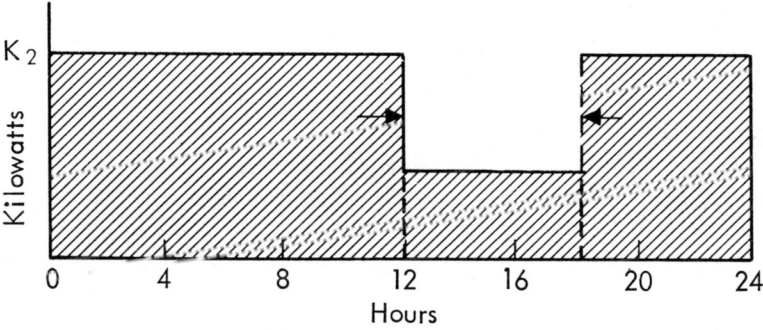

(b) Production expanded to capacity constraint
in the short run

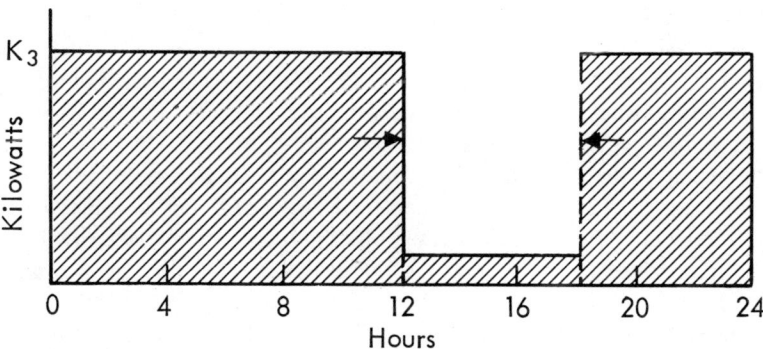

(c) Production capacity expanded in the long run

Figure 54. Case 5: Three-Shift Operation in which Capital Costs Are Significant

shapes of load curves after a peak-load tariff has been in effect for some time, there are several different initial patterns from which the ultimate load shapes may evolve. Since we are limited here to observing only the ex post load curves of European industrial customers some years after the introduction of time-of-day rates, we will generally tend to underestimate the shift in peak-period consumption that has taken place over time. Our measures of the effects of time-of-day rates on peak-period electricity consumption can therefore be regarded as conservative estimates of the potential load shifting that could be achieved in the United States.

DATA AND METHODOLOGY

Before describing our estimates of the potential response of U.S. industries to peak-load tariffs, the applicability of European load-curve data to U.S. conditions will be examined, and then the methods on which our estimates are based will be described.

Applicability

If industrial customers in the United States were in exactly the same economic position today that their French industrial counterparts occupied at the initiation of time-of-day pricing, one would expect that the shapes of the load curves for U.S. industries would eventually come to resemble closely those seen in France today. For these conditions to prevail, the terms of the tariffs would have to be identical, the technologies would have to be the same, and the relative prices of factor inputs—such as labor, capital, and energy—would have to be equal in both situations.

Despite the fact that not all circumstances in the United States are identical with those in France, the potential U.S. time-of-day tariffs appear to be very similar to French time-of-day rates. Although the overall price level and specific terms of U.S. peak-load tariffs (especially the peak hours and the relationship of kilowatt to kilowatt-hour charges) will vary from utility to utility, a basic similarity in tariff structure can be expected throughout much of the United States.

For instance, the structure of the time-of-day tariff that went into effect in early 1977 for the 120 largest customers served by the Pacific Gas & Electric Company (PG&E) in California closely resembles the French industrial tariff. Table 33 shows the terms of the two tariffs for the peak season (4 months in France, 5 months in PG&E's service territories). Each tariff has three distinct periods: peak, shoulder, and off-peak. Columns (1) and (2) show the actual prices under each tariff.[10] To make it easier to compare the cost savings from shifts in electricity

---

10. For purposes of comparing the two tariffs, the French subscribed demand charge is stated as a monthly amount, even though it applies to the maximum kilowatt demand in a 4-month period.

Table 33. Comparison of Peak Season Time-of-Day Rates in France and California

Period	Actual Tariff		Effective Price[a]
	$/kw/mo (1)	¢/kwh (2)	¢/kwh (3)
France[b] (November–February)			
Peak (4 hr, 6 days/wk)	5.08[c]	4.3	9.2
Shoulder (12 hr, 6 days/wk)	1.35[d]	2.6	3.0
Off-peak (8 hr, 6 days/wk; all day Sunday)	0.24[e]	1.3	1.4
California PG&E[f] (May–September)			
Peak (6 hr, 5 days/wk)	3.45	2.2	4.8
Shoulder (8 hr, 5 days/wk; 14 hr on Saturday)	0.28	2.0	2.1
Off-peak (10 hr, 6 days/wk; all day Sunday)	0.00	1.8	1.8

[a] Based on consumption of electricity at a constant rate during each period of time.
[b] General Tariff version of the Green Tariff (1976) for customers served at 60 to 90 kv, based on the rate of exchange prevailing on January 3, 1977.
[c] Monthly portion of the annual charge for subscribed power.
[d] Monthly portion of the annual charge for power subscribed during a shoulder period, which is billed at an amount no less than the amount subscribed during the peak period.
[e] Monthly portion of the annual charge for power subscribed during an off-peak period, which is billed at an amount no less than the amount subscribed during the shoulder period.
[f] Rates in effect February 1977.

use under different combinations of kilowatt and kilowatt-hour charges, column (3) restates the tariffs in terms of the equivalent price per kilowatt-hour in each time period.[11]

Both rate structures offer substantial inducements to shift load away from peak hours into either shoulder or off-peak periods. However, because the differences among the peak, shoulder, and off-peak rates are more extreme under the Green Tariff, a firm analyzing the merits of load shifting will find that benefit-cost comparisons of load adjustments will show a greater gross benefit under the French tariff than under this particular U.S. tariff.

11. The equivalent price is calculated by dividing the kilowatt charge by the total number of hours to which it applies, and adding this amount to the price per kilowatt-hour. This amount indicates the saving per kilowatt-hour when a customer reduces consumption by 1 kilowatt of demand throughout the time period.

Conservative Nature of the Calculations

There are three principal reasons to expect that the calculated responsiveness of French industrial customers will provide a conservative estimate of the long-run load changes that can be expected from U.S. industrial customers in corresponding industries.

First, as observed in discussing Cases 1 through 5 above, the measured load curves will frequently understate the long-term reduction in peak electricity use that has occurred in response to the introduction of time-of-day tariffs, particularly when the use of electricity during peak hours still exceeds that during off-peak hours (see Figure 53).

Second, most forms of energy have, for several years, been more costly in most European countries than in the United States. Consequently, many possibilities for economizing on energy consumption in the United States have already been exploited in European industries. Also, the relatively greater scarcity and higher cost of alternative forms of energy, such as natural gas and fuel oil, have meant that European industrial customers could not as readily substitute those sources of energy for electricity in their industrial processes.

Third, in calculating the degree of industrial load-shifting in the United States, we assume that total electricity use remains the same over the course of the day. In those instances in which the introduction of a time-of-day tariff lowers total electricity use, actual load reductions at peak hours will exceed those calculated. Furthermore, as described in Case 1, even in instances in which a customer's total use of electricity increases, the methodology will usually yield a conservative estimate.

The import of these three factors is that by applying evidence of load-shifting from French industrial customers to U.S. industrial customers, we will get minimum estimates of the potential for reducing peak-period electricity consumption.

Data Used

Our calculations of potential load-shifting among U.S. industrial customers are based on detailed load-study data for both French and California industrial customers. As described in Chapter 4, the French high-voltage tariff has two types of time-of-day charges: one is based on maximum kilowatt demand subscribed in each of three time periods in the winter (and two time periods in the summer); the other is a charge per kilowatt-hour consumed in each of these five time periods. From a study of a sample of some 250 French firms (about half of France's large industrial users), we have data available on both the industries' subscribed demand levels and their daily load curves, from which we calculate kilowatt-hour usage by period.[12] Based on the U.S. Standard Industrial Classi-

---

12. The dates for the load study were chosen in advance by EdF's analysts. The study covered the third Wednesday in December and the following Saturday and Sunday. The net system load was lower than the historical average on this Wednesday, but we have been un-

Table 34. Annual Electricity Use in U.S. Manufacturing Industries, 1976

Industry	SIC Code	Annual Use of Electricity (millions kwh)
Textile mill products[a]	22	31,125
Paper and allied products[a]	26	43,591
Industrial inorganic chemicals	281	94,094
Plastics[a]	282	17,005
Petroleum refining	291	28,125
Rubber and miscellaneous products	300	19,030
Cement (hydraulic)	324	10,632
Blast furnace and steel works	331	62,347
Iron and steel foundries[a]	332	9,829
Electric lighting and wiring equipment	364	2,506
Communication equipment	366	6,021
Electronic components and accessories	367	6,455
Motor vehicles and equipment	371	20,000
Ship and boat building and repairing	373	2,025
Miscellaneous transportation equipment	379	641
Engineering, laboratory, scientific and research equipment	381	589
Surgical, medical and dental instruments	384	959
Total of 17 industries		355,020
Other industries		287,546
Total		642,566

[a]Indicates load-study data available for the industry in the French sample but not in the California sample.

fication (SIC) codes, seventeen of these industries, listed in Table 34, closely correspond to the manufacturing industries found in our California sample. These seventeen U.S. industries accounted for slightly more than half of total electricity sales to the manufacturing industry sector. The data from the remaining French industries were not used for calculating the potential for load-shifting in the United States.

Data for U.S. industries are taken from load studies of individual industrial customers of two major utilities—one in Northern California and one in Southern California. Load data for a total of approximately 175 customers in thirteen industry groupings (based on 4-digit SIC coding) are available for either a 2- or 3-month period for each customer. For four additional industrial groupings, good load data for France are available, but there are no corresponding load

able to detect any systematic bias in the percentage difference between peak-hour and slack-hour demand. Analysis of a sample of industries taken the same day a year later showed similar responses to the ones reported here.

curves within the sample of California industries (although there are such industries located in California). For these groups we used the total amount of electricity consumed in the corresponding California industry, and based our estimates on the assumption that the initial load curves were flat.[13] (These four industrial groups are indicated by a note in Table 34.)

In the United States the seventeen industries on which we have detailed load data accounted for 355 billion kwh in 1976, slightly more than 55 percent of electricity sales to all manufacturing industrial customers.

Methods of Calculating Response to Peak-Load Pricing

To estimate the potential impact of peak-load pricing on all U.S. manufacturing industries, we will use four methods of calculating the changes in industrial load in France and the United States. Because of the variety of load shapes and types of industrial responses, no one method can satisfactorily capture the changes in load under all circumstances. From the French sample we use either subscribed-demand data or load-study data to calculate the magnitude of load reduction in foreign industries. In the United States we estimate the potential change in peak-period consumption either by assuming a reduction in energy use during peak hours, proportional to that in the French data, or alternatively by postulating that U.S. customers will alter production so that their load curve takes the shape of their foreign counterpart industry. These various assumptions combine, as shown in Figure 55, to yield the four separate methods of estimating impact. Two of these procedures, Method 1 and Method 4, will be discussed in detail to illustrate the steps used in our calculations. As noted earlier, throughout our calculations we assume that total industrial consumption in the United States remains the same and that only the time at which electricity is used is affected. In all cases we calculate the potential load changes that would result from introducing a time-of-day rate with a peak period of 6 hours per day, Monday through Friday. This compares with the peak period in the French tariff of 4 hours per day, 6 days per week.

Method 1. Method 1 is based on first determining the percentage difference (δ) between the subscribed kilowatt demand in off-peak periods and in peak periods in a French industry. This difference is illustrated in Figure 56(a), which shows the stylized load curve of a French industry. Part (b) of Figure 56 shows the stylized load curve of a corresponding U.S. industry with its maximum demand during daytime hours.

To estimate the reductions in energy that would be used during a 6-hour peak period in the U.S. industry, we multiply the amount δ by the average num-

---

13. This is a conservative assumption since the demands of most of these customers are likely to peak during the daytime. Consequently, their true response would be greater than we have calculated.

Peak-Load Pricing for Industry

	Basing the French calculation on data from	
Basing the United States calculation on	(a) Subscribed demand	(b) Load study
(a) Reduction in peak period consumption proportional to French data	Method 1	Method 2
(b) U.S. industries taking the load shape of French industries	Method 3	Method 4

Figure 55. Matrix Illustrating How Alternative Assumptions about French and U.S. Load Changes Yield Four Methods of Calculating Load Response in the United States

ber of kilowatts currently demanded in the U.S. industry during peak hours to obtain the shaded area (R) in graph (b).[14] Since we assume that the total amount of energy consumed remains unchanged, there is a corresponding increase in off-peak hours—the cross-hatched areas (S) in Figure 56(b); our estimates of the amounts of peak-period energy reductions are unaffected by the particular hours in which increased off-peak usage occurs.

In some French industries, subscribed demand in peak periods is as large as that subscribed in off-peak periods. In this case, our Method 1 calculation ascribes no response to the U.S. industry. As discussed in the context of Case 4 (Figure 53) above, this procedure imparts a conservative bias to the calculated response.

Method 4. At the other methodological extreme we assume that peak-load pricing will cause the load curve of U.S. industries to take the shape now observed in France. Method 4 uses data from the French load study of actual demands, rather than the levels of subscribed demand, to calculate the mean kilowatt demand in off-peak and peak periods. We then determine for each French industry the fraction of the total energy consumed during the day that is used in the four peak hours of the Green Tariff. That is, in graph (a) of Figure

---

14. For this calculation, the response from French data was estimated by using demand from midnight to 6 a.m. for off-peak, and 7 to 9 a.m. for peak hours. In the California data the period from noon to 6 p.m. was used to calculate the effect of a 6-hour tariff. This period covers the time of the system peak of utilities in California and many other states.

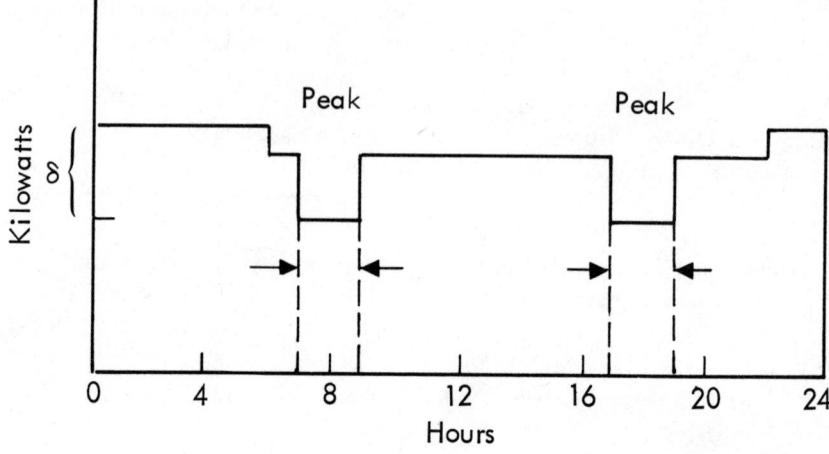

(a) France: Pattern of subscribed demand

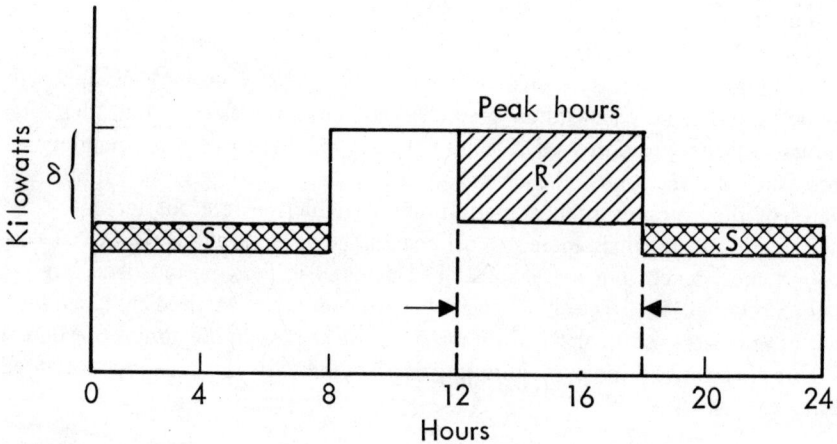

(b) United States: Estimated industrial response

Figure 56. Percentage Reduction in Peak-Period Energy Estimated by Method 1

57, we calculate the dotted areas (P) as a percentage of the total area under the French industry's load curve. We then assume that the proportion of peak-period electricity used in U.S. industry would match this same amount, but be scaled up for the greater number of hours covered by the assumed 6-hour peak-load tariff.[15] This new on-peak level of consumption is shown as the dotted area

---

15. The precise scaling factor was determined by the actual number of peak-period hours in a year under French and (assumed) U.S. conditions.

Peak-Load Pricing for Industry 171

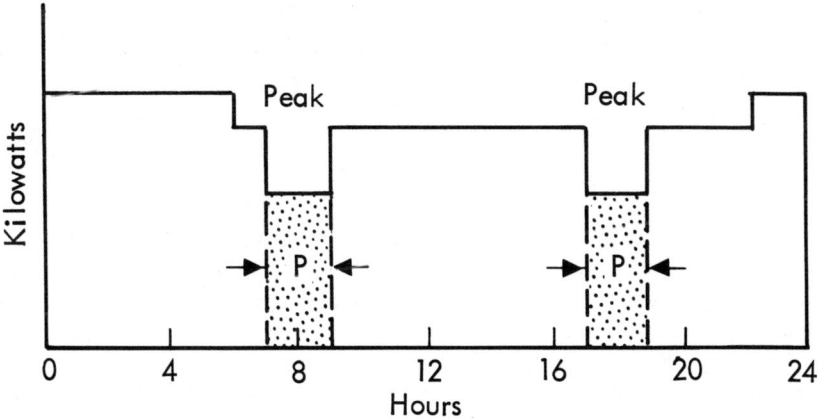

(a) France: Pattern of mean observed demand

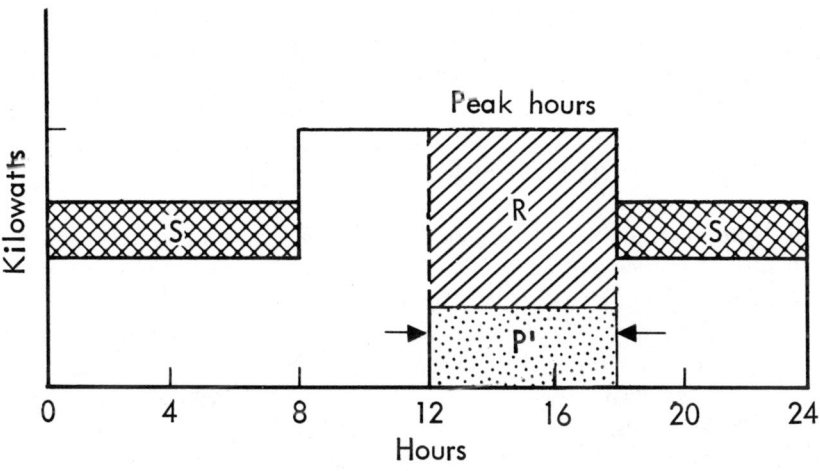

(b) United States: Estimated industrial response

Figure 57. Percentage Reduction in Peak-Period Energy Estimated by Method 4

(P') in Figure 57(b), and the estimated reduction in peak-period energy consumption obtained by this method is shown as the shaded area (R). Because total energy consumption is unchanged, there is again an increase in off-peak usage, which is shown as the cross-hatched areas (S).

In contrast to Method 1, this method of calculating change in response to a peak-load tariff can generally accommodate the case in which French demand (observed or subscribed) is greater during peak periods than during slack periods.

The only exception occurs when the U.S. industry is already observed to use a relatively lower portion of its total energy during the peak price period than that used by the French industry.[16] In this case the amount of reduction (R) in the U.S. is assumed to be zero.

The other two methods of calculating load changes can now be summarized by referring to Figure 55.

Method 2. The average values of demand observed during off-peak and peak periods from the French load study (rather than the subscribed-demand levels) are used to calculate the percentage reduction in maximum demand at the peak periods (instead of calculating the portion of total energy that is consumed during a peak period). That is, if graph (a) of Figure 56 were modified to show mean number of kilowatts demanded in each time period, then the percentage reduction (δ) would be applied to the corresponding U.S. industry as shown in graph (b) of Figure 56.

Method 3. The subscribed levels of demand in the off-peak and peak periods for French industry (rather than the observed mean kilowatt demand from the load study) are used to calculate the amount of energy used during peak hours as a proportion of total energy use (instead of calculating percentage reductions in energy use). That is, graph (a) of Figure 57 is reinterpreted to show subscribed levels of demand in each time period, and the rest of the calculation is made as illustrated in graph (b) of that figure.

A Note on U.S.-European Comparisons. The estimated relative reductions in industrial peak-period energy demand are specific to the United States and should not be interpreted as the reductions that would necessarily be calculated in any other country, including France. This follows from the fact that the estimated reductions (areas R in Figures 56 and 57) depend on the shape and size of the U.S. load curve. When the present U.S. industrial load shape is flat or very similar to the corresponding French industrial load shape, all four methods will yield similar inferences in both the United States and France. On the other hand, when the initial U.S. pattern is to have a disproportionate amount of energy consumed during peak hours, calculation in which U.S. industries take on the load shapes of their European counterparts (Methods 3 and 4) will yield a larger reduction from present peak-period consumption than appears to be the case from casual inspection of *present* French load shapes (compare Figures 57[a] and 57[b], for instance). Of course, if the counterpart French industrial customer started with a day-peaking load shape similar to that now observed in the

---

16. That is, when approximately four-fifths of the sum of areas R and P' in graph (b) of Figure 57 is a smaller proportion of the total area under the curve than are the areas P in graph (a).

United States, then the reduction in the French load over time is correctly given by the calculations in Methods 3 and 4.

THE NATIONAL EFFECT OF PEAK-LOAD PRICING

To estimate the potential nationwide effect of peak-load pricing, the data and methods described will be used to calculate the changes in industrial loads that could be expected from a tariff with a single 6-hour peak period on weekdays. Of course, generating resources, customer loads, and climatic conditions vary among both U.S. and European utilities, and the precise form of each utility's peak-load rate structure should be designed to reflect those local conditions. Most U.S. utilities rely on thermal generation from fuel oil for their marginal source of energy, and experience a single daily peak in their system loads. Furthermore, the differences between daily maximum and minimum loads are normally considerably larger than differences between monthly peaks. In these circumstances the time-of-day tariff should have a single peak period, with possibly different hours in summer and winter, rather than the twin morning and afternoon peak periods used in France and Britain. In many utilities an intermediate shoulder period rate would be justified. Nevertheless, we limit our calculations to the effects of a simple peak/off-peak tariff.

To carry out these calculations it must be assumed that customers in a given industry throughout the United States have a daily and seasonal load shape similar to their California counterpart industry, because industrial load-curve data are not readily available for other states. Such an assumption would be questionable in the case of commercial or residential customers, whose uses of electricity are often strongly affected by weather conditions. However, industrial patterns of electricity use are far less dependent on climatic factors and the use of California data is more justifiable.

All of our calculations are carried out for the levels and costs of electricity consumption prevailing in 1976. The estimates assume that industrial customers have fully adjusted to the incentives of peak-load rates. Of course, adaptation of industrial processes will take some time and peak-load rate structures will probably not achieve their full effect until perhaps 10 years after they are adopted. Furthermore, during this decade electricity consumption and peak loads will probably grow substantially. Our estimates are therefore to be regarded as measures of the *relative* potential for increasing efficiency in the electricity sector. In absolute terms the ultimate gains will undoubtedly be larger.

Industrial Use of Peak-Period Electricity

In 1976, electricity sales throughout the United States amounted to some 1835 billion kwh, of which 35 percent (643 billion kwh) went to manufacturing industrial customers (Table 34). If we define the peak period to include each utility's system peak for a period 6 hours per day, 5 days per week, throughout the year, then based on load profiles in California industries, U.S. manufacturing currently uses 126 billion kwh per year at peak hours, or about 20 percent of the total amount of electricity it purchases annually.[17] The 17 industrial groupings on which our principal calculations are based accounted for 355 billion kwh in 1976 or about 55 percent of the electricity consumed by all U.S. manufacturing industries.

In constructing estimates of the potential effect of peak-loading pricing in the United States, our first step was to assess, industry by industry, the potential changes in daily patterns of electricity consumption. To do this we used the information from the study of French industrial customers and applied it to the sample of California industrial customers, applying the four methods described above. We then estimated the potential national effect by scaling-up the estimates for this sample of California firms, using the total amount of electricity consumed nationally in each industry and assuming that the national response during peak hours would be proportional to that estimated for our sample.[18]

Impact of Time-of-Day Pricing on Seventeen Industries

The seventeen groups of industries for which we have French data are listed in Table 35. In the United States these seventeen industries consumed about 20 percent of their power, or 70 billion kwh during the weekday 6-hour (noon to 6 p.m.) peak period. Depending on which of our four methods is used to calculate the shift in energy use from peak to off-peak hours, between 10.1 and 24.5 billion kwh of annual peak-period energy is expected to be shifted to off-peak periods if U.S. manufacturing industries respond in a manner similar to that of their French counterparts. This amounts to a reduction of 15 to 35 percent of the energy now consumed by those customers during that 6-hour daily peak period.

Generally speaking, of the four methods used, Method 2 yields the least expected change, and Method 3 the greatest. This is in part due to the fact that for the industries in the right side of Table 35, Method 3 is the only one for which the estimated change in peak-period consumption is positive. In these cases the zero impact calculated under the other methods occurs because the subscribed

---

17. These values are calculated using data from the U.S. Bureau of the Census, *Census of Manufactures, 1972, Special Series: Fuels and Electric Energy Consumed (Supplement)*, MC72(SR)-6S, Table 8, p. SR-89 (Washington, D.C.: GPO, Sept. 1974). The 1971 data were updated to 1976 levels by applying a factor of 1.25 to reflect the increase in electricity use by all customers between 1971 and 1976. The *Census of Manufactures* is needed to provide industry-specific information on electricity use.

18. Because our sample of California load curves is drawn from the largest industrial customers, there is a possibility that the national extrapolations overstate the total impact of peak-load pricing if the (proportionate) response of the smaller consumers is not as great as that of the larger ones. However, the comparison of customer-specific and systemwide impacts in subscribed kilowatt usage in France suggests that this is not a major source of bias (see Chapter 5).

peak demand equals the subscribed off-peak demand, or because, on the day of the load study, these French industries used a greater proportion of electricity during peak hours than their counterparts in the United States. Consequently, under Methods 1, 2, and 4 we assign a zero value to the expected change in U.S. industry, even though the long-term effect of the tariff may have been to reduce the level of the peak load from an unobserved, but still higher, level. In contrast, Method 3, which is based on the subscribed—rather than the observed—load of French industries, results in a positive estimate when a French industry subscribes to the same or greater level of demand in the off-peak than the peak period, and its counterpart U.S. industry has a flat or day-peaking load shape.

In both relative and absolute terms, the industry that yields the greatest expected reduction in peak-period energy use is the blast furnace and steel works industry. Depending on the method used, we calculate the potential reduction in peak-period use of electricity in this industry should be between 33 and 73 percent. The lower amount will result if the U.S. firms reduce their current peak-period load by just the proportional load difference now observed between peak and off-peak hours in the French blast furnace and steel industry, whereas the larger reduction will occur if the load curves of U.S. firms eventually take the actual shape now observed in France. The size of potential load response is due both to the amount of electricity consumed by this industry in the United States and the major response shown in the French data. Other industries that are expected to make large reductions (each with over 1 billion kwh per year shifted from the peak period) include: rubber and miscellaneous products, cement, motor vehicles, industrial inorganic chemicals, petroleum refining, and paper and allied products. The first two industrial groups are expected to reduce their peak-period energy use in excess of 50 percent. The motor vehicles, industrial inorganic chemicals, petroleum refining, and paper and allied products industries account for large contributions even though their percentage reduction is smaller, because they use very large amounts of electricity.

Impact on Other Industries

The calculations reported above for seventeen groups of industrial customers involve somewhat more than half of the electricity consumed by all manufacturing industrial customers in the United States. Since we do not have French load data for other manufacturing groups, we cannot make detailed estimates of the potential impact of peak-load pricing for every industry. However, we can roughly estimate the potential effect of peak-load pricing for the remaining industrial groups by assuming that those industries will, on average, have the same percentage response to peak-load pricing that characterizes the seventeen industries covered by our sample.[19]

19. In making these calculations, we assume that the remaining industries consume the same proportion of energy during peak-price hours as do the industries in our sample. (We tested the hypothesis of equality of the proportions and accepted it at the 0.005 level of

Table 35. Projected Effects of Time-of-Day Pricing on Annual Electricity Use in U.S. Manufacturing Industries, 6-Hour Peak Period (millions kwh)

Industry	Total Current Weekday Consumption Noon to 6 p.m.	Estimated Annual Reduction in Peak Period Consumption				Total Reduction When Method Giving Greater Impact is Used for each Industry
		Method 1	Method 2	Method 3	Method 4	
Textile Mill products[a]	5,540	776	–	776	–	776
Paper and allied products	7,759	1009	853	1009	853	1009
Industrial inorganic chemicals	16,655	2165	2998	1999	2998	2998
Plastics[a]	3,036	273	122	273	122	273
Petroleum Refining	4,894	1172	686	749	290	1172
Rubber & miscellaneous products	4,415	662	–	3002	–	3002
Cement (hydraulic)	2,190	701	657	1555	1533	1555
Blast Furnace and Steel Works	12,843	4238	4631	9119	9376	9376
Iron & Steel Foundries[a]	1,750	402	192	402	192	402
Electric Lighting & Wiring Equipment	466	–	–	33	–	33
Communication Equipment	1,734	–	–	676	676	676

[a]Indicates load study data available for the industry in French sample but not in California sample. See text for basis of calculating impact of time-of-day pricing in the United States.

The results of this calculation appear at the end of Table 35. We estimate that the remaining industrial groups will reduce their peak-period use of energy by 8.2 billion to 19.9 billion kwh under a 6-hour tariff.

National Savings from Peak-load Pricing

Nationwide implementation of peak-load pricing for manufacturing industries will have the long-term effect of reducing both the energy consumed and the maximum rate of demand during peak periods. These responses will lower utilities' fuel burn and maintenance expenses, savings that will be reflected in lower short-run marginal costs of supplying electricity. Over time these changes in the shapes of system load curves will also permit utilities to use a more efficient

significance). For each of the four methods, we then applied the percentage reduction in peak-energy use calculated for the 17 industries in our sample.

Table 35. Continued

Industry	Total Current Weekday Consumption Noon to 6 p.m.	Estimated Annual Reduction in Peak Period Consumption				Total Reduction When Method Giving Greater Impact is Used for each Industry
		Method 1	Method 2	Method 3	Method 4	
Electronic Components & Accessories	1,381	–	–	746	–	746
Motor Vehicles and Equipment	5,760	–	–	2246	–	2246
Ship & boat building & repairing	518	–	–	36	–	36
Miscellaneous Transportation Equipment	171	–	–	65	–	65
Engineering, Laboratory, Scientific & Research Equip.	130	–	–	25	–	25
Surgical, Medical & Dental Instruments	326	–	–	150	–	150
Total of 17 Industries[b]	69,568	11,399	10,138	22,860	16,040	24,540
Other Industries	56,346	9,232	8,211	18,515	12,991	19,876
Total	125,913	20,631	18,349	41,375	29,031	44,415

[b] Items may not sum to total because of rounding error.

combination of generating units and thus reduce their long-run marginal costs. Since each of the measures provides a different perspective on the potential nationwide savings, we will evaluate the savings according to four criteria: (1) reductions in energy consumed in peak periods; (2) reductions in maximum demand; (3) savings in short- and long-run marginal costs; and (4) reductions in the need for peak generating capacity. All these calculations are at 1976 levels of electricity costs and demands. The full magnitude of these changes will be realized over several years.

Reduced Energy Consumption in Peak Periods. A 6-hour peak-load tariff for all U.S. manufacturing industries would reduce electricity used during the peak period by an estimated 18.3 billion kwh to 44.4 billion kwh per year

Table 36. National Effects of Peak-Load Pricing of Electricity for U.S. Manufacturing Industries, Calculated at 1976 Levels of Prices and Demand

Type of Effect	Magnitude
Electric Energy Use	
Reduction in peak period usage	44.4 billion kwh
Peak Electricity Demands	
Reduction in maximum demand	28.4 million kw
Proportion of peak demand in manufacturing industry	35%
Proportion of U.S. noncoincident peak demands	7.5%
Annual Cost Savings	
Reduction in short-run costs (fuel and operating costs)	$0.4–1.8 billion
Reduction in long-run costs (fuel, operating, and capital costs)	$1.3–3.5 billion
Construction of Peak Generating Units	
Reduction in 200 MW units	142 units
One-time saving in capital expenditure	$5.7 billion

(Table 35). This amounts to a reduction of 15 to 35 percent of the electricity used by U.S. manufacturing industry at peak hours.

The range of estimated energy reductions is due to the use of the four alternative methods of calculation. As pointed out above in describing this methodology, these measures generally produce a conservative estimate of the full impact of peak-load pricing. In the following discussion, therefore, we will base our national projections on the method that yields the maximum potential impact in each industry. The results are summarized in Table 36.

Reductions in Peak-Period Maximum Demand. There are no readily available data on the demands of individual U.S. manufacturing industries during peak periods. Therefore to construct an estimate of industry-specific rates of demand, each industry's kilowatt-hour consumption during the peak period is divided by the number of hours to which the peak rate applies. By using this projection it is assumed implicitly that industrial firms will reduce energy use equally at every moment during the peak period. But individual firms do not generally have completely flat load curves during these hours. If a time-of-day rate were introduced that included a significant charge based on the consumer's maximum demand, firms would have an incentive to reduce their maximum demand during peak hours by a proportionately greater amount than their reduction of kilowatt-hour usage during the same period. Our estimate may therefore understate the likely reduction in peak demands. On the other hand, because the peaks of individual customers' demands occur at different times, the reduction of the collective maximum demand will generally be somewhat less than the sum of the reductions in individual demands.

We estimate that the current level of maximum demand would be reduced under nationwide peak-load pricing by some 35 percent (Table 36). The currently estimated (noncoincident) demand of 80.5 million kw for U.S. industry is 21 percent of the noncoincident peak demand projected for all U.S. utilities in 1976.[20] Thus the lower peak demand of industrial customers would result in an average reduction of about 7.5 percent in the system peaks of U.S. utilities.

Reductions in Marginal Costs. Shifts in industrial load curves that reduce peak-period energy consumption and maximum demands will immediately reduce utilities' operating costs and eventually allow further savings to be realized by adjusting the mix of generating plants. We estimate that about 44.4 billion kwh will be shifted from the peak period each year. The value of these reductions is measured by differences in the values of short- and long-run marginal costs, between peak and off-peak periods. These values will vary from one utility to another depending on current generating resources, costs of fuels, interconnection arrangements with other utilities, and the shapes of system load curves.

Because of the diversity of marginal-cost conditions across the country, the estimated cost savings from peak-load pricing are based on a range of values. In 1977 the minimum difference between short-run marginal costs in the peak and off-peak period was estimated to be about 1 cent per kwh, while a reasonable upper bound was 4 cents per kwh.[21] Table 36 shows that the expected reduction in utilities' operating costs range between $0.4 and $1.8 billion per year.

The eventual savings in long-run marginal costs will also vary because of the wide differences among utilities in the amount of current capacity, environmental constraints, commitments to new construction, and the lumpiness of investments in new generating units.[22] A reasonable range of values may be inferred from two time-of-day electricity tariffs now available to industrial customers. The recent tariff applied to the largest 120 customers in California's Pacific Gas and Electric Company has an effective price differential of 3 cents per kwh between peak and off-peak periods, and the high-voltage tariff in effect for French industrial customers has an effective differential of 7.8 cents per kwh.[23] Using these two values, it is found that peak-load pricing results in a potential reduction of long-run operating and capital costs of between $1.3 and $3.5 billion per year in 1976 dollars (Table 36).

20. Projected from *EEI Statistical Year Book of the Electric Utility Industry for 1975*, Table 6S (excludes Alaska and Hawaii), using a growth rate of 5.6 percent.
21. The minimum value is calculated by taking the difference between the operating cost per kwh of the most efficient nonnuclear baseload plants in the country (about 1.0 to 1.2 cents per kwh generated) and the marginal costs of intermediate oil-fired cycling plants (about 2.2 to 2.4 cents per kwh). The difference is about 1 cent per kwh. The upper bound is based on the same baseload plant and a gas-fired turbine (about 5 cents per kwh), for a difference of 4 cents per kwh.
22. However, interconnections between utilities mitigate these factors in many cases.
23. See Table 33.

Reduction in Peak Generating Capacity. The opportunities for savings in long-run marginal costs will be realized when utilities that experience reduced peak-period demands postpone or eliminate the construction of some new peak generating capacity that would otherwise be needed.[24] In some cases, peaking units such as gas turbines or pumped storage facilities can be eliminated. In other cases, a base-load plant will be substituted for a planned peaking unit. This type of substitution will require a smaller increment in the kilowatt size of a baseload plant because it will be in operation over a greater number of hours each day.

If the entire effect of the projected 28.4 million kw reduction in maximum demand across the country is to postpone the construction of peaking units, then peak-load pricing would permit a nationwide saving of 142 peaking plants of 200 megawatts (200,000 kw) capacity each.[25] The construction and installation costs of such plants are at least $200 per kw. Consequently, such a reduction in peak demands would permit a one-time saving of a minimum of $5.7 billion; this is more than one-third of the annual rate of capital expenditure for new or improved generation facilities in all U.S. utilities in recent years.[26]

Initial Response to the First U.S. Peak-Load Rates

Because U.S. conditions influencing industrial production and the use of electricity may differ importantly from those in Europe, the estimates presented in the previous sections of the potential effects of peak-load pricing for U.S. industries are subject to a degree of uncertainty. It has been necessary to base our assessment of the long-term industrial adaptation of electrical loads primarily on European data since there has been no extended U.S. experience with peak-load rates.

But by early 1977, rate structure proceedings in state regulatory commissions had led to the first use of time-of-day rates for limited numbers of very large electricity consumers in California, Michigan, New York, and Wisconsin. The initial results from these new rates provide the first indications of how large U.S. customers react to time-of-day pricing. Of course, these reactions are necessarily of a short-run nature, limited almost entirely to changes in production practices that can be accomplished without altering plant and equipment.

In Wisconsin, peak-period electricity rates between 8 a.m. and 10 p.m. have already induced firms that manufacture plumbing fixtures, refrigeration equipment, marine products, and stainless-steel cookware to establish night-shift operations for foundry processes. One large firm expects such adjustments to

---

24. Utilities will also be able to realize savings in new transmission and distribution capacity. However, this effect is much more difficult to estimate due to the spatial and temporal diversity of demand within each utility.

25. To the extent that these reductions permit a saving in reserve capacity as well, the total effect would be greater.

26. In 1975 new capital expenditure in U.S. electricity utilities was variously reported to be $15 billion (*EEI Statistical Year Book,* Table 50S) and $17 billion (*Electrical World,* March 15, 1976).

Table 37. Rate Structures for the Largest PG&E Customers (February 1977)

Conventional Rate		Peak-Load Rate				
				Demand Charge		
Demand Charge	Energy Charge[a]	Customer Charge	Tariff Period	Winter (Oct-April)	Summer (May-Sept.)	Energy Charge[a]
$2465 first 1000 kw	3¢/kwh, first 100 kwh/kw	$715/ month	Peak[b]	$2.30/kw	$3.45/kw	2.2¢/kwh
$1.75 over 1000 kw	2.6¢/kwh next 200 kwh/kw		Shoulder[c]	0.28/kw	0.28/kw	2.0¢/kwh
	2.4¢/kwh all other		Off-Peak[d]	0	0	1.8¢/kwh

[a]Net of fuel and energy adjustments.
[b]Peak hours are 4:30-8:30 p.m. weekdays winter; 12:30-6:30 p.m. weekdays summer; except holidays.
[c]Shoulder hours are 8:30 a.m.-4:30 p.m. and 8:30-10:30 p.m. weekdays winter; 8:30 a.m.-12:30 p.m. and 6:30-10:30 p.m. weekdays summer; 8:30 a.m.-10:30 p.m. Saturdays all year; except holidays.
[d]Off-peak hours are 10:30 p.m.-8:30 a.m. Monday through Saturday, and all day Sunday and holidays, all year.

reduce its annual electricity bill by some $450,000. To do so it has rescheduled about 5 percent of its work force and paid additional night wage premiums of $25,000.[27]

As noted earlier, in February 1977 the Pacific Gas and Electric Company (PG&E) established mandatory seasonal and time-of-day rates for 130 industrial and commercial customers in northern and central California having maximum annual demands exceeding 4000 kw. Before 1977 these large customers were supplied under a conventional maximum-demand tariff which still applies to other large customers. Now, under the new peak-load tariff, there is one peak period—4 hours long in winter and 6 hours in summer—and two shoulder periods on weekdays, as well as an overnight off-peak period. Furthermore, higher maximum-demand rates apply during the peak hours of the summer (May-September) season. The terms of both rate structures are shown in Table 37.

The load curves of these customers prior to 1977 and for the first six months that the new rate structure was in effect are the first available data measuring the speed with which industrial loads adjust to peak-load pricing.[28] A few firms have adapted rapidly to the new rates. Load curves for firms in the cement, chemical, and paper products industries and for a large shopping and office com

27. *Wall Street Journal*, August 12, 1977.
28. These data are included in Pacific Gas and Electric Company, prepared testimony of Stephen P. Reynolds, before the California Public Utilities Commission, Application No. 57666 pursuant to Decisions No. 85359, 86543.

182 Peak-Load Pricing for the United States

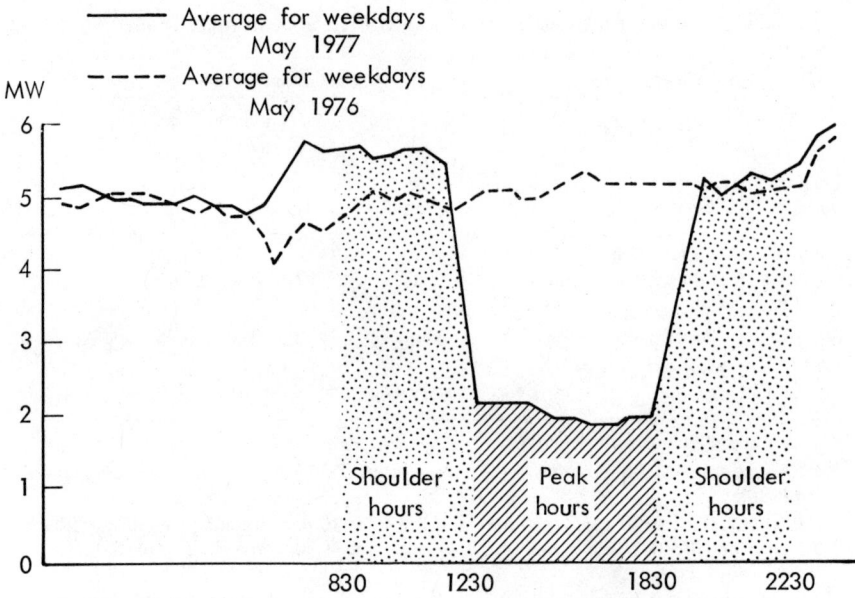

Source: Prepared Testimony of Stephen P. Reynolds, Pacific Gas & Electric, before The Public Utilities Commission of California, Application 57666.

Figure 58. California Cement Firm before and after the Introduction of Peak-Load Rates

plex are shown in Figures 58 through 61. In each case the firm's average weekday load during the peak season is compared for one month in 1977 with the same month during the previous year. The qualitative nature of the load response seen for these selected firms is quite similar to the hypothetical cases discussed earlier in this chapter, and to the load curves for comparable industries in France and England discussed in Chapter 5.

A mixed pattern emerges, with some firms responding only to the peak price and others reacting during the shoulder period as well. The cement firm shown in Figure 58 went from an almost flat load curve before the introduction of peak-load pricing, to a load shape in which shoulder use was increased slightly and the peak-period use was reduced by over 50 percent. The reduction in peak-period use parallels closely that of cement firms in both France and England. Before the introduction of time-of-day rates, the chemical firm shown in Figure 59 showed a drop of about 20 percent in energy use during part of the daytime hours. With the introduction of peak-load pricing, the reduction has been

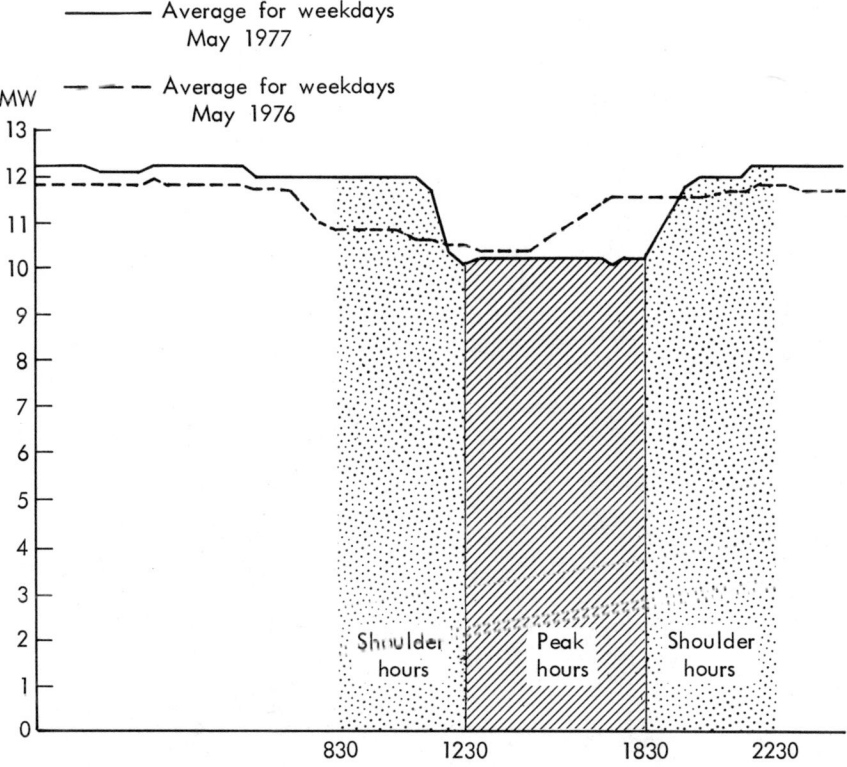

Source: Prepared Testimony of Stephen P. Reynolds, Pacific Gas & Electric, before The Public Utilities Commission of California, Application 57666.

Figure 59. California Chemical Plant before and after the Introduction of Peak-Load Rates

adjusted to match very precisely the beginning and end of the peak charge hours.

The paper products firm in Figure 60 illustrates several features of load response to price schedules discussed throughout this book. Under the conventional kw/kwh tariff, the firm had a flat load curve (an almost ideal response to a tariff with a kw charge and a block-extender feature that additionally rewards level load curves). With the introduction of peak-load pricing, the firm cut back on its use of energy across the entire shoulder and peak periods, while increasing its off-peak usage more than one-third. This latter feature of its response illustrates the rapid adjustment possible in a firm that has unused production capacity available. Furthermore, the net effect of the firm's adjustment was to increase daily electricity use by about 8 percent in 1977 over 1976.

184 Peak-Load Pricing for the United States

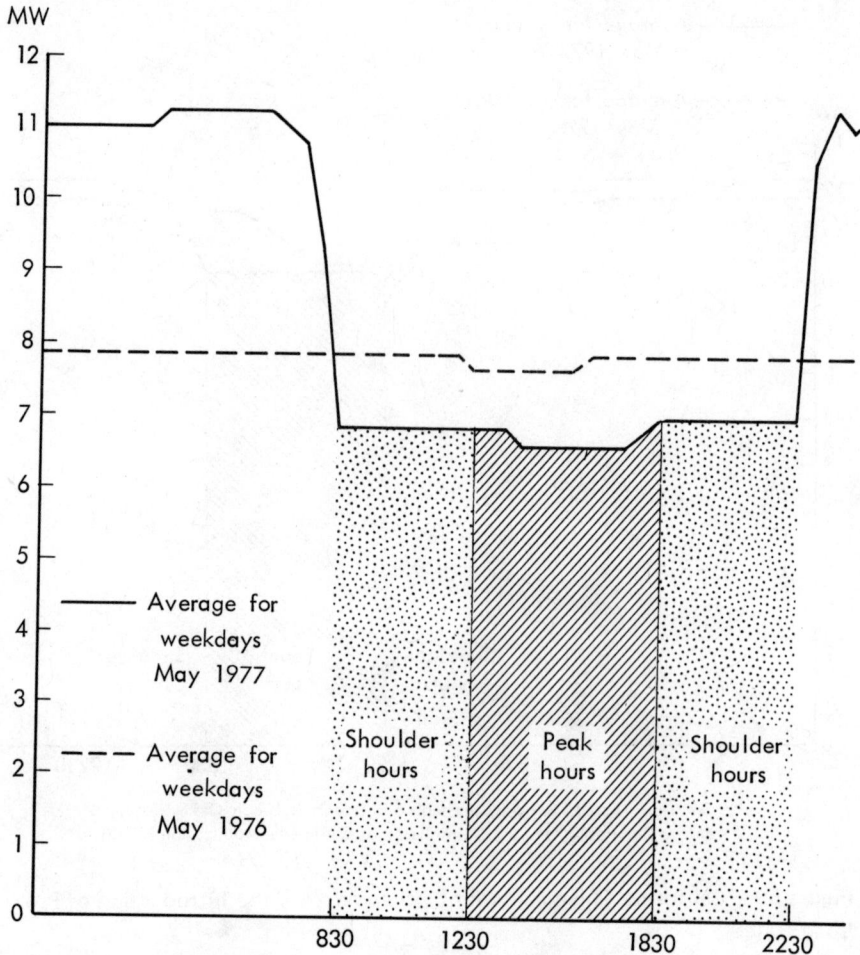

Source: Prepared Testimony of Stephen P. Reynolds, Pacific Gas & Electric, before The Public Utilities Comission of California, Application 57666.

Figure 60. California Paper Products Firm before and after the Introduction of Peak-Load Rates

Finally, the shopping and office complex (Figure 61) provides an interesting bit of evidence for a major sector of electricity use in the United States, whose scope for adjustments are chiefly limited in the short run to changes in lighting and air conditioning. Commercial customers use about one-third of U.S. electricity, and this example suggests that under peak-load pricing large office buildings can contribute measurably to reducing system peak loads.

Only a few of PG&E's customers have made such extensive short-run changes in load. Nevertheless, for the group of consumers who are subject to peak-load rates, the amount of load reduction during peak hours has increased from month

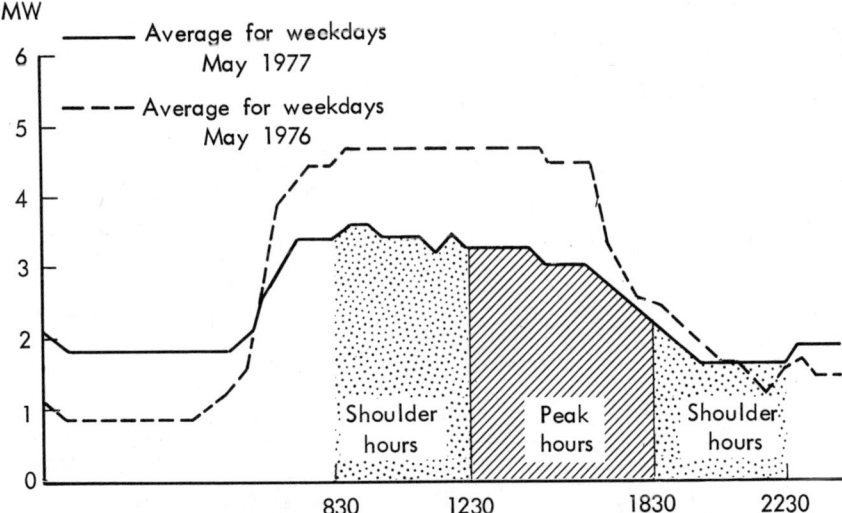

Source: Prepared Testimony of Stephen P. Reynolds, Pacific Gas & Electric, before The Public Utilities Commission of California, Application 57666

Figure 61. California Shopping and Office Complex before and after the Introduction of Peak-Load Rates

to month. During the first month of the new rate structure, the aggregate normalized load of this class of consumers was 1.25 percent below that of the previous February. By May, the first month of the summer peak rates, the effect had increased to 2.15 percent, and by July to a 2.6 percent reduction compared to the previous year. The aggregate load curve of these 130 customers, shown in Figure 62, illustrates the shift of load out of the peak period and into the off-peak hours.

During the initial months of the first U.S. peak-load tariffs, customer responses were no doubt accomplished by adjustments in the operation and scheduling of existing production facilities. The trend of growing responsiveness illustrates learning and increased adaptability over time. It is equally a reminder that only a small proportion of the full effect of peak-load pricing will occur during the first year of a basic change in rate structures. The full impact of time-of-day pricing incentives estimated in the previous section will only be attained after several years, when firms have had the opportunity to adjust capital stocks and other inputs to the new configuration of energy costs.

RELATED CHANGES IN ELECTRICITY USAGE

Peak-load pricing in European utilities has been accompanied by related changes in industrial uses of electricity. Self-generation of power by industrial firms and interruption of high-voltage deliveries to selected customers is practiced

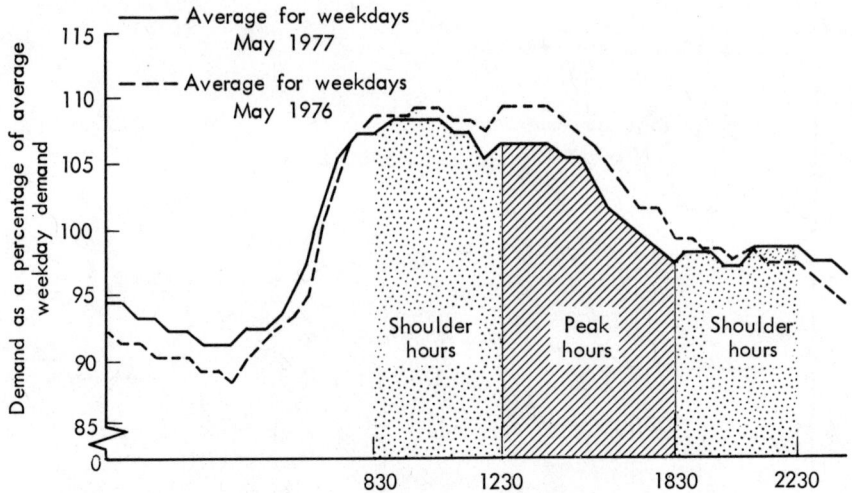

Source: Prepared Testimony of Stephen P. Reynolds, Pacific Gas & Electric, before The Public Utilities Commission of California, Application 57666.

Figure 62. Response of 130 Large California Electricity Consumers to the Introduction of Peak-Load Rates

much more extensively in Europe than in the United States. A reexamination of U.S. rate structures logically extends to investigating the potential for increasing energy efficiency by these means.

Cogeneration of Electricity

Peak-load rate structures have given rise to substantial use of self-generation and cogeneration of electricity in Europe. As noted in Chapter 5, rate structures based on marginal costs encourage European industries to recover waste heat and to use by-product fuels to drive their own turbines. Because of the greater amount of self-generation by industrial firms, many European utilities offer tariffs that provide for the supply of emergency power from the utility. Other provisions of these tariffs frequently enable an industrial customer to sell excess electricity to the utility or to rent the latter's transmission facilities for "wheeling" self-generated power from one location to another.

Recent exploratory studies have noted that there is room for a sizable increase in the by-product generation of electricity in conjunction with U.S. industrial production activities. In the United States, industry-generated power has declined from 40 percent in the mid 1930s, to 21 percent of electricity consumed in 1960, to 17 percent in the early 1970s.

The potential for significant increases in self-generation is concentrated in a few U.S. industries—petroleum refining, pulp and paper, chemicals, and steel—which together account for an estimated 40 percent of the total by-product

Table 38. Estimated Potential for Generating By-Product Electricity in U.S. Industry

Industry	Power Generated as a Percent of the Potential for By-Product Power Generation
Petroleum refining	13
Pulp and paper	53
Chemicals	33
Steel	41
Average of four industries	35
Projected potential for all industry	30

Source: Spencer et al. (1977).

power potential.[29] Currently these industries generate about one-third of that potential (Table 38). Taking into account the fact that by-product generation is generally not economically attractive unless the industrial steam load is at least 400,000 pounds per hour at a single location, Spencer et al. (1977) estimate that by 1980 the potential for new by-product power generation is some 33,000 MW. The significant efficiency gains that are possible with increased cogeneration can be appreciated from their estimate that such installations would result in a net saving of generating plant investment by utilities (after allowing for increased industry investments) of $19.2 billion, and an increase in fuel efficiency equivalent to roughly 680,000 barrels of oil per day.

Interruptible Tariffs

Further increases in the efficiency of the U.S. electricity sector could be achieved by more widespread use of special rates for interruptible service to industrial customers willing to curtail loads on short notice. As described in Chapter 5, England and Wales have used the Potential Peak Warning system with considerable success, achieving 11 percent reductions in industrial peak loads on days of impending system peaks.

To date, U.S. utilities have instituted interruptible service to only a limited extent. Firms engaged in processes that involve crushing coal, crushing minerals and rocks in mining and for manufacturing cement, rolling mills, ferro-alloy furnaces, arc furnaces, electric melting operations, induction-heating applications, electrochemical processes, and the production of industrial gases are occasionally able to obtain power under interruptible contracts at reduced rates.[30] However, in many U.S. utilities no such rates are presently available. In other utilities the terms of interruptible service are unrelated to marginal

29. See Spencer et al (1977).
30. See Sherry (1975).

costs and are sufficiently inferior to the standard industrial tariff that they are of no interest to customers. Consequently, increased use of special tariffs that are keyed to the few hours per year of actual system peak conditions or unusual equipment outages is likely to achieve important savings in peak-load capacity.[31]

SUMMARY

Proceedings in state regulatory commissions and proposed national legislation foreshadow the widespread adoption of peak-load rate structures for industrial customers in the United States over the next several years. Data from load studies of European industries indicate that time-of-day tariffs will lead to sizable long-run changes in industrial load curves. Using these data and comparable load studies of California industrial firms served under conventional tariffs, we have estimated the potential effects of nationwide adoption of time-of-day rates for U.S. industry.

We calculate that peak-load pricing would lead manufacturing industries to reduce their electricity usage during a 6-hour peak period by an average of 35 percent, shifting consumption to lower-cost hours and permitting utilities to achieve a 7.5 percent reduction in their system peak loads. These estimates of the long-run load shifts at peak hours are consistent with the increasing amounts of load shifting observed during the first months that peak-load rate structures have been in effect for large industrial and commercial consumers in California and Wisconsin.

Reductions in peak-period electricity use will permit utilities to supply the same quantity of electricity at off-peak hours more efficiently and therefore to lower the average cost per kilowatt-hour supplied. Our calculations are based on electricity costs and consumption prevailing in 1976. We estimate that the national savings in operating costs range from $0.4 to $1.8 billion per year.

Over the long term, reductions in electricity demand during peak periods will permit utilities to postpone or eliminate additions to peaking capacity and to achieve a more efficient mix of generating units. Including the savings in operating costs, the potential long-run cost savings range from $1.3 billion to $3.5 billion per year. These capacity savings correspond to eliminating or postponing the construction of 28.4 million kilowatts of capacity. At current construction costs, this amounts to a one-time savings in capital investment of almost $6 billion. Over time, the growth of the economy and increased use of electricity will result in correspondingly greater savings.

Additional increases in the efficiency of the U.S. electricity sector can be achieved by more extensive use of industrial cogeneration of electricity and by special tariffs for selling interruptible power to selected industrial customers.

31. An exception to the almost total absence of such special tariffs in the United States is the San Diego Gas and Electric Company, which introduced in late 1977 a peak-load tariff for its largest customers modeled after the British Bulk Supply tariff.

This chapter has assessed the potential effects of peak-load pricing for industrial customers in the United States. For U.S. commercial and residential customers the costs and benefits of peak-load rate structures are more problematic and form the subject of Chapter 9.

Chapter 9

Rate Reform for Commercial and Residential Customers

As noted earlier, much of the impetus for restructuring U.S. electricity rates has resulted from an increasing public awareness that the incentives contained in conventional electricity rate structures do not encourage U.S. consumers to use resources efficiently. This growing understanding of the importance of price incentives may eventually provide the political support required for the adoption of new rate structures based on the true economic costs of energy.

For electricity supplied at high and medium voltage, even very small percentage changes in customer loads are more than sufficient to repay the costs of the more complex time-of-day meters. Thus, for most industrial customers and for large office buildings and other commercial establishments served at high or medium voltage, the economic case for time-of-day pricing is not seriously in doubt. Indeed, the preliminary evidence available in California, discussed in Chapter 8, suggests that some commercial customers may make significant adjustments to time-of-day pricing (see Figure 61). However, for smaller commercial and residential customers served at low voltages the economic issue is whether the benefits from more efficient use of energy that would be fostered by time-of-day rate structures would outweigh the additional costs they would impose.

At the residential level, there are some 73 million electricity-consuming U.S. households. Depending on the complexity of the tariff, a time-of-day rate structure can require an investment of from approximately $100 to $350 per customer for multiple-register, time-of-day meters.[1] Nationwide conversion to

---

1. These estimates reflect installed costs of currently manufactured meters. With large-scale production, and perhaps the use of integrated circuits, the price per meter could be well under $100 even for quite complicated equipment. McKay (1977) has considered some

residential time-of-day pricing could therefore result in additional one-time capital investments of as much as $7 billion. Furthermore, the introduction of advanced load-management technologies that would remotely control heating and air conditioning loads could substantially increase the required expenditure.

Moreover, European utilities have used residential time-of-day tariffs on a large scale, primarily in conjunction with storage space-heating and water-heating devices. The extent to which this experience is directly transferable to U.S. conditions is open to question because of significant differences in climate, ownership of household appliances, prices and availability of alternative fuels, and general life style. The European experience with peak-load pricing for residential customers is therefore unlike the situation for industrial users, where the international similarity of technological processes makes the load responses of European industries directly relevant to U.S. conditions.

A systematic examination of the benefits of new residential rate structures is, therefore, a necessary prelude to any statewide or national decision to change low-voltage electricity tariffs. The relevant economic analysis requires an assessment of benefits, measured from consumers' demand curves for electricity, net of the added metering and administrative expenses. However, because of the almost complete absence of peak-load pricing in the United States, no data on consumers' demands for electricity under time-of-day rates have been available in this country.

INFORMATION REQUIREMENTS

Several types of information will be required in order to reach a reliable assessment of the merits of adopting alternative rate structures for residential customers.

Seasonal tariffs, in which the peak period lasts for several months, can be implemented with existing residential meters and minor changes in billing and meter-reading procedures. Thus the major policy issue with respect to seasonal tariffs is not to establish the precise magnitudes of changes in demand, but to determine whether there is any significant effect of raising the price per kilowatt hour for several months during the high-cost season and lowering it during the rest of the year. If consumers respond to seasonal variations in price, this limited form of peak-load pricing will necessarily result in a net welfare gain over nonseasonal rates, since there are no important costs of converting to such a rate structure.

In contrast with seasonal pricing, the policy question for time-of-day pricing is not whether there is a change in consumption, but how large the response to

---

aspects of the engineering and economic potential offered by low-cost, sophisticated metering options and the associated tariffs and load control they would permit.

such rate structures is Dividing the day into two or more rate periods will require replacing existing kilowatt-hour meters with more sophisticated meters incorporating at least two registers and a time switch (or a remotely controlled switch). Unless the gain in economic efficiency from reducing usage at high-cost peak hours and increasing it during the low-cost off-peak period is sufficiently large, the higher metering costs will produce a net loss in economic welfare.[2] For example, for many customers who have low usages of electricity, it will not pay to introduce time-of-day pricing until metering costs have fallen substantially. To analyze the policy question of peak-load pricing for residential consumers, measurements are needed of the period-by-period changes in electricity usage under time-of-day pricing.

A related requirement in assessing net benefits is to measure the sensitivity of consumer response to the length of time that the peak price is in effect. Since the utility's operation of a mix of electricity-generating plants with different capital/fuel ratios results in marginal costs that vary continually over the day, there is no well-determined peak period surrounding the system peak demand. If the peak period of a peak-load tariff is defined too narrowly, it may cause consumption to shift to adjacent periods and create a new demand peak. Conversely, a peak period that is too long may inhibit shifting and diminish the potential gain from smoothing the load curve.

Data for U.S. conditions are also needed to determine at which rates and under what circumstances residential customers will choose to be billed under a time-of-day rate structure if it is made available as an option to the standard tariff. Without exception, time-of-day tariffs are optional in all European utilities that we studied and in the United States time-of-day rates for households are also likely to be introduced on an optional basis.

Finally, there is a need for data that can be used to make reliable forecasts of period-by-period *levels* of load under both conventional tariffs and under peak-load rate structures. Both investment planning for capacity expansion and the design of a particular rate structure that will recover historical costs require accurate predictions of load by period. Data are therefore required on consumer responses to a variety of possible structures and levels of electricity rates.

Not surprisingly, the first systematic study of consumer responses to peak-load electricity tariffs was conducted in Europe when the Electricity Council of London undertook a five-year residential tariff experiment. Subsequently, growing U.S. interest in new rate structures has produced a number of field trials of residential load-management technologies and time-of-day and seasonal tariffs. In the following sections the nature and findings of the British rate-

2. The appropriate economic comparison is the increase in consumers' plus producer's surplus from switching to the time of day structure from the next most efficient rate structure, versus the additional metering and billing costs. Calculation of the change in surplus when prices of several related services are changed requires knowledge of the *change* in usage in both the peak and off-peak periods. See Besen and Mitchell (1975).

structure experiment are reveiwed, and the first U.S. efforts at testing residential peak-load rates are examined.

THE BRITISH EXPERIMENT

From 1966 to 1972 the Electricity Council of London conducted a 5-year experiment with peak-load and maximum-demand tariffs;[3] 3420 residential customers in England and Wales from six of the twelve area boards took part. The participants were selected by stratified random sampling of all customers who used at least 3000 kilowatt-hours of electricity annually.

Experimental Tariffs

Two types of peak-load rate structures were tested—a seasonal tariff and a time-of-day tariff. The rates are shown in Table 39 as a percentage of the then-prevailing household rate of about 2.8¢ per kwh. In order to measure the demand elasticities for small changes in prices, two alternative rate levels were used for each tariff form. Under the seasonal tariff, the peak rates applied at all hours of the winter season, December through February; these winter rates were slightly more than double the summer rates.

The experimental time-of-day tariff also had a seasonal component—during the same winter months the peak rate applied on weekdays from 8:00 a.m. to 1:00 p.m. and 4:30 p.m. to 7:30 p.m. Nighttime electricity, from 11:00 p.m. to 7:00 a.m., was billed at the off-peak rate, 12 months a year. All other hours (including all daytime hours in March-November) were priced at an intermediate rate.

In all, 840 customers were assigned to seasonal tariffs, another 840 were placed on time-of-day rates, and 900 acted as controls.[4] Consumers were not given a choice of tariffs, but were offered a modest payment for their cooperation. It is important to note that during the period of the experiment most British households had the option of purchasing electricity under the "restricted-hour" tariff—the first rate structure used in Britain to promote residential storage space-heating and water-heating (see Chapter 6). Since some of the control households had such facilities and made use of the restricted-hour rate, the quantitative differences between control and experimental tariff groups are narrower than the differences that might be expected in a U.S. comparison of similar experimental tariffs with conventional declining-block rates.

Results

Table 40 shows that customers in both experiments responded to the price signals of the tariffs in the expected directions. The apparent anomaly of a de-

---
3. See Electricity Council of London (no date).
4. A fourth group of 840 customers received a load-rate tariff similar to the Norwegian subscribed-demand tariff for residential customers described in Chapter 4.

Table 39. Peak-Load Tariffs in the British Experiment

	Rate per kwh as Percentage of Standard Domestic Rate[a]		
	Alternative Tariffs		Average of (1) & (2)
	(1)	(2)	
Seasonal Tariff			
Winter (December-February)	146.2	164.2	155.2
Summer (March-November)	77.1	67.0	72.1
Time of Day Tariff			
Peak Hours (weekdays 8 a.m.-1 p.m., 4:30 p.m.-7:30 p.m., December-February)	301.0	347.7	324.4
Shoulder (all except peak and off-peak hours)	81.3	74.5	77.9
Off-Peak (11 p.m.-7 a.m. all year)	40.0	40.0	40.0

Source: Electricity Council of London (no date).
[a] These percentages applied to each area board's follow-on, or tail-block rate for regular domestic customers of about 2.8¢/kwh at the time of the study. Experimental customers also continued to pay the area board's standard fixed monthly charge.

Table 40. Changes in Electricity Consumption in the British Experiment

	Change in Consumption per household[a]	
Period	kwh	percent
Seasonal Tariff		
Summer	-47	-1.1%
Winter	-186	-9.7%
Restricted hours[b]	+651	—
Time-of-Day Tariff		
Peak hours	-116	-23.7%
Shoulder hours	+52	+1.4%
Off-peak hours	+168	+9.6%

Source: Electricity Council of London (no date).
[a] Changes in consumption are 5-year averages measured relative to the control group average.
[b] Customers on experimental seasonal tariffs increased their installed storage heating load by an average of 15 percent. The average increase of 651 kwh per year is 10.7 percent of the annual consumption per customer in the control group.

crease in summer consumption under the seasonal tariff is explained by the increased use by experimental households of storage heating during the restricted hours, which is separately metered. Since some heating is needed during several months of the summer tariff period, which covers the months of March through November, overall consumption during the off-peak period did, in fact, increase under this tariff.

Customers on the experimental time-of-day rates decreased their consumption during peak hours and increased it at night. In addition, electricity usage increased to a small extent during the shoulder hours, and had the effect of raising annual daytime load factors. The comparative patterns of the load curves for experimental time-of-day customers and for control-group households are shown in Figure 63. Both experimental rates, therefore, were effective in discouraging peak-period consumption and increasing usage at off-peak periods. Both tariffs also induced consumers to increase their total use of electricity compared to control households.

Evaluation

The British tariff experiment represents the first thorough and scientific attempt to systematically study the behavior of consumers in response to changes in electricity rate structures. The British investigators measured the gains in the efficiency of resource use by evaluating benefits in terms of changes in consumers' surplus for all experimental households. They concluded that, when set against the additional metering and billing costs of the technology then available, peak-load pricing for residential consumers resulted in net losses[5] to the economy, on average.[6]

It should be remembered, however, that the British utilities already offered optional restricted-hour tariffs that were intended to encourage the adoption of storage heating. The tariff experiment, therefore, was a test of what *additional* gains might be achieved by the more extensive use of peak-load tariffs, and its results do not constitute an evaluation of the benefit of replacing a conventional rate structure by a peak-load tariff.

The negative and pessimistic findings of the British experiment should also be tempered by observing that the gains from the introduction of peak-load tariffs

---

5. The load-rate tariff also produced net losses.

6. For two technical reasons, the British methodology for measuring welfare gains understates the possible gains from peak-load pricing. First, the formula for measuring net benefit assumes that there is no cross-price effect, especially between day and night periods. To correct for substitution in electricity usage between periods, one needs to know the cross-price elasticities, which are unfortuantely unmeasurable in the British experiment. Second, the formula does not reflect the effect of long-run interfuel substitution, except to the extent that it occurred during the course of the 5-year experiment. As the British experience with storage heating suggests, a substantial part of the gain from time-of-day rates may be associated with long-term changes in the ownership of appliances.

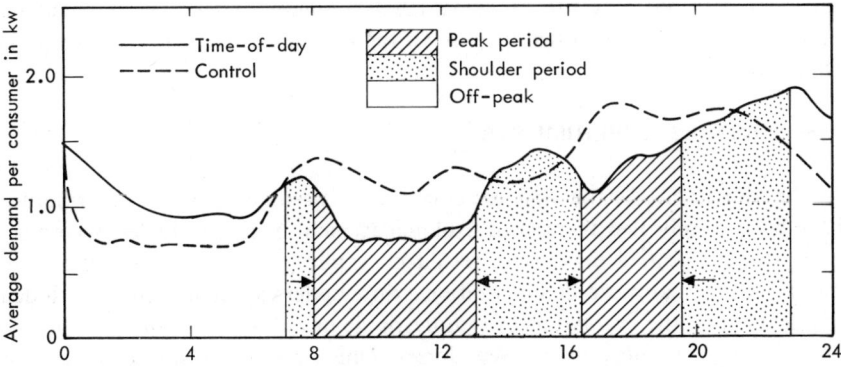

Source: J. G. Boggis, personal communication. Copyright Electricity Council of London. Used by permission.

Figure 63. Time-of-Day and Control-Group Load Curves in the British Experiment, Average Winter Weekday Loads, 1969/70

increase with the customer's annual amount of electricity use, while the metering cost remains the same. Using the British data, a more recent calculation[7] finds that the experimental British time-of-day tariff yields positive net benefits if limited to large customers. Furthermore, an important part of the added metering cost for the seasonal tariffs resulted from more frequent meter-reading than the prevailing British practice of reading residential meters only once every three months. These observations suggest that the prospects for residential peak-load tariffs could be brighter in many regions of the United States where average electricity consumption is much higher than in Britain, and where most utilities read meters at least every 60 days.

Despite the large scale of the British experiment—some 3400 customers over a five-year period—it was focused on the study of just three specific alternatives to the standard rate structure, all of which used rates justified by the prevailing cost conditions. No attempt was made to measure demand curves over a broad range of prices. By the time the experimental results were available, changes in the world oil market had made the experimental rate levels obsolete. Reflecting on the outcome of the study, Boggis (1975) has observed:

> With the aid of hindsight, the experiment might have been better directed to a more primitive problem. What are the price elasticities and cross elasticities of electricity demand by time-of-day, day-of-week and season-of-year? Such primitive, component information could be patched together to form views of the effectiveness of composite price structures without having settled those beforehand by somewhat arbitrary judgment.

7. National Economic Research Associates, Inc. (1977).

THE FIRST U.S. EXPERIMENTS

The value of collecting the fundamental data suggested by this comment has been recognized in the design of some of the subsequent rate experiments in the United States.

In the United States the first experimental trials of peak-load rate structures have been closely tied to tests of load-management hardware. In 1974, German-built storage heating units were tested on a pilot basis in ten homes in Vermont.[8] Other hardware demonstrations, now underway or recently concluded, are devoted to the evaluation of remote ripple or radio control of water heating and storage space-heating (in New Jersey, Ohio, and Wisconsin), cycling of air conditioning loads (in Arkansas, Georgia, Detroit, and California), and the use of solar heating (in Arizona). These demonstration projects should provide useful engineering experience with load-control technologies and indicate the willingness of consumers to relinquish to the utility the control of selected appliance loads.

Several U.S. utilities are now exploring the use of time-of-day and seasonal rate structures for residential customers by offering trial rates for all uses of electricity in the household, rather than tariffs that apply only to selected appliance loads under particular remote load-management controls. To varying degrees, the first U.S. residential time-of-day experiments will obtain the information needed to answer the major policy questions about peak-load pricing for residential customers.

Characteristics of several of the initial projects are summarized in Table 41. Some of these trials, such as those in Arkansas, Connecticut, New Jersey, and Ohio, involve comparisons of the load responses under one or two experimental rate plans with the loads of a control group on the utility's conventional domestic declining-block rate schedule. Most experiments are also testing seasonal variation in rates, and in most cases the average level of the experimental rates are based on the utility's current costs. These projects can be expected to provide useful new information about the level of loads under tariffs that are more or less appropriate to the initial cost conditions of the particular utilities in which the trials are being held.

THE LOS ANGELES EXPERIMENT

To provide greater generality of results, more complex peak-load rate experiments can be undertaken. In 1976, Los Angeles began a 4-year study with 2200 households on a total of forty-one experimental and conventional rates.[9] The

---

8. See de Grasse (1977).
9. The study is being conducted by the Los Angeles Department of Water and Power in collaboration with the Rand Corporation and is funded in part by the Department of

Table 41. U.S. Residential Time-of-Day Experiments

Project	Number of Customers		Number of Experimental Tariffs	Range of Rates (c/kwh)			Length of Peak Period (hrs)	Date	Duration of Experimental Rates
	Experimental	Control		Peak	Shoulder	Off-Peak			
Connecticut	199	200	1	16	3	1	4	1976	12 months
Arkansas	1033 (1 town)	244	2	4 to 8	—	1	8	1976	12 months
New Jersey	666	334	2	5 to 6	—	1	12	1977–1978	24 months
Ohio	100	100	2	9	3	0.4	6	1976–1977	18 months
Arizona	140	10	28	8 to 16	3 to 7	1 to 4	3 to 8	May–Oct. 1976	6 months
Los Angeles	2000	200	41	5 to 13	—	1 to 2	3 to 12	1976–1980	30 months

Source: FEA, Electric Utility Rate Design Proposals, Interim Report, FEA/D-77/063, February 1977.

experiment has been designed to anticipate changing circumstances so that the results will be applicable not merely to the current cost structure of the Los Angeles utility, but to a wide variety of plausible conditions, including future cost increases and peak-load conditions found in several types of electric utilities. The number and variety of tariffs used in this experiment are intended to meet the objective of obtaining measurements of the fundamental component information necessary to estimate own- and cross-price elasticities for electricity by time of day, time of week, and time of year.

The set of tariffs in the Los Angeles experiment consists of three general categories of rate structures: (1) time-invariant tariffs; (2) seasonal tariffs; and (3) time-of-day tariffs, which necessarily require special meters. Rate levels for each type of tariff are shown in Tables 42 and 43.

Time-Invariant and Seasonal Tariffs

Two groups of related rate structures comprise the time-invariant category of rate structures: (a) conventional declining-block tariffs, labeled "controls"; and (b) flat-rate tariffs, under which the price per kilowatt is constant for all levels of consumption year-round. The seasonal tariffs have separate flat rates in effect in the summer and the winter. When appropriately analyzed, load data from all of these rate structures can be used to estimate separate electricity demand curves for summer and winter seasons. To provide additional load data, about 20 percent of the households with seasonal and time-invariant tariffs are equipped with continuously recording meters. (See Table 42.)

Time-of-Day Tariffs

The time-of-day tariffs were selected by using statistical models to represent the load response within five pricing methods: 9 a.m.–noon; noon–3 p.m.; 3–6 p.m.; 6–9 p.m.; and 9 p.m.–9 a.m. Since a question of major interest is whether consumer response to peak-load pricing is sensitive to the time of the peak pricing period, the set of experimental tariffs encompasses variations in both the levels of peak and off-peak rates, the periods in which they apply, and the length of the peak period. The seventeen experimental time-of-day tariffs are shown in Table 43.

Each of the time-of-day tariffs is further distinguished according to whether the peak price applies for 5 or 7 days per week. In many utilities the marginal costs of electricity supply on weekends are at intermediate or off-peak levels, suggesting that peak rates should apply only 5 days a week. However, if day-of-week as well as time-of-day variations must be measured, the costs of metering are increased. In order to obtain data to permit an assessment of the benefits

---

Energy. Acton, Manning, and Mitchell (1977) provide a general description of the objectives and features of the study and Manning, Mitchell, and Acton (1976) provide a detailed discussion of the experimental design.

Table 42. Time-Invariant and Seasonal Tariffs in the Los Angeles Experiment

Type of Tariff	Price (¢/kwh)	Number of Households
Controls	Declining Block (4¢/kwh average)	400
Flat rate	2¢	350
	5¢	110
Seasonal (summer/winter)	5/2	140
	8/2	50
	2/5	150
	2/8	20
Total	–	1220

Table 43. Time-of-Day Tariffs in the Los Angeles Experiment

Peak Period[a]	Prices Off-Peak/Peak (¢/kwh)	Approximate Number of Households
9 a.m.–noon	2/5	80
	2/9	60
	2/13	20
Noon–3 p.m.	2/9	40
	2/13	20
3 p.m.–6 p.m.	2/5	20
	2/9	80
	2/13	80
6 p.m.–9 p.m.	2/5	20
	2/9	60
	2/13	60
3 p.m.–9 p.m.	2/7	40
Noon–9 p.m.	1/5	120
	1/9	20
9 a.m.–9 p.m.	1/5	20
	1/9	80
9 p.m.–9 a.m.	2/5	160
Total	–	980

[a] For each tariff shown, one-half of the customers pay peak prices every day and the other half pay peak rates on weekdays only.

of exempting weekends from peak charges, the Los Angeles experiment divides the sample of time-of-day households so that one-half of the customers are assigned to tariffs with all weekend hours billed at the off-peak rate.

SUMMARY

Large commercial customers served at high and medium voltage levels can be placed on time-of-day electricity rates with the expectation that even very modest changes in patterns of energy use will offset additional metering and administrative costs.

For small commercial customers and for residential customers in the United States, peak-load rate structures will be advantageous only if the value of the changes in electricity use exceed the additional costs of metering and administration that such rate structures require. European utilities have successfully used a variety of optional time-of-day tariffs for low-voltage customers to encourage the installation of storage space-heating and water-heating appliances. However, the direct applicability of this experience to U.S. conditions is tempered by significant differences in climate, ownership of appliances, energy costs, and life-styles.

Experimentation with peak-load tariffs for small samples of residential consumers offers the opportunity to obtain data relevant to local conditions. Following the pioneering research in England and Wales, U.S. utilities have begun field trials to evaluate new rate structures. These studies promise to provide important new information needed to evaluate the desirability of implementing residential peak-load pricing throughout the United States. Because time-of-day pricing would require sizable additional investments for new meters, any policy decision to adopt time-of-day rates at the residential level should be taken only after the benefits and costs of such an action can be carefully weighed.

Fundamental changes in the structure of U.S. electricity rates will have wide-ranging impacts on customers, utilities, and regulatory bodies. How the transition to peak-load rates can be accomplished is the subject of Chapter 10.

Chapter 10

The Transition to Peak-Load Pricing in the United States

The first declining-block and maximum-demand rate structures were adopted by U.S. utilities over 70 years ago. Since that time, conditions in the electricity sector have changed markedly. New sources of low-cost hydroelectricity have now been largely exhausted. Most of the economies of constructing large-scale generating plants have been realized. The prices of fossil fuels have doubled and tripled and at the same time the expectations of economical sources of nuclear power have evaporated. Finally, rising concern to preserve the natural environment has curtailed the expansion of generating facilities. These changes have brought an end to the "benign era" of declining electricity prices.[1]

In the search for a coherent national energy policy, a fundamental reassessment of U.S. electricity pricing is of pressing importance. The experience of electric utilities in several European countries indicates that new rate structures can contribute significantly to increasing the efficiency with which energy is used. This experience, accumulated over several decades, establishes the feasibility of using peak-load pricing under a wide variety of conditions. This final chapter draws together the principal lessons of this experience and considers the issues raised by the transition to peak-load pricing in the United States.

ELECTRICITY PRICING AND ENERGY POLICY

Electricity prices, if appropriately set, can make a major contribution to achieving the goals of an effective energy policy. Rate structures based on marginal-cost principles permit society to rely on the economic self-interest of buyers and

---

1. See Joskow (1974).

sellers to promote efficient uses of energy. Such rates insure that each consumer will use only that amount of electricity whose value to the individual is at least equal to the costs of its supply. At the same time, marginal-cost rates do not deprive anyone of electricity when that person is willing to pay its full costs.

Since the costs of electricity vary by the hour of the day and also frequently by season, any pricing structure that does not reflect these cost differences necessarily underprices energy at the very time it is most expensive, and overprices it when it is least costly. The current U.S. practice of averaging high-cost and low-cost periods into a single, time-invariant price has two consequences. First, it encourages overuse of electricity during high-cost periods and unnecessarily deters consumption when costs are below average. Second, charging a single price at all times forces consumers who use electricity during low-cost periods to support others who consume power in high-cost periods.

Increases in Efficiency

Electricity rate structures based on peak-load principles will lead to both immediate and longer-term increases in the efficiency with which energy is used. In the short run, the introduction of peak-load pricing will discourage those uses of electricity that are of less value to consumers than the costs of supplying power. Some activities that use electricity will be shifted to less costly periods, and others may be eliminated. For example, by rescheduling maintenance activities, setting load-limiting devices on compressors and pumps to reduce peak-hour loads, and installing storage heating and cooling units having flexible charging times, industrial and commercial firms can readily make significant adjustments in their electricity-consumption patterns. More extensive changes in industrial activities may also occur, including staggering of working hours and higher employment in off-peak periods.

Over a period of years the introduction of peak-load pricing will further affect energy efficiency by influencing a wide variety of investment decisions throughout the economy. For example, nationwide use of peak-load pricing will encourage the development of low-cost electronic circuitry for controlling heating and cooling equipment and other electrical processes in plants and office buildings. Similar devices may eventually be developed for use with specific residential appliances or for the control of all electrical loads in a household. Peak-load rates can be expected to influence the architectural standards for designing larger buildings as well as the equipment for heating and cooling them. In diverse industries the capacity of selected processes will be expanded to permit storage of intermediate products or higher rates of production at off-peak hours. In plants requiring large amounts of process heat, peak-load rate structures will enhance the attractiveness of industrial cogeneration of electricity, which lowers the combined energy bill for electricity and the production process.

Summary of the European Experience

Most electric utilities in Western European countries have historically been confronted with higher operating costs than those in the United States. Because of limited capacity, many of these utilities have also faced shortage conditions at times of peak demands. These circumstances have stimulated the introduction of peak-load tariffs.

Peak-load rate structures are found in European electric utilities operating under a variety of forms of ownership and control: nationalized, municipal, and privately-owned. All these enterprises operate under financial constraints similar in character to those of U.S. utilities: they must cover their operating costs and pay a return on invested capital out of revenues from electricity sales. For industrial customers in these systems, either mandatory or optional time-of-day rates are in use, depending on the utility. At the residential level, simplified day/night rates are offered at the customer's option.

In supplying electricity to residential customers, European utilities have employed methods of load management that extend the direct effects of market prices. In some cases utilities participate in the design or marketing of particular appliances having favorable load characteristics. Many systems limit the connection of new appliances such as electric storage heaters to avoid undesirable system effects, such as a shift in the time of the system peak load. Utilities in several countries have used methods of remote load control (by airwave or over the wire) to shed certain residential loads when capacity shortages or unusually high operating costs occur. In each case, active load management in European electric utilities is accompanied by rate incentives, usually in the form of alternative tariffs offered on an optional basis.

Although U.S. utilities have rarely used peak-load rates, several systems have practiced remote load-shedding. In a few areas, utilities have employed radio control of residential water heaters in conjunction with a special tariff. And a number of utilities have supplied certain industrial users with power under special rates that permit interruptions of service.

The full effects that peak-load pricing has had on the operating expenses and capital outlays of European utilities are not easily measured. Aggregate data are available only on changes in system load curves before and after the introduction of peak-load electricity rates. There are no direct measurements of the pattern of system-wide demand that would have occurred in the absence of peak-load pricing, but some British and French analysts have concluded that peak-load rate structures are responsible for reductions in system peak loads of as much as 14 percent. Despite the difficulty of measuring the complete effect of peak-load pricing, the load curves of individual industrial plants and groups of customers provide dramatic evidence of demand elasticity in a variety of industries, and there can be no doubt that seasonal and time-of-day pricing has significantly modified system loads.

INTRODUCING NEW RATE STRUCTURES IN THE UNITED STATES

The case for selling electricity under seasonal and time-of-day rates has been well established in economic theory for many years. Electric utilities in Europe have been the first to develop practical methods for using peak-load tariffs to reflect differences in the marginal costs in an electrical system. Their experience demonstrates that peak-load pricing is a workable means of promoting energy efficiency.

For American utilities the policy issue of peak-load pricing reduces to a comparison of the benefits and costs of introducing new rate structures. The benefits from peak-load pricing will consist of the increases in economic efficiency that occur when electricity usage is reduced during peak hours and increased at off-peak periods. These changes in consumption can be evaluated in terms of the prices and marginal costs of supplying power in the peak and off-peak periods. These gains in efficiency must then be compared with the extra costs of introducing and using a more complex process for metering electricity usage and billing consumers. Although the economic circumstances of individual utilities in the United States differ, some general conclusions about the desirability of introducing peak-load rates can nevertheless be drawn.

Industrial Tariff Reform

The evidence presented in earlier chapters has made clear that peak-load rate structures are feasible for large consumers of electricity—predominantly industrial plants served at high voltages—and are effective in shifting electricity loads away from peak periods. Although industrial customers account for about one-third of the electricity sales of U.S. utilities, they constitute only a tiny proportion of all customers served by electricity distributing companies. Peak-load rates will therefore require only limited increases in administrative expenses and expenditures for time-of-day meters. Given the demonstrated capability of industrial customers to reduce and shift peak loads in significant amounts, the savings to utilities in operating and capacity costs will surely exceed the extra costs of metering and implementation. In Chapter 8 we estimated that at 1976 prices and demand, the nationwide benefits in increased efficiency could amount to $3.5 billion per year in the long run.

Commercial and Residential Tariff Reform

In the commercial and residential sectors, European evidence of the effects of peak-load pricing is less readily transferable to the United States. Comparisons of responses to tariffs in these sectors are complicated by major differences in climate, customary patterns of electricity use, and the availability of specific appliances. Nevertheless, for the largest commercial customers in most U.S. utilities, peak-load pricing should lead to net increases in economic efficiency.

In terms of electricity service, large commercial customers are similar to major industrial customers; they are often supplied at high voltage and they are few in number, so that there will be a relatively small cost of implementing time-of-day tariffs. Even very small percentage changes in load patterns will produce sufficient cost savings to offset the costs of additional meters and billing.

For smaller commercial customers and for all residential customers the case for peak-load pricing of electricity requires more detailed analysis. Seasonal pricing—because it can be accomplished by merely changing the dates at which meters are read and by modifying automated billing procedures—is likely to be cost-effective for most utilities and result in positive, although modest, gains in overall efficiency. In some parts of the country where the climate and the costs of electricity and other sources of energy are similar to conditions in Western Europe, storage heating devices may prove highly desirable to both customers and utilities.

Time-of-day pricing, however, would significantly increase the cost of serving each residential customer. If implemented for all of a utility's customers, time-of-day rates would require a major multiyear program of purchasing and installing new meters. It is unlikely that the efficiency gains from time-of-day pricing will be sufficiently large to justify such investments on a mandatory basis for even the majority of U.S. residential households. Instead, the benefits are likely to be largest for consumers who use substantial quantities of electricity and who are served by utilities having pronounced daily variations in marginal costs.

Policy decisions to proceed with time-of-day pricing for residential and small commercial customers will require additional data on changes in customer loads in response to different levels of peak and off-peak prices and to different peak-pricing periods. Such fundamental information will be forthcoming from analyses of experiments with new rate structures, from trial implementation of time-of-day rates in selected utilities, and by offering new tariffs on an optional basis to regular customers.

SOME NECESSARY RESEARCH

In addition to experimental studies now underway on the responses of U.S. consumers to new rate structures, public policymaking in the electricity sector can be advanced by research into the structure of marginal costs in an electricity supply system, and the economic effects of interconnection between utilities and the cogeneration of power by industrial customers.

Marginal Cost Structures

To improve the efficiency with which energy resources are used, new electricity tariffs and load-management decisions should be based on sound measures of the marginal costs of supplying service under different conditions. For example, if consumers' incentives are to be consistent with supply costs, the level of peak and off-peak rates as well as the timing and length of one or more peak periods must be closely matched to the incremental costs of delivering additional electricity during each period.

European electric utilities, especially those in Sweden and France, have conducted detailed studies of marginal costs as a basis for planning system expansion and setting tariffs. But comparable analyses of marginal costs have not been undertaken by U.S. utilities. Instead, they have used cost-of-service studies to allocate common costs on a historical, fully distributed basis to various classes of customers.

Fortunately much of the data needed to carry out a study of marginal costs is routinely collected by utility engineers. In daily operation, power-system personnel rely on measurements of the short-run marginal costs of generating units to dispatch the system economically. For long-run planning, utilities attempt to minimize the discounted value of total system costs by using computer models to study variations in plant mix, availability of fuel and water, environmental restrictions, and growth in system loads.

These data can provide the starting point for establishing the marginal costs of electricity. But in order to carry out empirical studies of the structure of costs in U.S. utilities, new research will be needed to develop the methodology necessary to analyze these data in terms of economic principles.[2] Moreover, although based on a common principle of marginal-cost pricing, the peak-load rate structures appropriate for individual utilities can differ markedly because of variations in the nature of generating resources available, the cost of fuel, the pattern of system demand, and interconnection with other utilities. The level of peak rates, the time at which they are effective, and the length of the peak period will all be affected, for example, by the extent to which thermal rather than hydroelectric generating units are employed.

Interconnection

The interconnection of separately managed utilities can potentially increase the efficiency of the electricity sector. Interconnection reduces the generating capacity required to maintain a given standard of reliability for each utility's customers and permits the regular exchange of energy between systems at times when their short-run marginal costs are significantly different. When electricity rate structures include seasonal or time-of-day variations, the availability of interconnected resources becomes an important determinant of the level and

---

2. A beginning has been made by Cicchetti, Gillen, and Smolensky (1976), who describe a simple method for approximating marginal costs and apply it in case studies of three utilities in California and Wisconsin. Turvey and Anderson (1977) provide additional methodological examples of basic calculations in several developing countries. Scherer (1977) illustrates the use of a programming model applied to New York conditions. Vardi, Zahavi, and Avi-Itzak (1977) discuss means of including loss-of-load probability in the calculation of marginal costs.

structure of a peak-load tariff. For example, access to the hydroelectric or pumped-storage capacity of another utility can substantially modify both the length of the optimal peak-pricing period and the magnitude of the difference between peak and off-peak marginal costs in an otherwise all-thermal system.

To calculate the benefits from interconnecting disparate systems, the analyst needs to assess both short- and long-run marginal costs for each utility. He must then determine the peak-load tariffs that would be appropriate if each system were operated independently and calculate how these rate structures would be modified by interconnection.

European utilities have achieved a generally high degree of interconnection, both within national systems and among countries. U.S. practice is quite diverse, and preliminary investigation of the opportunities for greater interconnection between U.S. systems have foreseen only limited benefits when conventional rate structures are used.[3] However, these tentative conclusions deserve careful reexamination in the context of peak-load tariff structures and load-management techniques.

Cogeneration

In several industries in Europe, electrical power generated in the plants of industrial customers from waste heat (or heat used first to generate electricity and then applied to the process), by-product fuels, and oil accounts for significant reductions in the peak loads of electric utilities. Higher overall levels of energy efficiency can frequently be obtained by producing power and industrial heat in a single plant than would be realized by operating these two processes separately. By and large the tariffs of U.S. electricity utilities have not encouraged the development of self-generated power, despite the significant potential that exists in U.S. industry.[4]

Peak-load tariffs will encourage firms to harness waste heat and other by-products in those industries in which co-generation of electricity is economically advantageous. As long as the utility sells electricity at its marginal cost, decisions by industrial customers to produce some of their own power in order to reduce their own electricity costs will lower overall costs to society as well.

Cogeneration does, however, raise two related issues. First, it is possible that decentralizing the production of electricity could lead to increased environmental pollution, unless industrial generating units are subject to emission standards similar to those applicable to utility plants. The second issue involves the sale of surplus electricity generated by industrial firms to the electric utility. In some cases the attractiveness of investing in cogeneration facilities will be affected by the market for excess power. At the same time, unless industrially generated power is supplied to the utility on a regularly scheduled basis, it will

3. See Neville et al. (1976); and Congressional Research Service (1971).
4. See Dow Chemical Company (1975); and Thermo Electron Corporation (1976).

be of lower reliability than utility-generated power. The utility will therefore tend to value cogenerated power at less than the marginal cost of running its own generating units.[5]

Two areas of new research would be useful: first, to establish for selected industrial production processes the cost conditions under which it would become economically effective to engage in cogeneration; and second, to investigate the opportunities and difficulties of allowing larger industrial firms to both buy and sell electricity.

THE OUTLOOK FOR PEAK-LOAD PRICING

Although substantial benefits would be achieved by shifting large U.S. industrial and commercial electricity consumers to peak-load rates without delay, several institutional factors may inhibit a rapid reform of electricity rate structures. The division of regulatory authority among a multitude of agencies, the consequences of increased working hours at off-peak periods, and public sensitivity to environmental conditions are likely to result in a pattern of diverse tariff structures across the United States.

Regulatory Complications

The regulation of electric utilities in the United States is divided in piecemeal fashion among a wide variety of state and federal agencies. Broadly speaking, the sale of electricity to wholesale customers and across state boundaries is regulated by the Federal Power Commission (recently transferred to the Federal Energy Regulatory Commission). Under the Federal Power Act the states have been delegated the responsibility for setting retail electricity rates. Thus, rates for the sale of electricity by privately-owned utilities are also regulated by state public utility commissions. Most publicly-owned electric utilities—municipally-owned systems or rural cooperatives—are regulated by specific governing boards or political bodies charged with reviewing and approving retail pricing policies.

A number of other regulatory bodies have jurisdiction over some aspects of electricity supply and indirectly affect rates. At the national level, the Nuclear Regulatory Commission licenses nuclear power plants and the Environmental Protection Agency sets air and water pollution standards. In some states other government agencies oversee the siting of generating or transmission facilities and set standards for discharging effluents into the air or water.

The consequence of this complex framework of regulation is likely to be an uneven pace of tariff reform across the country. The existence of state-by-state regulation of electricity prices may also hinder the adoption of new rate structures. Public utility commissions, legislatures, and municipal governments have

---

5. The utility may also prefer to have its own units in order to have a greater capital base on which its allowed rate of return is calculated.

occasionally used preferential electricity rates to attract new business enterprises. To the extent that peak-load pricing is perceived—nowever incorrectly—as being anti-business, individual states may be reluctant to introduce tariff reforms that would otherwise be regarded as good policy. Such interstate pricing rivalry would, of course, be reduced if all states move in concert to offer peak-load pricing, and recent congressional and administration proposals for nationwide rate reform are a means of overcoming this obstacle.

Other Constraints

The introduction of peak-load electricity rates may be retarded by perceived complications in labor markets and possible effects on environmental quality. Although for the economy as a whole peak-load electricity rates are unlikely to cause major shifts in hours of work, in selected industries the availability of electricity at off-peak rates will encourage employers to rearrange work assignments. Today, in most manufacturing industries only modest wage premiums are needed to attract workers to second and third shifts. However, large increases in demand for labor at off-peak hours could require larger pay differentials and perhaps changes in union work rules to induce a sufficient number of employees to work at off-peak periods.

Public concern to preserve the quality of the environment has increasingly affected planning and construction of electricity generating plants. Fortunately, the net effect of peak-load pricing would have beneficial environmental effects. More efficient use of generating capacity will mean that fewer plants are required to satisfy a given total demand for electrical energy. Shifts in demand away from peak hours will increase the proportion of energy supplied by baseload plants and thus increase the use of those generating units that are most efficient in converting fossil fuels into electricity. Some increase in the rate of construction of baseload plants may result, but this will be more than offset by the reduced need for capacity supplied by peaking and cycling units.

Phasing-in New Rate Structures

The transition to peak-load pricing in the United States can be eased by introducing new rate structures in a series of phases. It is difficult to forecast how rapidly system load conditions will change when peak-load rates are established. More extensive information on consumers' load responses and on utilities' marginal costs can help to reduce this uncertainty. To provide further information, peak-load rates can be established first for the largest high-voltage customers. Then as experience is gained and more time-of-day meters become available, these rates can be extended to the larger numbers of medium- and lower-voltage consumers. This is the pattern of rate development that was followed, for example, in France. It is also the pattern adopted in several states where a statewide commitment to peak-load pricing has been made.

The utilities' customers will also be uncertain about how new rate structures will affect their electricity bills and to what extent they will be able to adjust their electricity-using activities. Acceptance of new rate structures by consumers—particularly those facing higher payments—can be facilitated by either of two measures. One approach is for the utility to announce its intention to shift to cost-based peak-load rates and to publicize a program of phased implementation. The first peak-load rates can be introduced with a relatively small rate differential between time periods; this will permit rate structures to send a clear signal about high- and low-cost periods without creating large changes in consumer bills. The rate differential can later be increased to bring it into line with differences in marginal costs.

The second measure for phasing-in new rate structures is to offer peak-load rates as an *option* to the conventional tariff. In this case those customers who are able to shift electrical loads or find it advantageous to install load-regulating equipment or storage devices will select a peak-load rate, while customers with inelastic demands will continue on the standard tariff. Optional tariffs have been extensively used by European utilities. They are particularly attractive when, as in the case of residential customers, a peak-load tariff causes significant added metering costs. In this case a charge for the incremental metering costs can be included in the optional peak-load rate. The consumers who select the peak-load rate will automatically be those who expect their savings to exceed the extra costs, and metering expenses need only be incurred for this group of customers.[6]

Peak-load pricing, long the esoteric interest of the theoretical economist, has been practiced by major European electricity utilities for many years. Their accumulated experience with time-of-day and seasonal pricing is compelling evidence that rate structures, when appropriately set to reflect marginal costs, increase economic efficiency.

The policies of U.S. utilities and regulatory commissions have traditionally supported selling electricity at a single, time-invariant price. Today, the potential benefits of shifting to peak-load pricing are substantial. Fundamental reform of electricity rate structures can realize these benefits and contribute to an effective energy policy for the United States.

6. The introduction of an optional peak-load rate may require a small increase in the level of the conventional rate. This situation would arise if the electricity usage of customers remaining on the standard rate is particularly concentrated at peak hours.

 *Appendix*

French and British High Voltage Electricity Tariffs

This appendix provides additional details of the terms of the French and British high-voltage tariffs.

FRENCH TARIFFS

The present structure of the Green Tariff (*Le Tarif Vert*) has been in effect since 1958. The tariff consists of a series of schedules in which prices vary by season of the year and time of day for each geographical area, supply voltage, and range of load duration. As depicted in Figure 64 the customer is charged for demand (kw) and energy (kwh) in each of five time periods:

1. Winter peak hours from 7 to 9 a.m. and 5 to 7 p.m., Monday through Saturday, November through February.
2. Winter shoulder hours from 6 a.m. to 10 p.m., October through March, with the exception of Sunday and the winter peak hours.
3. Winter off-peak hours from 10 p.m. to 6 a.m. and all day Sunday, October through March.
4. Summer shoulder hours from 6 a.m. to 10 p.m., May through September, except Sunday.
5. Summer off-peak hours from 10 p.m. to 6 a.m. and all day Sunday, May through September.

Variants. Five versions of the Green Tariff are offered at the customer's option. The version appropriate to a particular customer is usually determined by his hours of utilization, which are equal to his annual kilowatt-hours of consumption divided by his annual maximum kilowatt demand:

Very long utilization: over 5500 hours.
Makeup, or long utilization: 3500 to 5500 hours.
General: appropriate for most customers.
Short utilization: less than 700 or 800 hours.
Security, or emergency supply to self-generators.

Demand Charges. Customers are charged for their effective amount of subscribed power. This "reduced power" P_R is calculated from subscribed capacity P_i in each of the five tariff periods according to the formula

$$P_R = P_1 + \sum_{i=2}^{5} c_i(P_i - P_{i-1})$$

where

P_i = subscribed power in period i.
c_i = coefficient for the tariff variant chosen.

In this calculation, no discount is given if a customer subscribes to a lesser amount of power during a shoulder period rather than during the peak period (or an off-peak period rather than a shoulder period), so that $P_1 \leq P_2 \leq \ldots \leq P_5$.

The coefficients depend on which tariff variant the customer selects. The values are given in Table 44.

Each tariff variant consists of one price per kw for reduced power P_R plus five prices for the energy consumed in each of the tariff periods. Tables 45 and 46 contain typical values for 1975. The demand charge is further subject to a percentage rebate based on the magnitude of actual, rather than subscribed, demand, computed using actual demand levels in the P_R formula (1):

Demand (kw)	Rebate (%)
First 100	0
Next 200	4
Next 700	8
Next 2000	13
Next 7000	18
Remainder	24

Demand in Excess of Subscription

1. Electricité de France (EdF) has the right to instill circuit-breakers that cut off the customer's power when demand exceeds subscribed levels by more than 10 percent.
2. Actual demand is measured monthly and converted to an "effective" demand $\hat{P}_R$ using the P_R formula (1). Excess demand $\hat{P}_R - P_R$ is billed monthly at the

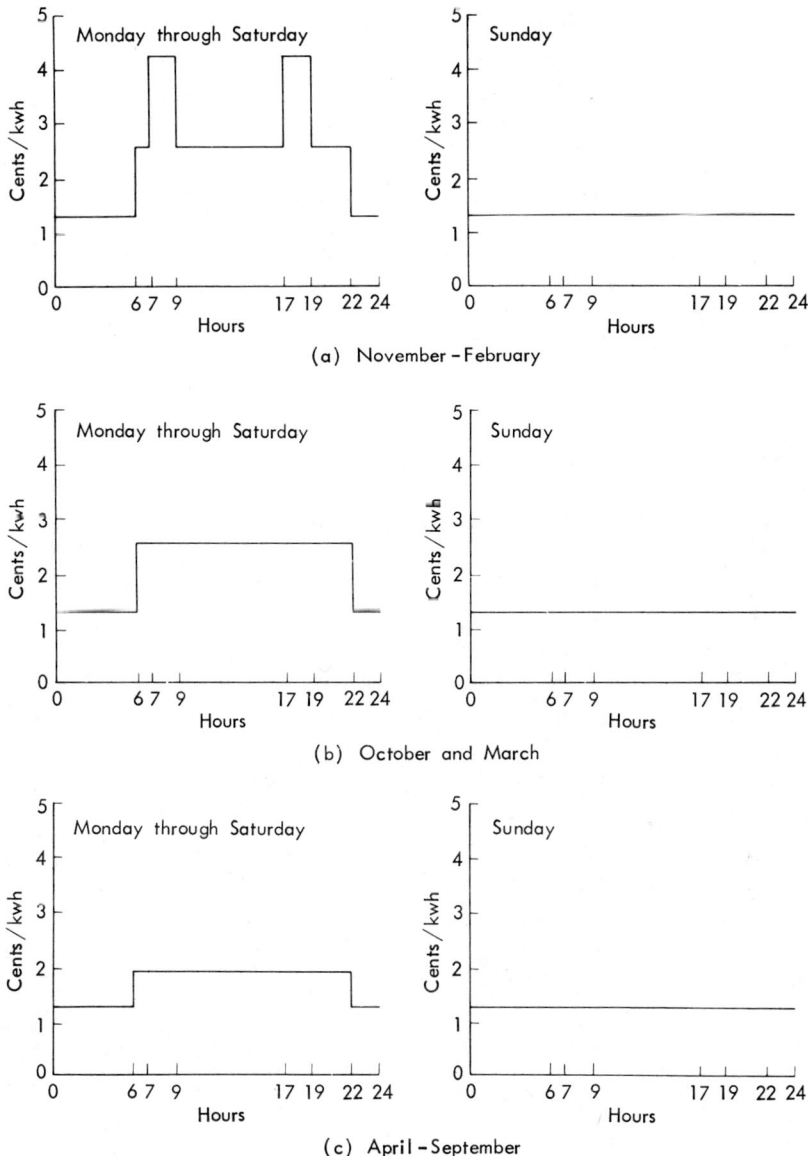

Source: Mitchell, Manning, and Acton (1977).

Figure 64. Energy (kwh) Charges in the French Green Tariff, 1975

Table 44. Subscribed Power Coefficients for the Green Tariff

		Version of Tariff		
Period	i	Make-up and General	Very Long Utilization	Short Utilization and Emergency
Peak	1	1.0	1.0	1.0
Shoulder winter	2	0.4	0.65	0.60
Shoulder summer	3	0.2	0.35	0.30
Off-Peak winter	4	0.07	0.08	0.21
Off-Peak summer	5	0.02	0.03	0.06

Source: Electricité de France, *Tarification de L'Energie Electrique*, (1974).

rate of 70 percent of the annual charge per subscribed kw. The effect is to penalize overruns of subscribed power that occur more than one month in twelve.

3. If the customer exceeds subscribed power by more than 20 percent, EdF will automatically increase the subscribed power level for that customer's contract. Green Tariff contracts are for a 5-year term, and subscribed power levels are for the duration of the contract. If the subscribed level is increased, the new subscribed power level is in effect for 5 years. However, in certain instances—notably shipbuilding—EdF will enter into a shorter-term contract if the customer pays an additional demand charge.

Billing for Reactive Energy. The Green Tariff rates for kw and kwh are set on the assumption that, during peak and shoulder hours, the consumption of

Table 45. Green Tariff at Medium Voltage, 5/15/30 kv, 1976

Tariff Version	Demand Charge (francs per kw)	Energy Charges (centimes per kwh)				
		Winter			Summer	
		Peak	Shoulder	Off-Peak	Shoulder	Off-Peak
Very long utilization	345.66	13.96	10.34	6.32	6.97	6.08
Makeup	200.97	21.19	14.44	6.80	9.46	6.48
General	128.62	30.84	16.77	6.89	10.66	6.56
Short utilization	51.45	49.94	26.60	6.89	12.85	6.56
Emergency	57.88	49.94	26.60	6.89	12.85	6.56
Reactive energy						
Surcharge (at all hours)			2.10		1.33	
Discount (at all hours)			0.83		0.53	

Note: Prices exclude the 17.6 percent value-added tax. Tariffs apply in all except selected areas.

Table 46. Green Tariff at High Voltages, 1976 (Bouches-du-Rhone Department)

Voltage (kv)	Tariff Version	Demand Charge (francs per kw)	Energy Charge (centimes per kwh)				
			Winter			Summer	
			Peak	Shoulder	Off-Peak	Shoulder	Off-Peak
220	Very long utilization	254.25	6.53	6.53	5.86	6.28	5.59
	Makeup	120.05	11.57	9.02	6.45	8.65	6.15
	General	100.19	16.38	9.94	6.51	9.47	6.21
	Short utilization	40.08	25.95	15.25	6.51	11.37	6.21
	Emergency	60.12	25.95	15.25	6.51	11.37	6.21
	Reactive energy Surcharge (at all hours) Discount (at all hours)			1.24 0.50			1.19 0.48
150	Very long utilization	274.19	7.21	7.21	5.88	6.31	5.61
	Makeup	131.74	13.04	10.09	6.46	8.70	6.16
	General	100.19	18.32	11.04	6.53	9.54	6.23
	Short utilization	40.08	29.16	17.08	6.53	11.46	6.23
	Emergency	60.12	29.16	17.08	6.53	11.46	6.23
	Reactive energy Surcharge (at all hours) Discount (at all hours)			1.39 0.55			1.19 0.48
60/90	Very long utilization	298.84	8.25	8.25	5.89	6.36	5.63
	Makeup	149.29	15.26	11.67	6.50	8.77	6.20
	General	100.19	21.22	12.71	6.56	9.65	6.26
	Short utilization	40.08	33.98	19.85	6.56	11.59	6.26
	Emergency	60.12	33.98	19.85	6.56	11.59	6.26
	Reactive energy Surcharge (at all hours) Discount (at all hours)			1.59 0.63			1.21 0.48

Note: Prices exclude the 17.6 percent value-added tax.

reactive energy is 60 percent of the consumption of active energy. When the reactive/active proportion exceeds 60 percent, the excess is billed by adding a surcharge rate per kwh. If the proportion is less than 60 percent, a discount per kwh is allowed; however, the discount is limited to not more than 40 percent of the active energy used in peak and shoulder hours.

ENGLISH AND WELSH TARIFFS

The retail tariffs of an area board are based on retail distribution costs and the payments which the board must make under the Bulk Supply Tariff to the Central Electricity Generating Board (CEGB) for generating and distributing elec-

218 Peak-Load Pricing for the United States

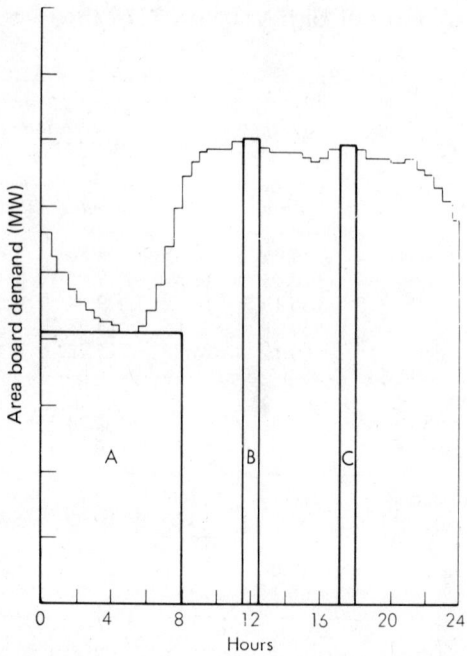

Figure 65. Load Curve for a Hypothetical Area Board

tricity at the wholesale level. The CEGB rates include two demand charges, three energy rates, a fixed charge, and a fuel escalation clause (see Table 47). The Bulk Supply Tariff's energy charges are complex and can best be understood with the aid of a hypothetical area board's load curve, as shown in Figure 65. Energy consumed in rectangle A has a price of 0.51 p/kwh; the area is limited in size by the area board's minimum demand between midnight and 8 a.m. Therefore, area A corresponds to the energy consumed overnight at a demand no greater than the area board's minimum demand for that day. The Bulk Supply Tariff charges 1.81 p/kwh for consumption during the CEGB's daytime peak half hour before 4 p.m. and for the peak half hour between 4 p.m. and midnight, rectangles B and C, respectively. The two half hours that define these rectangles are determined retrospectively for each day. All other energy consumption is billed at 0.85 p/kwh.

The Bulk Supply Tariff gives an indirect discount to the area board's nighttime consumption. If an area board can shift 1 kw of demand from the rest of the load curve and raise the minimum kw during the midnight to 8 a.m. period, then it receives an effective discount on 8 kwh by increasing the size of rectangle A and reduces its expense in the higher cost areas. If the 1 kw comes from the peak, the savings is 1.30 p per corresponding kw (e.g., 1.81 - 0.51). If the

Table 47. Central Electricity Generating Board Bulk Supply Tariff, 1976/77

Fixed by the Central Electricity Generating Board (the Generating Board) pursuant to Section 37(1) of the Electricity Act, 1947, for the year ending 31st March 1977.

Bulk Supply Points

Service Charge

1. Each Area Board will pay a sum equal to the ascertained annual charges and expenses of providing the bulk supply point capacity to meet its electricity requirements.

Demand Charges

Peaking Capacity Charge or Rebate

2. £8 charge (or rebate) for every kilowatt by which the Area Board's peak demand exceeds (or falls short of) its basic demand.

Basic Capacity Charge

3. £20-55 for every kilowatt of the Area Board's *basic demand* subject to:
 a) a minimum payment by each Area Board equal to that proportion of 705 million which the Area Board's *basic demand* bears to the sum of the *basic demand* of all Area Boards;
 b) a maximum payment by each Area Board equal to that proportion of £740 million which the Area Board's *basic demand* bears of all Area Boards.

4. For the purpose of the above capacity charges:
 (i) *"peak demand"* means the sum of kilowatt-hours supplied to the Area Board during the half-hour of maximum *system demand* before 16.00 hours and the half-hour of maximum *system demand* after 16.00 hours during *potential peak warning periods;*
 (ii) *"system demand"* means twice the number of kilowatt-hours sent out from the Generating Board's power stations and purchased by Generating Board from other sources for supply in England and Wales within a single half-hour;
 (iii) *"potential peak warning periods"* means those periods for which the Generating Board has by 17.00 hours on the previous day issued a warning that the maximum *system demand* may occur. Such period shall not exceed 60 hours in aggregate and shall be confined to the period 1 November 1976 to 28 February 1977 inclusive, but excluding Saturdays, Sundays, Christmas Day, Boxing Day and New Years Day.

 (iv) *"basic demand"* means twice the average number of kilowatt-hours supplied to the Area Board in each half hour when the *system demand* during the year is within plus or minus 1 per cent of 90 per cent of the average of the two maximum *system demands* specified in (i) above.

Energy Charges

Peak Rate

5. 1-81 per kilowatt-hour supplied to the Area Board each day during the two half-hours of highest *system demand* occurring between midnight and 16.00 hours and the two half-hours of highest *system demand* occurring between 16.00 hours and midnight.

Night Rate

6. 0-51p per kilowatt-hour supplied during the period midnight to 08.00 hours each day (unless charged under the Peak Rate above) *plus* 0.34p for every kilowatt-hours which would have been supplied had the Area Board's *night valley demand* on that day been maintained in all half-hours during that period (excepting for any half-hours in the period charged under the Peak Rate above).
 "Night valley demand" means twice the number of kilowatt-hours supplied in the half-hour of minimum *system demand* on each day.
 "System demand" is defined in 4(ii) above.

Standard Rate

7. 0-85p per kilowatt-hour supplied throughout the year other than the kilowatt-hours supplied at Night and Peak Rates.

Fuel Cost Adjustment

8. The above kilowatt-hour rates shall be increased or reduced by 0-000 415p for each 1p (0-5 or any greater decimal part of a penny being treated as 1p) by which the *national fuel cost per tonne* in the year differs from 1430p.
 "The national fuel cost per tonne" means the total delivered cost of coal, coke, oil or gaseous fuels consumed at all the Generating Board's stations in the period in the year multiplied by 26 and divided by the gross heat content of such fuels in gigajoules.

shift comes from other hours, the gain is 0.34 p (e.g., 0.85 - 0.51). This indirect incentive in the Bulk Supply Tariff is reflected in the off-peak energy rates area boards charge their industrial customers under the maximum demand tariffs.

The area boards pay two distinct demand charges to the CEGB. These charges are based on the "peak demands" and "basic demand" of each board, and are defined as follows. The peak demand kw_p is the sum of the kwh consumed by the board during the two half hours when the CEGB demand is at the annual maximum observed during a potential peak warning (PPW) period before 4 p.m. and, similarly, at the maximum for a PPW period after 4 p.m. PPWs can only occur between October 27 and February 29. The basic demand kw_b is the board's average kw demand when the CEGB system load is at 90 percent (± 1 percent) of the system annual peak demand. The area board is then billed for peak capacity (or receives a rebate) equal to £8 · ($kw_p - kw_b$). In addition, the board pays a basic capacity charge equal to £20.55 · kw_b. Subject to two constraints, the payment cannot be less than £705,000,000 · $kw_b/\Sigma kw_b$ or greater than £740,000,000 · $kw_b/\Sigma kw_b$, where Σkw_b is the sum of all area boards' basic demands.

The basic capacity charges are supposed to recover the incremental costs of providing and maintaining most of the CEGB's generation and transmission plant. The peak capacity charge is intended to recover the costs of using gas turbines and older plants to meet peak demands.

The Bulk Supply Tariff also charges fixed fees, which vary by area board, and a fuel-escalation clause. The exact language of the Bulk Supply Tariff for 1976-1977 is reproduced in Table 47.

Because demand and energy charges in the Bulk Supply Tariff are determined ex post, differences in expectations among the area boards about their own and the CEGB's load curves lead to some heterogeneity in individual area board tariffs. Typical industrial and residential tariffs are shown in Tables 17, 18, and 19 in Chapter 4.

Bibliography

Acton, Jan Paul, Morlie H. Graubard, and David J. Weinschrott. 1974. *Electricity Conservation Measures in the Commercial Sector: The Los Angeles Experience.* Santa Monica: Rand (R-1592-FEA), September.

Acton, Jan Paul, Willard G. Manning, and Bridger M. Mitchell. 1977. "Lessons from the Los Angeles Rate Experiment in Electricity." In J.L. O'Donnell, ed., *Adapting Regulation to Shortages, Curtailment, and Inflation.* East Lansing, Mich : Michigan State University.

Acton, Jan Paul, and Bridger M. Mitchell. 1975. *Economic Principles and the Structure of Electric Rates: Cost of Service, Allocation of Costs, and Rate Design.* Santa Monica: Rand (P-5545), November.

Acton, Jan Paul, Bridger M. Mitchell, and Ragnhild S. Mowill. 1976. *Residential Demand for Electricity in Los Angeles: An Econometric Study of Disaggregated Data.* Santa Monica: Rand (R-1899-NSF), September.

Acton, Jan Paul, and Ragnhild S. Mowill. 1976. "Regulatory Rationing of Electricity Under a Supply Curtailment." *Land Economics* 52 (November): 493–508.

Acton, Jan Paul, and Ragnhild S. Mowill. 1975. *Conserving Energy by Ordinance: A Statistical Analysis.* Santa Monica: Rand (R-1650-FEA), February.

Aigner, Dennis J. 1975. "A Sampling Design Model for an Electricity Pricing Experiment." Working paper, University of Wisconsin, Madison, May.

Anderson, Kent P. 1975. *A Simulation Analysis of U.S. Energy Demand, Supply and Prices.* Santa Monica: Rand (R-1951-NSF/EPA), October.

———. 1974. *The Price Elasticity of Residential Energy Use.* Santa Monica: Rand (P 5180), February.

Anderson, Kent P. 1973. *Residential Energy Use: An Econometric Analysis.* Santa Monica: Rand (R-1297-NSF), October.

———. 1972. *Residential Demand for Electricity: Econometric Estimates for California and the United States.* Santa Monica: Rand (R-905-NSF), January.

Anderson, Kent P., and J.C. De Haven. 1975. *The Long-Run Marginal Costs of Energy.* Santa Monica: Rand (R-1590-NSF), February.

Asbury, J.G., 1974. "The Econometric Approach to Electricity Supply and Demand: Review and Analysis." Argonne, Ill.: Argonne National Laboratory, May.

Asbury, J.G., and A. Kouvalis. No date. *Electric Storage Heating: The Experience in England and Wales and in the Federal Republic of Germany.* Argonne, Ill.: Argonne National Laboratory (No. ANL/ES-50).

Asbury, J., et al. No date. *Assessment of Energy Storage Technologies and Systems Phase I: Electric Storage Heating, Storage Air Conditioning and Storage Hot Water Heaters.* Argonne, Ill.: Argonne National Laboratory (No. ANL/ES-54).

Averch, Harvey, and Leland L. Johnson. 1962. "Behavior of the Firm under Regulatory Constraint." *American Economic Review* 52 (December); 1053-69.

Axelsson, Bo. 1974. *Study of Price Electricity at the Request of the Swedish State Power Board.* Stockholm, Sweden: Bergman and Co., February 11. Mimeo.

Bailey, Elizabeth E. 1973. *Economic Theory of Regulatory Constraint.* Lexington, Mass.: D.C. Heath.

Bailey, Elizabeth E. 1972. "Peak-Load Pricing under Regulatory Constraint." *Journal of Political Economy* 80 (July-August): 662-79.

Bailey, Elizabeth E., and Lawrence J. White. 1974. "Reversals in Peak and Off-Peak Prices." *Bell Journal of Economics and Management Science* 5 (Spring): 75-92.

Balasko, Yves. 1976. "A Contribution to the History of the Green Tariff, Its Impact and Its Prospects" in Harry M. Trebing, ed. *New Dimensions in Public Utility Pricing.* Michigan State Public Utilities Studies. Michigan State University. East Lansing.

——. 1975. "Formes Optimales de Tarification l'Electricité." Madrid: Union Internationale des Producteurs et Distributeurs D'Energie Electrique, April.

——. 1974. "On Designing Public Utility Tariffs with Applications to Electricity." Working Paper IP-218. Center for Research in Management Science—Institute of Business and Economic Research, University of California, Berkeley, October.

Bates, Robin, and Neil Fraser. 1974. *Investment Decisions in the Nationalized Fuel Industries.* London: Cambridge University Press.

Baughman, Martin, and Paul Joskow. 1975. "The Effects of Fuel Prices on Residential Appliance Choice in the United States." *Land Economics* 51 (February): 41-49.

Baumol, William J., and David F. Bradford. 1970. "Optimal Departures from Marginal Cost Pricing." *American Economic Review* 60 (June): 265-73.

Baumol, William J., and Alvin K. Klevorick. 1970. "Input Choices and Rate-of-Return Regulation: An Overview of the Discussion." *Bell Journal of Economics and Management Science* 1 (Autumn): 162-90.

Baxter, R.E., and R. Rees. 1968. "Analysis of Industrial Demand for Electricity." *Economic Journal* 78: 277-98.

Bergman, Lars, Clas Bergstrom, and Anders Bjorklund. 1976. *An Energy Forecasting Model for Sweden.* Stockholm, Sweden: Swedish Industrial Board. Mimeo.

Berkowitz, Michael K., and Frank C. Jen. 1977. "A Note on Production Inefficiency in the Peak-Load Pricing Model." *Southern Economic Journal* 44 (October): 374-79.

Berlin, E., C.J. Cicchetti, and W.J. Gillen. 1975. *Perspectives on Power: A Study of the Regulation and Pricing of Electric Power*. Report to the Energy Policy Project of the Ford Foundation. Cambridge, Mass.: Ballinger.

Berman, Mort B., and Morlie H. Graubard. 1973. *A Model of Residential Electricity Consumption*. Santa Monica: Rand (P-5063), July.

Berman, Mort B., and Morlie J. Hammer. 1973. *The Impact of Electricity Price Increases on Income Groups: A Case Study of Los Angeles*. Santa Monica: Rand (R-1102-NSF/CSA), March.

Berman, Mort B., Morlie J. Hammer, and Dennis P. Tihansky. 1972. *The Impact of Electricity Price Increases on Income Groups: Western United States and California*. Santa Monica: Rand (R-1050-NSF/CSA), November.

Berrie, T.W. 1967. "The Economics of System Planning in Bulk Electricity Supply." *Electrical Review* 181 (September 15, 22, and 29, 1967). Reprinted in R. Turvey, ed., *Public Enterprise*. New York: Penguin, 1968.

Besen, Stanley M., and Bridger M. Mitchell. 1975. *On Measuring the Gains in Economic Welfare from Marginal Cost Pricing When a Related Market Is Important: The Case of Electricity and Natural Gas*. Santa Monica: Rand (P-5668), August.

Bessiere, F., and P. Masse. 1964. "Long-Term Programming of Electrical Investments." In J.R. Nelson, ed., *Marginal Cost Pricing in Practice*. Englewood Cliffs, N.J.: Prentice-Hall.

Blain, D. 1975. "Influence of Prices on the Consumption of Electricity." In C.J. Cicchetti and W.K. Foell, eds., *Energy Systems Forecasting, Planning, and Pricing*. Madison: Institute for Environmental Studies, University of Wisconsin.

Blakeley, P.W. 1974. "Household Electricity Consumption in New Zealand." Paper presented at the 9th World Energy Conference, Detroit, September.

Boggis, James G. 1975. "Some Practical Aspects of the British Experiment with Electricity Pricing." In C.J. Cicchetti and W.K. Foell, eds., *Energy Systems Forecasting, Planning, and Pricing*. Madison: Institute for Environmental Studies, University of Wisconsin.

———. 1974. "Field Trials Show Domestic Consumers Respond to Seasonal and kw Demand Tariffs." *Electrical Review*, No. 22, February.

Boiteux, Marcel. 1971. "On the Management of Public Monopolies Subject to Budgetary Constraints." *Journal of Economic Theory* 3 (September): 219-42.

———. 1964a. "The Choice of Plant and Equipment for the Production of Electric Energy." In J.R. Nelson, ed., *Marginal Cost Pricing in Practice*. Englewood Cliffs, N.J.: Prentice-Hall, pp. 199-214.

———. 1964b. "Electrical Energy: Facts, Problems, and Prospects." In ibid., pp. 3-28.

———. 1964c. "Marginal Cost Pricing." In ibid., pp. 51-58.

———. 1964d. "The 'Tarif Vert' of Electricité de France." In ibid., pp. 127-50.

———. 1949. "La Tarification des Démandes en Pointe." *Revue Générale de l'Electricité* 58: 321-40. Translated as "Peak-Load Pricing." *Journal of Business* 33 (April 1960): 157-79.

Boiteux, Marcel, and Paul Stasi. 1964. "The Determination of Costs of Expansion of an Interconnected System of Production and Distribution of Electricity." In J.R. Nelson, ed., *Marginal Cost Pricing in Practice*. Englewood Cliffs, N.J.: Prentice-Hall, pp. 91-126.

Boley, T.A. 1977. "Pricing Policy and Tariffs for Electricity in England and Wales." *Electronics and Power* (August): 636-40.

———. 1976. "British Electric Load Management for the Record." *Public Utilities Fortnightly* 78 (September 23): 10.

Boley, T.A., and D.L. Walker. 1974. "The Effect of Prices and Economic Growth on Consumers' Energy Requirements." Paper presented at the 9th World Energy Conference, Detroit, September.

Boyd, James W., ed. 1976. "Proceedings on Forecasting Methodology for Time-of-Day and Seasonal Electric Utility Loads." Electric Power Research Institute, March.

Brown, Gardner, Jr., and M. Bruce Johnson. 1969. "Public Utility Pricing and Output under Risk." *American Economic Review* 59 (March): 119-28.

Burchnall, J.A. No date. "The Supply Industry and Private Generation." London: Electricity Council.

Caille, P., and P.L. Lhermitte, 1971. "Marginal Cost Pricing in a Random Future as Applied to the Tariff for Electrical Energy by Electricité de France." In Harvey M. Trebing, ed., *Essays on Public Utility Pricing and Regulation*. East Lansing: Michigan State University.

California Energy Resources Conservation and Development Commission. 1977. "California Load Management Research, 1977." A First-year Report to the Federal Energy Administration on the FEA/California Electric Utilities Demonstration Project, October.

California Public Utilities Commission. 1974. "Investigation on the Commission's Own Motion into Electric Utility Rate Structures, and the Changes, if Any, That Should Be Made in Presently Constituted Rate Structures to Encourage Conservation of Electricity in the State of California." Case No. 9804. San Francisco.

Canal, M. 1976. "Campagne de Mésures BTT-GTI 27 Essai d'Application des Méthodes d'Analyse de Données à la Classification des Clients Basse Tension." Electricité de France, September 15.

Canal, M., and H. Fourati. 1977. "Campagne de Mesures BT-GTI 27, une Classification Naturelle des Clients BT Simple Tarif en Fonction de Leur Courbe de Charge." Electricité de France, January 10.

Cargill, Thomas F., and Robert A. Meyer. 1971. "Estimating the Demand for Electricity by Time of Day." *Applied Economics* 3: 233-46.

Chapman, D., T. Tyrell, and T. Mount. 1972. "Electricity Demand Growth and the Energy Crisis." *Science* 178 (November 17): 703-8.

Chiogioji, M.H. 1975. "Load Management: What Can Be Learned from European Experiences." McLean, Va.: MITRE, September 26.

Cicchetti, C.J., and W.K. Foell, eds. 1975. *Energy Systems Forecasting, Planning, and Pricing*. Madison: Institute for Environmental Studies, University of Wisconsin.

Cicchetti, Charles J., William J. Gillen, and Paul Smolensky. 1976. "The Marginal Cost and Pricing of Electricity: An Applied Approach." Unpublished draft, Planning and Conservation Foundation, Sacramento, January.

Cicchetti, Charles J., and V. Kerry Smith. 1974. "Alternative Price Measures and the Residential Demand for Electricity: A Specification Analysis." Unpublished, June.

Committee on Challenges of Modern Society. 1974a. *Minutes of the Electric Utility Load Management Conference, Brussels, 1974.* Federal Energy Administration.

———. 1974b. "Pilot Study on the Rationale Use of Energy." In ibid.

Committee on Supply Interruption Costs. No date. "Cost of Interruptions in Electricity Supply." Sweden.

Congressional Research Service. 1971. *National Power Grid System Study— An Overview of Economics, Regulatory and Engineering Aspects.* A study prepared at the request of Lee Metcalf, Chairman, Subcommittee on Minerals, Materials, and Fuels of the Committee on Interior and Insular Affairs, United States Senate.

Connecticut Public Utilities Control Authority. 1977. *Connecticut Peak Load Pricing Test.* Department of Planning and Energy Policy, Office of Consumer Counsel, Northeast Utilities, May.

Converse, A.O., and Thomas Laaspere. 1975. "Technical Alternatives for Load Management, with Implications for Rate Structures." In C.J. Cicchetti and W.K. Foell, eds., *Energy Systems Forecasting, Planning, and Pricing.* Madison: Institute for Environmental Studies, University of Wisconsin.

Craven, J. 1971. "On the Choice of Optimal Time Periods for a Surplus Maximizing Utility Subject to Fluctuating Demand." *Bell Journal of Economics and Management Science* 2 (Autumn): 495–502.

Crew, M.A., and P.R. Kleindorfer. 1978. "Reliability and Public Utility Pricing." *American Economic Review* 68 (March).

———. 1976. "Peak Load Pricing with a Diverse Technology." *Bell Journal of Economics and Management Science* 7 (Spring): 207–31.

———. 1975. "On Off-Peak Pricing: An Alternative Technological Solution." *Kyklos* 28: 80–93.

A Critique of *The Electricity Industry* by the Energy Research Group. 1976. Buckinghamshire: Open University, Research Report ERG 013, March.

Crowley, W.J. 1941. "Elasticity of Residential Demand for Electricity: A Reply." *Journal of Land and Public Utility Economics* 18 (November).

Cutler, Howard A. 1941a. "The Elasticity of Residential Demand for Electricity." *Journal of Land and Public Utility Economics* 18 (May).

———. 1941b. "Elasticity of Residential Demand for Electricity: A Rejoinder." *Journal of Land and Public Utility Economics* 18 (November).

Dansby, Robert E. 1977. "An Economic Evaluation of Interruptible Service Offerings." Paper delivered to American Economic Association, December 29.

———. 1975. "Welfare Optimal Peak-Load Pricing and Capacity Decisions with Intraperiod Time Varying Demand." Economics Discussion Paper No. 39. Holmdel, N.J.: Bell Laboratories, November.

De Alessi, Louis. 1974. "An Economic Analysis of Government Ownership and Regulation: Theory and the Evidence from the Electric Power Industry." *Public Choice*, Fall.

De Grasse, Richard V. 1977. "Electric Storage Heating after Two Years." *Public Utilities Fortnightly*, January 6.

Demsetz, Harold. 1968. "Why Regulate Utilities?" *Journal of Law and Economics* 11 (April): 55–65.

Dessus, G. 1964. "The General Principles of Rate-Fixing in Public Utilities." In J.R. Nelson, ed., *Marginal Cost Pricing in Practice*. Englewood Cliffs, N.J.: Prentice-Hall, pp. 31–50.

Doernberg, A. 1975. "Comparative Analysis of Energy Use in Sweden and the United States." New York: Brookhaven National Laboratory Informal Report, September.

Donatelli, Bruce Edmond. 1967. "Price Elasticity of Demand for Electricity: Residential Markets in Southern California." Unpublished master's thesis, University of California, Los Angeles.

Dreze, J. 1964. "Some Postwar Contributions of French Economists to Theory and Public Policy." *American Economic Review* 54 (June): 1–64.

Edblad, P.G., S. Gothe, B. Lantz, and E. Skalsky. 1975. "Cost Calculations behind the Swedish Electricity Tariffs." In International Union of Producers and Distributors of Electrical Energy, *Conference on Electricity Tariffs*. Madrid, April 21–23.

Electricité de France. 1975. *Statistiques de la Production et de la Consommation*. Paris.

———. 1974. "Tarification de l'Energie Electrique." January. Memorandum.

Electricity Council of London. 1975. *Annual Report, 1974/75*.

Electricity Council of London. No date. *Domestic Tariffs Experiment*. Load and Market Research Report No. 121.

Electric Utility Rate Design Study. 1977. "Rate Design and Load Control: Issues and Directions." A report to the National Association of Regulatory Utility Commissioners, November.

Erickson, Edward W., Robert M. Spann, and Robert Ciliano. 1974. "Substitution and Usage in Energy Demand: An Econometric Study of Long-Run and Short-Run Effects." In Milton F. Searl, ed., *Energy Modeling: Art, Science, Practice*. Baltimore: Johns Hopkins University.

Falck-Jorgensen, S. 1975. "Low Voltage Tariff System in Norway." In International Union of Producers and Distributors of Electrical Energy, *Conference on Electricity Tariffs*. Madrid, April 21–23.

Falck-Jorgensen, S., and R. Stromme. 1975. "Norwegian Tariff Development and Its Background." Ibid.

Faulhaber, Gerald, and John Panzar. 1977. "Optimal Two-Part Tariffs with Self-Selection." Bell Laboratories Economics Discussion Paper, No. 74, January.

Federal Energy Administration. 1976. *1976 National Energy Outlook*. Washington, D.C.: GPO, February.

FEA/California Electric Utilities Demonstration Project Master Plan. California Energy Resources and Development Commission, Utilities Office, Conservation Division, January 1977.

Felton, J.R. 1965. "Competition in the Energy Market between Gas and Electricity." *Nebraska Journal of Economics and Business* 4 (Autumn): 3-12.

Fisher, Franklin M., and Carl Kaysen. 1962. *A Study in Econometrics: The Demand for Electricity in the United States.* Amsterdam: North-Holland.

Fletcher, J., and B.O. Helzen. 1975. "The Swedish Six Hour Demand." In International Union of Producers and Distributors of Electrical Energy, *Conference on Electricity Tariffs.* Madrid, April 21-23.

Gabor, A. 1955. "A Note on Block Tariffs." *Review of Economic Studies* 23 (1955-1956): 32-41.

Gravelle, H.S.E. 1976. "The Peak Load Problem with Feasible Storage." *Economic Journal* 86 (June): 245-77.

Griffin, James M. 1974. "The Effects of Higher Prices on Electricity Consumption." *Bell Journal of Economics and Management Science* (Autumn): 515-39.

———. 1972. *A Long-Term Forecasting Model of U.S. Electricity Supply and Demand.* Unpublished manuscript, University of Houston, Texas.

Gujarti, D. 1969. "Demand for Electricity and Natural Gas." *Public Utilities Fortnightly,* January 30.

Häfele, Wolf, et al. 1976. *Second Status Report of the IIASA Project on Energy Systems, 1975.* Research Report RR-76-1. Laxenburg, Austria. IIASA.

Häfele, Wolf, and Alan S. Manne. 1975. "Strategies for a Transition from Fossil to Nuclear Fuels." *Energy Policy,* March.

Halvorsen, R. 1975. "Residential Demand for Electric Energy." *Review of Economics and Statistics* 57 (February): 12-18.

———. 1973. "Short-Run Determinants of Residential Electricity Demand." Discussion Paper No. 73-13. University of Washington, Seattle.

———. 1972a. "Residential Electricity: Demand and Supply." Paper presented at the Sierra Club Conference on Power and Public Policy, Vermont, January 1972.

———. 1972b. "Residential Demand for Electricity." Unpublished Ph.D. dissertation, Harvard University, December.

Harmsworth, J.A. 1975. "Interruptible Loads." In International Union of Producers and Distributors of Electrical Energy, *Conference on Electricity Tariffs.* Madrid, April 21-23.

Heinemann, G.T., B.A. Nordman, and E.C. Plant. 1966. "The Relationship between Summer Weather and Summer Loads: A Regression Analysis." *IEEE Transactions on Power Apparatus and Systems* 85: 1144-51.

Hirshleifer, J. 1958. "Peak Loads and Efficient Pricing: Comment." *Quarterly Journal of Economics* 72: 451-62.

Holth, H., and J. Tveit. 1975. "High-Voltage Tariffs at the Norwegian Water Resources and Electricity Board (NVE)." In International Union of Producers and Distributors of Electrical Energy, *Conference on Electricity Tariffs.* Madrid, April 21-23.

Houthakker, H.S. 1951a. "Electricity Tariffs in Theory and Practice." *Economic Journal* 61 (March): 1-25.

———. 1951b. "Some Calculations on Electricity Consumption in Great Britain." *Journal of the Royal Statistical Society* [Series A (General)] 114: 359-71.

Houthakker, H.S., P.K. Verleger, Jr., and D.P. Sheehan. 1974. "Dynamic Demand Analyses for Gasoline and Residential Electricity." *American Journal of Agricultural Economics* 56 (May): 412-18.

Institution of Electrical Engineers, Power Division. 1977. *Metering Apparatus and Tariffs for Electricity Supply.* Third International Conference, November 15-17, London.

Johnson, Leland L. 1973. "Behavior of the Firm under Regulatory Constraint: A Reassessment." *American Economic Review* 63 (May): 90-97.

Johnson, M. Bruce, and Gardner Brown, Jr. 1970. "Public Utility Pricing and Output under Risk: Reply." *American Economic Review* 60 (June): 489-90.

Johnston, J., and T.J. Tyrell. 1974. "Electricity Demand in the United States: An Econometric Analysis." In M.S. Macrakis, ed., *Energy: Demand, Conservation, and Institutional Problems.* Cambridge, Mass.: M.I.T. Press.

Jorgenson, Dale W. 1974. "Consumer Demand for Energy." Harvard Discussion Paper No. 386. Cambridge, Mass., November.

Joskow, Paul L. 1977. "Electric Utility Rate Structures in the United States: Some Recent Developments." Paper presented at the Seventh Michigan Conference on Public Utility Economics.

———. 1976. "Contributions to the Theory of Marginal Cost Pricing." *Bell Journal of Economics* 7 (Spring): 197-206.

———. 1975. "Applying Economic Principles to Public Utility Rate Structures: The Case of Electricity." In Charles J. Cicchetti and John L. Jurewitz, eds., *Studies in Electric Utility Regulation.* Cambridge, Mass.: Ballinger.

———. 1974. "Inflation and Environmental Concern: Structural Change in the Process of Public Utility Price Regulation." *Journal of Law and Economics* 17 (October): 291-327.

Kahn, Alfred E. 1971. *The Economics of Regulation: Principles and Institution.* 2 vols. New York: Wiley.

Katz, Myron B., et al. 1973. "Impact Study of BPA Proposed Rate Increases." Portland, Oregon: Bonneville Power Administration, U.S. Department of the Interior.

Kirchmayer, L.K. 1958. *Economic Operation of Power Systems.* New York: Wiley.

Kline, Phyllis H. 1974. "An Econometric Model for Residential Electricity Demand." In Federal Power Commission, *The Methodology of Load Forecasting,* Appendix B-1. Washington, D.C.: GPO.

Koenker, Roger. 1977. "Optimal Peak-Load Pricing with Time-Additive Consumer Preferences," in Anthony C. Laurence, ed. *Forecasting and Modeling Time-of-Day and Seasonal Electricity Demands,* Electric Power Research Institute, Palo Alto, December.

Laaspere, T. 1974. *On European Approaches to Managing the Electric Load.* Report No. DVE-2. Montpelier: Vermont Public Service Board, May.

Leland, Hayne E., and Robert A. Meyer. 1976, "Monopoly Pricing Structures with Imperfect Discrimination." *Bell Journal of Economics* 7 (Autumn); 449-462.

Lindquist, J. 1962. "Operation of a Hydro-thermal Electrical System: A Multi-Stage Decision Process." *IEEE Transactions,* April.

Little, J.D.C. 1955, "The Use of Storage Water in a Hydro-Electric System." *Journal of the Operations Research Society of America* 3 (May): 187-97.

Littlechild, Stephen C. 1972. "Maintenance Requirements and Peak-Load Pricing." *Metroeconomica* 24 (September-December): 291-98.

———. 1970. "Marginal Cost Pricing with Joint Costs." *Economic Journal* 80 (June): 323-25.

Lorgeou, J. 1976. "La Tarification de l'Electricité." Paris: Electricité de France, July.

Lublin, Joann S. 1977. "New Electricity Rates Could Have Big Effect on Prices and People." *Wall Street Journal,* August 12.

Lundberg, L. 1975. "Report of the Group of Experts on Quality of Service from the Consumer's Point of View." In International Union of Producers and Distributors of Electrical Energy, *Conference on Electricity Tariffs.* Madrid, April 21-23.

Lundberg, L., B.O. Helzen, O. Petterson, and S. Johansson. 1975. "Tariff Framing Principles Used in Sweden." In International Union of Producers and Distributors of Electrical Energy, *Conference on Electricity Tariffs.* Madrid, April 21-23.

Lyman, R. Ashley. 1972. "Demand Conditions in the Electrical Power Industry: An Econometric Study." Unpublished Ph.D. dissertation, Northwestern University, Evanston, Ill.

Macrakis, Michael S., ed. 1974. *Energy: Demand, Conservation, and Institutional Problems.* Cambridge, Mass.: M.I.T. Press.

Main, R.S. 1973. "Periodic vs. Demand-Layer Pricing for Utility Loads." Unpublished dissertation, Department of Economics, University of California, Los Angeles.

Manning, Willard G., Bridger M. Mitchell, and Jan Paul Acton. 1976. *Design of the Los Angeles Peak-Load Pricing Experiment for Electricity.* Santa Monica: Rand (R-1955-DWP), November.

Marchand, M.G. 1974. "Pricing Power Supplied on an Interruptible Basis." *European Economic Review* 5: 263-74.

Masse, P. 1964a. "Electrical Investments." In J.R. Nelson, ed., *Marginal Cost Pricing in Practice.* Englewood Cliffs, N.J.: Prentice-Hall, pp. 183-98.

———. 1964b. "Some Economic Effects of the 'Tarif Vert.'" In ibid., pp. 151-56.

Masse, P., and F. Bessiere. 1964. "Long-Term Programming of Electrical Investments." In ibid., pp. 235-52.

Masse, P., and R. Gibrat. 1964. "Application of Linear Programming to Investments in the Electric Power Industry." In ibid., pp. 215-34.

Mathiesen, Lars. 1977. "Marginal Cost Pricing in a Linear Programming Model: A Case with Constraints on Dual Variables." *Scandinavian Journal of Economics* 79: 468-77.

Meek, Ronald L. 1973. "An Application of Marginal Cost Pricing: The Green Tariff in Theory and Practice." *Journal of Industrial Economics* 11 (July): 217-36; 12 (October): 45-63.

Merford, R.B., and W.G. Michaelson. 1974. "Electricity Demand—One Utility's Econometric Model." In M.S. Macrakis, ed., *Energy: Demand, Conservation, and Institutional Problems.* Cambridge, Mass.: M.I.T. Press.

Meyer, Robert. 1975. "Monopoly Pricing and Capacity Choice under Uncertainty." *American Economic Review* 65 (June): 326-37.

Mitchell, Bridger M. 1977. "A Note on Economic Modeling of Peak Electricity Demands." In Anthony Laurence, ed., *Forecasting and Modeling Time-of-Day and Seasonal Electricity Demands,* Electrical Power Research Institute, December.

Mitchell, Bridger M., with Jan Paul Acton and R.S. Mowill. 1975. Testimony in California P.U.C. Case 9804, April 22 and May 2. Summarized in *Selected Econometric Studies of the Demand for Electricity: Review and Discussion.* Santa Monica: Rand (P-5544), July.

Mitchell, Bridger M., and Jan Paul Acton. 1977. *Peak-Load Pricing in Selected European Electric Utilities.* Santa Monica: Rand (R-2031-DWP), July.

Mitchell, Bridger M., Willard G. Manning, and Jan Paul Acton. 1977. *Electricity Pricing and Load Management: Foreign Experience and California Opportunities.* Santa Monica: Rand (R-2106-CERCDC), March.

Mohring, H. 1970. "The Peak-Load Problem with Increasing Returns and Pricing Constraints." *American Economic Review* 60 (September): 693-705.

Monig, Walter. 1975. "Determinanten des Elektrizitätsangebots und volkswirtschaftliche Kriterien zu seiner Beurteilung." R. Oldenbourg Verlag, Munchen.

Moore, T.G. 1970. "The Effectiveness of Regulation of Electricity Utility Prices." *Southern Economic Journal* 36 (April): 365-75.

Morlat, G. 1964. "Instructions for the Optimum Management of Seasonal Reservoirs." In J.R. Nelson, ed., *Marginal Cost Pricing in Practice.* Englewood Cliffs, N.J.: Prentice-Hall, pp. 158-80.

Mount, T.D., and L.D. Chapman. 1974. *Electricity Demand Projections and Utility Capital Requirements.* Cornell Agricultural Economics Staff Paper No. 74-24, Ithaca, N.Y., September.

Mount, T.D., L.D. Chapman, and T.J. Tyrell. 1973. *Electricity Demand in the United States: An Econometric Analysis.* Oak Ridge National Laboratory, Tennessee, June.

Mount, T.D., and T.J. Tyrell. 1974. "Electricity Demand in the United States: An Econometric Analysis." In M.S. Macrakis, ed., *Energy: Demand, Conservation, and Institutional Problems.* Cambridge, Mass.: M.I.T. Press.

Mow, C.C., W.E. Mooz, and S.K. Anderson. 1973. *A Methodology for Projecting the Electrical Energy Demand of the Residential Sector in California.* Santa Monica: Rand (R-995-NSF/CSRA), March.

Mowill, R.S. 1977. *Residential Energy Use: Combining Disaggregate Data Sources for Policy Analysis.* Santa Monica: Rand (P-5754), January.

———. 1976. *Recent Research on Residential Consumption of Electricity.* Santa Monica: Rand (P-5703), August.

National Economic Research Associates, Inc. 1977. "Analysis of Electricity Pricing in France and Great Britain." Electric Utility Rate Design Study, January 25.

The National Energy Plan. 1977. Executive Office of the President, Energy Policy and Planning, April 29.

95th Cong., 1st sess. H.B. 6381. National Energy Act 1977.

Nelson, D.C. 1965. "A Study of the Elasticity of Demand for Electricity by Residential Consumers: Sample Markets in Nebraska." *Land Economics* 41 (February): 92-96.

Nelson, James R., ed., 1964. *Marginal Cost Pricing in Practice.* Englewood Cliffs, N.J.: Prentice-Hall.

Nelson, James R. 1967, "Practical Problems of Marginal-Cost Pricing in Public Enterprise: The United States." In A. Phillips and O. Williamson, eds., *Prices: Issues in Theory, Practice and Public Policy.* Philadelphia: University of Pennsylvania Press.

Nerlove, Marc. 1963. "Returns to Scale in Electricity Supply." In *Measurement in Economics: Studies in Mathematical Economics and Econometrics in Memory of Yehuda Grunfeld.* Stanford, Calif.: Stanford University Press.

Neville, Thomas, et al. 1976. "Electric Power Transfers for California." Final report. Organization Analysis Corp., August 13.

Newman, D.K., and D. Day. 1975. *The American Energy Consumer.* Cambridge, Mass.: Ballinger.

Nguyen, D.T. 1976. "The Problems of Peak Loads and Inventories." *Bell Journal of Economics* 7 (Spring): 242-48.

Nguyen, D.T., and G.J. Macgregor-Reid. 1977. "Interdependent Demands, Regulatory Constraint and Peak-Load Pricing." *Journal of Industrial Economics* 25 (June); 275-93.

Nissel, Hans E. 1976. "The Electric Rate Question Revisited." Electricity Consumers Resource Council, November.

Nuclear Energy Policy Study Group. 1977. *Nuclear Power Issues and Choices.* Cambridge, Mass.: Ballinger.

On Electricity Forecasting and Planning. 1976. A preliminary report prepared by Energy Assessment Division, Energy Resources Conservation and Development Commission, October.

Pacific Gas and Electric Company. 1974. *A Quantitative Analysis of the Consumption of Gas and Electricity by Low-Income Consumers in PG&E Service Area.* San Francisco, September.

Panzar, J.C. 1976. "A Neoclassical Approach to Peak-Load Pricing." *Journal of Economics* 7 (Autumn): 521-30.

Panzar, J.C., and David S. Sibley. 1977. "Public Utility Pricing under Risk: The Case of Self-Rationing." Economic Discussion Paper No. 82. Holmdel, N.J.: Bell Laboratories, February.

Peddie, R.A. 1975. "Peak Loads and Load Shaping of the CEGB's Demand." Seventeeth Hunter Memorial Lecture, Institute of Electrical Engineers, January 9.

Pelleter, Y. 1977. "Application des Méthodes d'Analyse de Données à l'Etude d'un Echantillon de Courbes de Charge des Clients Moyenne Tension." Electricité de France, 20 April.

Peterson, H. Craig. 1975. "An Empirical Test of Regulatory Effects." *Bell Journal of Economics* 6 (Spring): 111-26.

Pioger, Y. 1977a. "Analyse des Courbes de Charge des Clients du Service National du C.I.M.E. Sud-Est: Essai de Classification." Electricité de France, 3 February.

———. 1977b. "Eléments de Reflexion sur la Déformation des Courbes de Charge Globales et Sectorielles: Evaluation de l'Effet Induit par la Tarification." Electricité de France, 8 July.

———. 1975. "Forecasting Power Consumption and Models for Construction Load Curves." In C.J. Cicchetti and W.K. Foell, eds., *Energy Systems Forecasting, Planning, and Pricing*. Madison: Institute for Environmental Studies, University of Wisconsin.

Pressman, I. 1970. "A Mathematical Formulation of the Peak-Load Pricing Problem." *Bell Journal of Economics and Management Science* 1 (Autumn): 304-26.

Primeaux, Walter J., Jr. 1975. "A Reexamination of the Monopoly Market Structure for Electric Utilities." In Almarin Phillips, ed., *Promoting Competition in Regulated Markets*. Washington, D.C.: Brookings Institution.

Puromaki, A. 1975. "Trends in the Unification of the Electricity Tariffs in Finland." In International Union of Producers and Distributors of Electrical Energy, *Conference on Electricity Tariffs*, Madrid, April 21-23.

Ramsey, F. 1927. "A Contribution to the Theory of Taxation." *Economic Journal* 37 (March): 4-61.

Rees, Ray. 1976. *Public Enterprise Economics*. London: Weidenfeld and Nicolson.

Requin, Andre, and Jean Lorgeou. 1975. "Experiences with French Tariff Structures: Technical Means for the Implementation of Tariff Structures." In C.J. Cicchetti and W.K. Foell, eds., *Energy Systems Forecasting, Planning, and Pricing*. Madison: Institute for Environmental Studies, University of Wisconsin.

Reynolds, Reed S. 1968. "A Cross-Section Analysis of the Residential Demand for Electric Power in Selected Ohio Cities: 1963." University of Toledo.

Rouchon, J. 1975. "Experience in Restructuring Low-Voltage Tariffs: Problems Involved in Introducing the Universal Tariff in France." In International Union of Producers and Distributors of Electrical Energy, *Conference on Electricity Tariffs*, Madrid, April 21-23.

Salkever, David S. 1970. "Public Utility Pricing and Output Under Risk: Comment." *American Economic Review* 60 (June): 487-88.

Sasson, A.M., and H.M. Merril. 1974. "Some Applications of Optimization Techniques to Power System Problems." *Proceedings of the IEEE* 62: 959-972.

Scherer, Charles R. 1977. *Estimating Electric Power System Marginal Costs*. Amsterdam: North-Holland.

———. 1976. "Estimating Peak and Off-Peak Marginal Costs for an Electric Power System: An Ex Ante Approach." *Bell Journal of Economics* 7 (Autumn): 575-601.

Schipper, L., and A.J. Lichtenburg. 1976. "Efficient Energy Use and Well-Being: The Swedish Example." Lawrence Berkeley Laboratory, April.

Scott, J.T., and J.A.G. Bonner. 1975. "South Western Electricity Board Experience of the Influence of Off-Peak and Similar Tariffs on the Development of Storage Heating Load." In International Union of Producers and Distributors of Electricity Energy, *Conference on Electricity Tariffs*, Madrid, April 21-23.

Searl, Milton F., ed. 1973. *Energy Modeling: Art, Science, Practice.* Washington, D.C.: Resources for the Future, March.

Sharefkin, Mark. 1974. "The Economic and Environmental Benefits from Improving Electrical Rate Structures." Maryland: Jack Faucett Assoc., November.

Shepard, W.G. 1966. "Marginal-Cost Pricing in American Utilities." *Southern Economic Journal* 33 (July): 58-70.

Sherman, Roger, and Michael Visscher. 1978. "Second-Best Pricing with Stochastic Demand." *American Economic Review*, March.

Sherry, Edward V. 1975. "Curtailable Service Rates Can Cut Peaks." *Electrical World* 184 (October): 68-69.

Sibley, David, M. Barry Goldman, and Hayne E. Leland. 1977. "Optimal Non-Uniform Pricing." Paper delivered to American Economic Association Meetings, December 29.

Smith, R.T., and D. Weinschrott. Forthcoming. *The Aggregation Problem and Empirical Analysis of Industrial Demand for Energy.* Santa Monica: Rand (R-1879-NSF).

Smith, V. Kerry, and C.J. Cicchetti. 1974. "Measuring the Price Elasticity of Demand for Electric Power: The U.S. Experience." in Cicchetti, C.J. and W.K. Foell, eds. *Energy Systems Forecasting, Planning, and Pricing.* Madison: Institute for Environmental Studies, University of Wisconsin.

Southern California Edison Company. 1974. "Response to California Public Utilities Commission Order Instituting Investigation: Case No. 9804." Rosemead, Calif., December 16.

Spencer, R.S., et al. 1977. "The Potential for Fuel Economies via Combined Steam-Power Production." *Energy Systems and Policy* 2: 59-84.

Stein, J.P. 1976. *The Determinants of Residential Appliance Possession and Fuel Choice in Los Angeles: A Cross-Section Analysis of 1970 and 1975 Data.* Santa Monica: Rand (P-5733), September.

Steiner, Peter O. 1957. "Peak Loads and Efficient Pricing." *Quarterly Journal of Economics* 71 (November): 585-610.

Stigler, George J. 1971. "The Theory of Economic Regulation." *Bell Journal of Economics and Management Science* 2 (Spring): 3-21.

Stigler, G.J., and C. Friedland. 1962. "What Can Regulators Regulate? The Case of Electricity." *Journal of Law and Economics* 5 (October): 1-16.

Streiter, Sally Hunt. 1975. "Marginal Costs and Electricity Prices." New York: National Economic Research Associates, January 27.

"Summary of Voluntary and Compulsory Measures for Reducing Electrical Energy Consumption in Sweden in 1970 and 1974." No date. Swedish State Power Board. Mimeo.

Tansil, John. 1973. *Residential Consumption of Electricity: 1950-1970.* Oakridge National Laboratory, Tennessee, ORNL-NSF-AP-51, July.

Tansil, John, and John C. Moyers. 1974. "Residential Demand for Electricity." In M.S. Macrakis, ed., *Energy: Demand, Conservation, and Institutional Problems.* Cambridge, Mass.: M.I.T. Press.

Taylor, Lester D. 1977. "On Modeling the Residential Demand for Electricity by Time-of-Day." In Anthony Laurence, ed., *Forecasting and Modeling Time-of-Day and Seasonal Electricity Demands.* Electrical Power Research Institute, December.

——. 1975. "The Demand for Electricity: A Survey." *Bell Journal of Economics* 6 (Spring): 74-110.

Telson, M.L. 1975. "The Economics of Alternative Levels of Reliability for Electric Power Generation Systems." *Bell Journal of Economics* 6 (Autumn): 679-94.

Thermo Electron Corporation. 1976. *A Study of Inplant Electric Power Generation in the Chemical, Petroleum Refining, and Paper and Pulp Industries.*

Treadway, Hamilton. 1974. "Electric Rates and the Energy Shortage." *Public Utilities Fortnightly* 94 (December 5): 17-21.

Turvey, Ralph. 1974. "How to Judge When Price Changes Will Improve Resource Allocation." *Economic Journal* 84 (December): 825-32.

——. 1971. *Economic Analysis and Public Enterprises.* Totown, N.J.: Rowman and Littlefield.

——. 1970. "Public Utility Pricing and Output under Risk: Comment." *American Economic Review* 60 (June): 485-86.

——. 1969. "Marginal Cost." *Economic Journal* 79 (June): 282-99.

——. 1968a. *Optimal Pricing and Investment in Electricity Supply.* Cambridge, Mass.: M.I.T. Press.

——. 1968b. "Peak-Load Pricing." *Journal of Political Economy,* pp. 101-113.

——. 1967. "Practical Problems of Marginal-Cost Pricing in Public Enterprise: England." In A. Phillips and O. Williamson, eds., *Prices: Issues in Theory, Practice and Public Policy.* Philadelphia: University of Pennsylvania Press.

Turvey, Ralph, and Dennis Anderson. 1977. *Electricity Economics: Essays and Case Studies.* Baltimore, Md.: Johns Hopkins University Press.

Tveit, J., and H. Holth. 1975. "High-Voltage Tariffs at the Norwegian Water Resources and Electricity Board (NVE)." In International Union of Producers and Distributors of Electrical Energy, *Conference on Electricity Tariffs,* Madrid, April 21-23.

Tyrell, T.J. 1974. "Projections of Electricity Demand." In M.S. Macrakis, ed., *Energy: Demand, Conservation and Institutional Problems.* Cambridge, Mass.: M.I.T. Press, pp. 342-59.

UNIPEDE [International Union of Producers and Distributors of Electrical Energy]. No date. "The Study of Load Curves in Electricity Supply Economics: Manual of Theory and Practical Procedure." Paris.

United Nations. 1973. Department of Economic and Social Affairs. *Problems of Meeting Peak Electricity Demands: A General Study.* New York.

United Nations. 1972. Department of Economic and Social Affairs. *Electricity Costs and Tariffs: A General Study.* New York.

Vardi, Joseph, Jacob Zahavi, and Benjamin Avi-Itzhak. 1977. "Variable Load Pricing in the Face of Loss of Load Probability." *Bell Journal of Economics* 8 (Spring): 270-88.

Visscher, Michael L. 1973. "Welfare-Maximizing Price and Output with Stochastic Demand: Comment." *American Economic Review* 6 (March): 224-29.

Walker, David L. 1975. "Design of Electricity Tariffs in England and Wales and Experience in Their Application." In C.J. Cicchetti and W.K. Foell, eds., *Energy Systems Forecasting, Planning, and Pricing*. Madison: Institute for Environmental Studies, University of Wisconsin.

Waverman, Leonard. 1975. "Peak-Load Pricing under Regulatory Constraint: A Proof of Inefficiency." *Journal of Political Economy* 83 (June): 645-54.

Webb, Michael G. 1977. "The Determination of Reserve Generating Capacity Criteria in Electricity Supply Systems." *Applied Economics* 9: 19-31.

Weidenbaum, Murray L. 1975. "The Future of the Electric Utilities." *Challenge* (January-February): 46-52.

Wenders, J.T. 1976. "Peak-Load Pricing in the Electric Utility Industry." *Bell Journal of Economics* 7 (Spring): 232-41.

Williamson, Oliver E. 1966. "Peak-Load Pricing and Optimal Capacity under Indivisibility Constraints." *American Economic Review* 56 (September): 810-27.

Willig, Robert, and Elizabeth Bailey. 1977. "Methods of Public Interest Pricing." Paper delivered to American Economic Association Meetings, December 28.

Wilson, John W. 1971. "Residential Demand for Electricity." *Quarterly Journal of Economics and Business* 2 (Spring): 7-22.

Wilson, John W., and Robert G. Uhler. 1974. "Inverted Electric Utilities Rate Structures: An Empirical Analysis." Washington, D.C.: Federal Power Commission, March 18.

Zajac, Edward E. 1970. "A Geometric Treatment of Averch-Johnson's Behavior of the Firm Model." *American Economic Review* 60 (March): 117-25.

Zenegaglia, F. 1977. "Un Essai de Classification de la Clientèle Moyenne Tension en Fonction de la Forme de la Courbe de Charge." Electricité de France, 29 April.

———. 1975. "High-Voltage Tariffs (Tariffs for Interruptible Supplies)." In International Union of Producers and Distributors of Electricity Energy, *Conference on Electricity Tariffs*. Madrid, April 21-23.

Index

Activity analysis models, 40–41
Appliances, for residential load management, 122–24, 136, 204
Arizona, 198–99
Arkansas, 198–99
Average costs, 38, 43
 and economies of scale, 44–45
 and peak-load pricing, 39

"Backward-charging" units, 130
Baseload plant, and cost, 25–28, 36
Benefits
 of peak-load pricing, 206–207, 212
 of residential tariffs, 201–202, 207
Billing, 193
 costs, 196, 207
 in English and Welsh tariffs, 217–20
 in Green Tariff, 216–17
Bivalent residential heating, 132
Blast furnace, 175–76
Boiteux-Steiner model, 38–40, 44, 49
British Experimental Tariffs, 194–97
Bulk Supply Tariff, 75–79, 107, 188n, 217–20
By-product generation, in U.S., 186–87

California
 and potential load shifting, 166–72
 rate structure cases, 15
 time-of-day tariff for, 15, 151, 164–68, 180–85
California Energy Resources Conservation and Development Commission, xix
Capacity charge, 36, 66, 76

Capacity costs
 vs. energy costs, 24, 28, 66
 and interruptible power, 59
 and peak-load pricing, 38–39, 41, 49, 136
 and subscribed demand charges, 56, 87
 and supply of electricity, 24–28
Capacity requirements
 for distribution systems, 24, 34–35
 and effect of peak-load pricing, xx, 1, 38–39, 137–43, 148, 155–64
 for generation systems, 24–27, 31–32, 38, 177, 180, 188
 and load curve, 16–18
 social costs of, 6
Capacity shortages
 in England and Wales, 112–13
 in France, 67, 69
 vs. peak-load pricing, 37n
 and pricing, 56, 58–59
Capital costs
 in European utilities, 146
 and inflation, 46–47
 and peak-load tariffs, 155, 179, 188
 and storage, 29
 and supply of electricity, 24–27
 in thermal systems, 31
Carter administration, 4
Cement industry, and load curves
 in California, 181–82
 in England, 108–109, 112
 in France, 92–94, 119
 in U.S., 167, 175–76
 in West Germany, 81–82

237

Central Electricity Generating Board
  (CEGB), 75-79, 113, 142, 147,
  217-20
Chemical and allied industries
  in California, 183-84
  in England, 110-11
Circuit-breaker charge, 74-75, 87, 214
Climate control, 23, 122-23
Clock control, and load management,
  123, 131, 133, 136
Cogeneration, 148, 185-89, 209-10.
  See also Self-generation
Cold storage plants, 100, 119
Commercial customers. *See* Industrial
  customers; Residential customers
  in California, 183-85
Connecticut, 198-99
Conservation of energy, 1, 4-5
Construction costs, 25, 180, 188
Consumers
  in British experiment, 196
  and declining-block rate, 12-13, 15
  and distribution costs, 23-24, 34-36
  and generation costs, 23-24, 31-32
  and Green Tariff, 71-72, 213-217
  and Hopkinson rate, 13
  and load management, 121-23, 192,
    211
  and marginal cost, 43-44
  and peak-load pricing, 37, 42, 49-50,
    154, 184-85
  and price, 4-6, 23, 37-38, 49-50,
    147-48, 191-92
  and rate reform, 20-22, 53, 57-58,
    89-90, 210-12
  and storage, 29-30, 36
Consumption of electricity
  in British Tariff experiment, 194-97
  in Bulk Supply Tariff, 75-77, 218-20
  vs. efficiency, 30
  vs. energy, 21
  vs. environment, 149
  and generation system, 25-27
  in Green Tariff, 107, 216-17
  and load shifting, 29-30, 169, 172
  vs. peak-load pricing, 119, 159-62, 164,
    166-68, 169, 173-79, 188
  and prices, 9, 37-38, 43, 49-50
  and residential load management, 122-23,
    125-26, 133
Cost of electricity, 9, 23-30
  and economies of scale, 44-45
  and European tariffs, 7-8, 56-57, 71-73,
    86-87
  and inflation, 46-47
  and load shifting, 89, 92
  and marginal cost, 42-44
  vs. peaking plant, 25-26, 36

  and peak-load pricing, 1-2, 38-42,
    49-50, 152, 179-80, 188
  and price, 4-5, 9-10, 28, 204
  and rate structure, 7-8, 15-16, 19-22,
    37-38, 43, 56-59, 71-73, 86-87
  and supply, 23-30
  in U.S., 9, 152, 188
Cross-price effect, 196n
Customers. *See* Consumers; Industrial
  customers; Residential customers

Daily cycles, and marginal cost, 35-36,
  56-57
Daily demand, and load curves, 90-107,
  107-13
Daily load curves, 122-23
  in England, 142-43
  in France, 138-39
  in U.S., 173
Declining-block rate tariff, 10-13, 194,
  198, 203
  in England and Wales, 77
  in Los Angeles experiment, 200-201
  in Norway, 61
  in West Germany, 80-81
Demand charges, 87. *See also* Maximum
  demand; Subscribed demand
  in Bulk Supply Tariff, 218-19
  in England, 76
  in Green Tariff, 213-17
  in Sweden, 62-64
  in West Germany, 81-82
Demand for electricity, 16-18, 23-24, 151
  in Europe, 51, 56, 58-59, 86-87
  in France, 69-71, 73
  vs. generation plant, 27-28, 31
  and peak-load pricing, 1, 3, 151, 176-81
  and storage, 28-30
Department of Water and Power,
  See Los Angeles DWP
Direct control systems, 122-23, 131
Direct-resistance heating systems, 123,
  125-26
Distribution system
  and costs, 23-24
  and economies of scale, 44-45
  vs. inflation, 46
  and load curve, 16-18
  marginal cost of, 33-35, 56-57
  and rate structures, 43-44
  and supply of electricity, 23, 36, 58-59
  in West Germany, 128-32

Economic dispatching models, 42
Economic theory
  of electricity rates, 37-38, 42-43,
    191-92
  of peak-load pricing, 1-2, 20-22, 38-42,
    191-92

Economies of scale
  and declining-block rates, 13
  and marginal cost pricing, 44-45, 50
Economy, U.S., 3-5, 6-8, 20-22, 211-12
Efficiency, 5, 30
  and peak-load pricing, 1-2, 16, 22, 148-49, 152, 173, 206-207
Electricaire heating, 125
Electric arc furnaces, 95, 113
Electricité de France (EdF), 65-66, 69-74, 91, 102, 104-107, 138-40, 214
Electricity Council of London, 126, 193-96
Electricity tariffs, 7-8, 37-38, 51-59, 86-87
  defined, 9
  effect on load curves, 29-30, 48-49, 147-48
  in England and Wales, 75-80, 107-13, 124-27, 217-20
  in Europe, 53-87, 89-90, 118-23, 147-48, 155
  in Finland, 84-86, 117-18, 133-36
  in France, 65-74, 90-107, 133, 164-68, 213-17
  industrial, 13-15, 89-90, 118-20, 147-48
  and marginal costs, 35
  in Norway, 60-61, 117-18, 133-36
  rate reforms for, 16-22, 43-44, 210-12
  residential, 10-13, 121-23, 147-48
  in Sweden, 62-64, 113-16, 133-36
  in U.S., 10-15, 155, 164-68
  in West Germany, 80-84, 128-32
Electricity rate, defined, 9
Electricity sector
  and conservation, 4
  and market price, 5
  and peak-load pricing, xx, 1-2, 21-22, 149, 188-89
  role of, 2, 6-8
Electrochemical process, 119
  in France, 95-97
  and self-generation, 104
Electrometallurgy industry, 94-95, 119
Energy, vs. electricity, 1-2, 21, 24-25, 28
Energy charges, in electricity tariffs, 53-55, 86-87
  in Bulk Supply Tariff, 75, 218-20
  in England, 75, 78, 218-20
  in Finland, 85
  in France, 66, 69-70, 213-17
  in Green Tariff, 70, 73-75, 213-17
  in Norway, 60-61
  in Sweden, 62-64
  in West Germany, 81-82
Energy loss, 34-36
Energy policy, U.S., 3-6, 21-22, 146-47, 149, 203-205

Energy Resources and Development Administration (ERDA), xx
Engineering models, 41-42, 49
England and Wales
  electricity tariffs, xx, 53-54, 57, 75-80, 142-43, 217-20
  experimental tariffs in, 194-97
  industrial tariffs, 54, 75-77, 79-80, 107-13, 119, 142, 187
  and interconnection, 33
  load curves, 107-13, 119, 142-43, 145-47, 187
  load management, 53, 77, 123-27, 136, 202
  residential tariffs, 75, 77-79, 123-27, 136, 142, 194-95, 202
  and shifting peaks, 145-47
Environment
  effects on electricity consumption, 149
  effect on electricity sector, 5n, 6, 203
  and peak-load pricing, 1, 209, 211
Europe
  and cogeneration, 209-10
  electricity tariffs, 53-87, 147-48, 155
  and electricity usage, 185-86
  generation systems in, 56-57
  industrial tariffs, 89-90, 118-20, 147-48
  and interconnection, 208-209
  and marginal cost, 207-209
  and peak-load pricing, 18, 42, 50, 137-47, 205, 212
  rate structures in, 7-8, 50-59, 86-87
  residential tariffs, 121-23, 136, 147-48, 191-93, 202
  vs. U.S., 162-68
Experimental tariffs
  in England, 194-97
  in Los Angeles, 198-202
  in U.S., 198-99

Federal Energy Administration, xix
Federal Energy Regulatory Commission, 7, 210
Federal government, 6-7, 210
Federal Power Act, 7, 210
Federal Power Commission. See Federal Energy Regulatory Commission
Ferro-alloy plants, 94-95
Financial incentives. See also Incentives
  in England, 79-80
  in France, 70
  and load curves, 48-50, 70
  for load shifting, 104, 107, 121
  and rate structure, 37, 43, 49-50
Financial institution, in France, 100, 102
Finland
  electricity tariffs, xx, 54, 84-85
  and load curves, 117-18

and load management, 133–36
    residential tariffs, 133–36
Finnish State Power Board, 84–86
Fixed capital, 23
Fixed charge, 84–85, 218
Fixed costs, 12, 34
Flat load curves, 104, 106, 110, 122
Flat rate tariff
    in England, 77
    in Finland, 85
    in France, 74–75, 175
    in Los Angeles experiment, 200–201
    in Norway, 61
    in U.S., 175
Floor radiant heating, 132
"Forward charging" devices, 129–30
France
    Double Tariff, 74
    electricity tariffs, xx, 53–54, 57, 65–74,
        152–53, 155
    Green Tariff, 65–74, 90–91, 102, 104,
        107, 138–41, 162, 213–17
    industrial tariffs, 152–53, 155, 162,
        164–72, 213–17
    load curves, 90–107, 119, 147, 162,
        164–72
    and load management, 133
    residential tariffs, 133
    and shifting peaks, 145–46
    Universal Tariff, 66, 74
Fuel adjustment clause, 47, 218–20
Fuel costs, 25

General Tariff, 70
Generating capacity
    and peak-load pricing, 30–33
    and interconnection, 208
    and load curves, 16
    in U.S., 177, 180, 188
Generation system. See also Hydroelectric
    systems; Mixed systems; Thermal
    systems
    and costs, 23–28
    and economies of scale, 44–45
    and inflation, 46
    marginal costs of, 30–33
    and peak-load pricing, 38, 40, 42
    and prices in Europe, 56–59
    in U.S., 57, 177, 180, 188
Georgia, 198
Green Tariff, 65–74, 162, 213–17
    effects on industrial loads, 90–91, 102,
        104, 107, 138–41

Heat loss, 126n
Helsinki Electricity Works, 85

High-voltage tariffs, 53–56, 86–87, 89
    in England, 77, 107–13, 217–20
    in Finland, 85, 117
    in France, 65, 67–70, 91, 104–106,
        213–17
    in Norway, 60, 116
    in Sweden, 62–63, 114, 116
    in U.S., 151–52, 191, 202, 211
    in West Germany, 80–83
Historic costs, 19, 38, 46, 193
Hopkinson rate, 13–15
Hydroelectric systems
    and load curve, 16–18
    marginal cost of, 32, 36, 57
    in Norway, 59–61
    and residential load management, 133
    and shortages, 58
    in Sweden, 62–64, 114, 116

Incentives. See also Financial incentives
    for load shifting, 90, 92, 121–23, 147–48,
        205
    price, 48, 123, 136, 191–92. 194–95
Industrial customers, European
    and electricity tariff, xx, 28, 53, 56,
        86–87, 89–90, 118–20, 147–48
    in England, 79–80, 107–13, 217–20
    in Finland, 85, 117–18
    in France, 67–72, 90–107, 213–17
    in Norway, 60, 116–17
    in Sweden, 113–16
    in West Germany, 80–84
Industrial customers, U.S., 4n
    and electricity usage, 185–88
    vs. Europe, 164–68
    vs. France, 174–78
    national effects of, 173–85
    and peak-load pricing, 151–64, 168–72,
        206, 210
Industrial economy, 6, 23
Industrial gas production plants, 110, 113,
    119, 175
Industrial tariffs. See also High-voltage
    tariffs
    and Hopkinson rate, 13–15
    and PPW contract, 113
    and voltage, 9
Inflation, 19, 21, 46–47, 149
Insulation, 125–26, 136
Interconnection, 33, 208–209
    and tariffs, 59, 80–84, 86
Interruptible tariffs, 142
    and capacity costs, 59
    in England, 79–80, 113
    in Europe, 185, 187–88
    in France, 104

Index 241

in Norway, 60, 116
and peak-load pricing, 58-59
in U.S., 185, 187-89
in West Germany, 82-83
Inverted-block rate structure, 43
Investor-owned companies, 6-7
Iron and steel industry
 and load management, 94-95, 119
 in England, 110
 in France, 94-95
 in U.S., 167, 175-76

Kilovolts, 9n
Kilowatts, 9

Labor costs, 25, 155-62
Lifeline tariffs, 43
Liquids and gases transportation, 97-100, 119
Load curve, 16-18, 39, 41-42, 48-52, 89n
 in British experiment, 196-97
 in California, 181-85
 in England, 107-13, 152-53
 and European industrial tariffs, 89-90, 118-20, 205
 in Finland, 117-18
 in France, 90-107, 152-53, 166-72
 and industrial tariffs, 89-90, 118-20
 in Norway, 116-17
 and peak-load pricing, 151-53, 154-64, 166-72, 173-78, 188
 in Sweden, 113-16
 in U.S., xx, 151-64, 166-78, 188
Load duration curve, 26-27, 30-31, 46, 140
Load factor, 71-72
Load levels, 193
Load management
 in England, 77, 79-80
 in Europe, 51-59, 87, 121-22, 147-48, 205
 in France, 70, 133
 and load curves, 49
 and residential tariffs, 121-36
 in Scandinavia, 133-36
 and time-of-day tariffs, 192-93, 198
 in West Germany, 80, 128-32
Load-rate tariff, 61
Load shifting
 in California, 181-86
 vs. consumption, 29-30, 169, 172
 and costs, 28-30
 in England, 125-26
 in France, 133, 153, 165-72
 incentives for, 90, 92, 104-107, 118-21, 121-23, 147-48, 205

in Scandinavia, 136
in U.S., 15-16, 152-53, 164-66, 180-86, 206, 211-12
in West Germany, 128-32
Long-run marginal costs
 in distribution system, 35
 and peak-load pricing in U.S., 177, 179-80
 vs. short-run marginal costs, 47-48
 and type of generation plant, 27, 209
Los Angeles Department of Water and Power, xix, 14, 198-202
Los Angeles experiment, 198-202
Low-voltage tariff. *See also* Residential tariff
 in Europe, 202
 in France, 66
 in U.S., 191-92, 211
 in West Germany, 83-84

Madison Gas and Electric case, 15n
Manufacturing industries, 167, 174-78, 188
Marginal-cost pricing, 18-19, 21, 39-40, 42-48, 203-204
 in Europe, 7-8
 and resources, 5
 in U.S. residential tariffs, 10, 13
Marginal costs
 of distribution, 33-35, 36
 in England, 75-79
 and European utilities, 143-45, 148
 in France, 65-74
 of generation, 30-33, 36
 in Los Angeles experiment, 200
 and load management, 122, 133, 136
 vs. market price, 5
 and peak load in Europe, 52-59
 and peak-load pricing, 179, 207-208, 212
 rate structures, xx, 16-22, 37-50, 203-204, 212
 role of, 30-36
 and supply of electricity, 27-28, 30-35
Market price, 3, 5, 205
Markets, competitive, 5, 21, 89
Maximum demand, 28, 38
 vs. peak-load pricing, 157, 176-81, 203
Maximum demand charge, 53-56, 87
 and distribution system, 135-36
 in England, 77-78
 in Finland, 85, 117
 in France, 69-71, 74, 214, 216
 in Norway, 117
 in Sweden, 113
 in U.S., 71
Medium-voltage tariffs, 89
 in France, 70-71, 92

and single-shift load curves, 155n
  in West Germany, 81
Megawatts, 9n
Metering
  in England, 77-79
  in Europe, 56, 89
  for residential load management, 122-23
  in Sweden, 64
  in U.S., 151-52
Metering costs
  in British experiment, 196-97
  in Los Angeles experiment, 200
  and U.S. time-of-day tariff, 192-93, 206-207, 212
Michigan, 151, 180
Mixed systems, 179, 188
  in Finland, 84-85
  and marginal cost, 32-33, 36, 57
  and marginal cost tariffs, 59-60, 80-85, 87
  and shortages, 59
  in West Germany, 60, 80-84
Motor vehicles, 175, 177
Municipally-owned companies, 6-7

National energy policy, 3-6, 21-22
  role of pricing, xx
Nationalization, 75, 146-47
Natural gas transportation, 99-100, 119
Net benefit, 196n
New Jersey, 198-99
New York, 15, 151, 180
New York City, 11-12, 14
Norway
  electricity tariffs in, xx, 53, 55, 57, 60-61
  and interconnection, 33
  load curves, 116-17
  and load management, 133-36
  residential tariffs, 133-36
Norwegian Water Resources and Electricity Board (NVE), 60
Nuclear generating plants, 25-27, 210
Nuclear Regulatory Commission, 210

Off-peal period, 28, 67-70, 77-78, 81-82
  and consumption, 126, 133
  in England, 107-13, 126
  in Finland, 117
  in France, 90-92, 102-104, 104-107, 133
  and load curves, 90-92, 104-107, 107-13, 117, 119
  and load management, 122-23
  and self-generation, 102-104
Off-peak rates, 155-65
Ohio, 198-99
Oil embargo, xix, 3, 147, 149

Operating costs
  in Europe, 146-47, 205
  and generation plants, 27
  and load curve, 16n
  and peak-load, 41-42, 179, 188
  and storage, 29
  in thermal systems, 31
  in U.S., 179, 188

Pacific Gas and Electric Company (PG&E), 164-65, 179, 181-84
Paper products industry, 175-76, 182-84
Peak demand period, 28, 67-70, 76-78
  in California, 182-84
  and costs, 24-28, 81-82, 122-23
  in distribution system, 35, 36
  in England, 107-13
  in Finland, 117
  in France, 90-92, 104-107
  in hydroelectric systems, 32, 36
  in mixed systems, 32, 36
  and self-generation, 102-104
  in Sweden, 114
  in thermal systems, 31, 36
  in U.S., 176-80
Peaking plant, 25-28, 36
Peak-load tariffs, 37, 49-50, 86-87. See also Marginal-cost pricing; Seasonal rate structure; Time-of-day tariffs
  theory of, 38-42
Peak rate, 155-65, 194-95, 200-202
Periodicity of demand, 23-25, 38-42, 56-57. See also Seasonal demand; Time period
Petroleum refining
  in England, 109
  in France, 102-104, 119
  and self-generation, 102-104, 119
  in U.S., 167, 175-76
Petroleum transportation, 99-100, 119
Potential peak warnings, (PPW) periods, 76-80, 112-13, 187, 219
Power system equipment, 23
Power systems
  and marginal costs, 30-36
  types of, 25-27, 33, 36, 56-59
Price elasticity of demand, 12n, 45, 50n, 151
Prices for electricity, 6
  vs. costs, 4-5, 9-10, 28, 204
  and declining-block rate, 12-13
  economic purposes of, 37-38, 49-50
  and economies of scale, 44-45
  and energy policy, 2-5, 203-205
  in England, 107
  in Europe, 51-59, 86-87, 89-90, 147-48
  in France, 73, 107

and generation system, 32, 56-59
and inflation, 46-47
and load curves, 90-91
vs. marginal costs, 30, 37-40, 43-44, 47-48, 143-45
and rate structure, 9-10, 15-22, 192-93
and supply of electricity, 30, 51, 56-59
Production processes
and load management, 89, 95, 102-104
and peak-load tariffs, 37, 155-63
Public policy, and rates, 149, 191, 207-12
Public utility commissions, 21, 210

Ramsey price, 45, 73-74
Rate levels, 37, 49
Rate reforms, 15-16, 19-22, 38, 43-44, 186-88, 210-12
  in England, 194-97
  for residential customers, 191-93, 202
Rate structure. *See also* Electricity Tariffs
  in California, 181-85
  declining-block, 10-13, 194, 198, 200-201, 203
  defined, 9
  and economies of scale, 44-45
  in England, 75-80, 217-20
  in Europe, xix-xx, 7-8, 42, 50-59
  in Finland, 84-85
  in France, 65-74, 213-17
  Hopkinson, 13-15
  load curve, 16-18, 48-49
  marginal-cost pricing, 18-19, 21, 39-40, 42-48, 203-204
  new, 16-22, 202, 206-207, 211-12
  in Norway, 60-61
  peak-load pricing as, 1-2, 18, 21-22, 38-42, 147-48, 173-78, 188, 204-205, 212
  in Sweden, 62-64
  in U.S., xix-xx, 2, 5, 7-16, 38, 50, 149, 151-52, 188, 202, 206-207, 210-12
  in West Germany, 80-84
Regulatory commissions, 5, 7, 9, 19n, 20, 210-11
Remote control, 15, 193
Replacement costs, 19, 46-47
Residential customers
  declining-block rates for, 10-13
  and electricity tariffs for, 56-57, 86-87
  and voltage, 9
Residential tariffs. *See also* Low-voltage tariff
  in England, 77-79, 124-27, 145
  in Europe, 121-23, 147-48, 205
  in Finland, 85, 133-36
  in France, 73-74, 133, 145
  in Norway, 61, 133-36

and shifting peaks, 145-46
in Sweden, 64, 133-36
in U.S., 191-202, 206-207, 210
in West Germany, 83-84, 128-32
Resources, energy
  and competitive markets, 5, 21, 89
  and peak-load pricing, xx
  and supply of electricity, 6, 24, 36
Restricted-circuit approach, 123-24
Revenues
  in European utilities, 146
  and inflation, 46-47
  and marginal-cost pricing, 42-45
  and peak-load pricing, 41
  and rate levels, 37, 49
Ripple-controls systems, 131, 136
Rubber products industry, 175-76
Running costs
  in distribution system, 34
  in French systems, 67, 69
  in Norwegian system, 60-61
  and peak-load pricing, 38, 49
  and supply of electricity, 25-27
  in thermal systems, 31
"Run-of-the-river" installations, 32, 57

San Diego Gas and Electric Company, 188n
Savings
  from mixed systems, 27
  from peak-load pricing, 176-77, 179-80, 188
Seasonal charges, 81-82
Seasonal demand, 24-25, 27-28, 119
  and costs, 23-25, 56-57
  in England, 107-13
  in France, 90-107, 141
  and generation system, 31-33, 36
  in Norway, 116-17
  pricing, 53, 62-64, 67-69, 75-76
  in U.S., 173
Seasonal rate structures, 18, 20, 192, 212
  in England, 194-97
  in France, 67-69, 74
  in Los Angeles experiment, 198-202
  in U.S., 198, 206-207
Self-generation
  in England, 109
  in Europe, 185-86
  in France, 95, 97, 100-104
  in Sweden, 116
  in U.S., 186-87, 209-10
Shifting peaks, 40, 143-47
Short-run marginal costs
  vs. long-run marginal costs, 47-48
  and peak-load pricing, 176-77, 179
  and type of generation plant, 27-28, 42
Shoulder period, 28, 67-70, 82
  in British experiment, 195

in California, 182-84
in France, 90-92, 102-107, 164-65
and self-generation, 102-104
in U.S., 164-65
Single-shift firms, 155, 159-62
Social costs, 7, 20, 43
Solar heating, 198
State regulatory agencies, 5, 7, 19, 151-52, 180, 210-12
Steel works industry, 175-76
in West Germany, 82
Storage, 28-32, 36, 116
Storage radiators, 77, 79, 123-24
Storage space-heating, 16, 57, 207
effect on system load curve, 142-43
in England, 124-26, 196
in France, 133
and load management, 122-24, 136
and shifting peaks, 145-46
in Sweden, 64
in U.S., 198
in West Germany, 80, 84, 128-32
Storage water-heating, 136, 142-43
Subscribed demand charges, 56
in France, 69-71, 73, 168-72
in Green Tariff, 141-42, 214-17
in Norway, 60-61
in Sweden, 62-64
Supply of electricity
and costs, 23-30
and marginal costs, 30-35
and peak-load models, 40-42
and prices, 30, 51, 56-59
Sweden
electricity tariffs in, xx, 55, 57, 62-64
and load curves, 113-16
and load management, 133-36
residential tariffs, 133-36
Swedish State Power Board, 62-63, 113, 116
System load curves
in England, 142-43, 147
in France, 138-41, 147
and load management, 122-23
in mixed systems, 32-33, 36
and peak-load pricing, 137-39, 146-48
in thermal systems, 31, 36
in West Germany, 142-43, 147

Tariffs. *See* Electricity Tariffs
Tennessee Valley Authority (TVA), 7, 11-12, 14
Thermal systems
in England, 60, 75-80
in France, 65-74
marginal cost of, 31-32, 36

and marginal cost tariff, 60, 65-80, 87
and pricing, 57
rate structures for, 16, 18
and residential load management, 128, 134, 136
and shortages, 58-59
in U.S., 173
Time-invariant rates, 200-202, 204, 212
Time-of-day rate structure, 18, 20, 53
in California, 181-85, 188
in England, 77, 79, 107-12, 125, 142-43, 194-97
in Europe, 164-68
in Finland, 85, 117, 136
in France, 67-70, 74, 104-107, 137-39, 164-68
and industrial load management, 151-52, 155-64, 164-68, 174-78, 188, 206
interruptions, 53, 79-80
in Los Angeles, 198-202
and load curves, 119, 137-39, 142-43
in Norway, 116-17, 136
pricing, 56-57, 62-64, 74-75, 77-80, 85-87
and residential load management, 123, 136, 191-92, 202, 206-207
in Sweden, 62, 64, 114-16, 136
in U.S., 151-52, 191-92, 198, 212
in West Germany, 80-82, 84, 142-43
Time periods
and cost, 23, 27
and load curve, 16-17
and peak-load pricing, 38-42, 49-50, 193
and rate structure, 7-8, 15, 20-21
Total costs, of electricity supply, 25-27, 30, 146-47
and economies of scale, 44-45
and inflation, 46
and marginal-cost pricing, 44
in Norway, 60
vs. peak-load tariffs, 40-41, 155, 159

United States
and electricity usage, 185-88
vs. Europe, 164-68
generation systems in, 24-28, 57, 177, 180, 188
industrial tariffs, 152-64, 174-78, 188, 206
and interconnection, 208-209
and load curves, 151-64, 166-78, 188
and marginal cost, 207-209
mixed systems in, 32-33, 36, 57
and peak-load pricing, xix-xx, 18, 51n, 151-64, 166-78, 188

potential load shifting, 166-72
rate structures in, xix-xx, 7-16, 19-22, 38, 50-51, 149, 203-204, 206-207, 210-12
and seasonal demand, 173, 198
U.S. energy policy, 3-5, 21-22, 149
vs. Europe, 51, 146-47
and pricing, 203-205
U.S. Standard Industrial Classification (SIC) codes, 167
Universal Tariff, 66, 74
Usage, electricity
in British experiment, 197
in Europe, 153
in France, 162
and load management, 122, 125
and marginal-cost pricing, 18-19, 30
and peak-load pricing, xx, 1, 16, 18, 89, 168-72, 185-86, 188
and pricing, 1-4, 19-22
and rate reforms, 20
and rate structures, 7-8, 9-10, 10-15
in U.S., 9-10, 15, 154, 162, 167, 173-78, 185-88
Utilities
and economies of scale, 44-45
European, 146-48, 205
and generation plants, 25-28, 31-33

load curves, 41-42, 48-52
and load management, 121-22, 130
and marginal-cost pricing, 43, 47-48, 207-209
and market price, 5-6, 21, 205
and peak-load pricing, 42, 151-52
and rate structures, 9, 15-16, 19, 37-38, 49-50
and storage, 28-30

Value-added, 89, 92
Value-of-service pricing, 43, 45n
Vermont, 198
Voltage levels, 56, 60, 70-71
and marginal cost, 35
and rate structures, 7-9
and supply of electricity, 9, 23, 36

West Germany
electricity tariffs in, xx, 53, 57, 80-84
and interconnection, 33
and load curve, 147
and load management, 128-32, 136
and peak-load pricing, 142-43
residential tariffs, 128-32, 136
and shifting peaks, 145-46
White meter tariff, 77, 79, 123-26
Wholesale tariff, 75-77
Wisconsin, 15, 151, 180, 188

Selected Rand Books

Aumann, R.J., and L.S. Shapley. *Values of Non-Atomic Games*. Princeton, New Jersey: Princeton University Press, 1974.
Averch, Harvey A., et al. *How Effective Is Schooling? A Critical Review of Research*. Englewood Cliffs, New Jersey: Educational Technology Publications, 1974.
Baer, Walter S. *Cable Television: A Handbook for Decision Making*. New York: Crane, Russak & Company, Inc., 1974.
Bagdikian, Ben H. *The Information Machines: Their Impact on Men and the Media,* New York: Harper and Row, 1971.
Becker, Abraham S., Bent Hansen, and Malcolm H. Kerr. *The Economics and Politics of the Middle East*. New York: American Elsevierr Publishing Company, 1975.
Becker, Abraham S. *Military Expenditure Limitation for Arms Control: Problems and Prospects. With a Documentary History of Recent Proposals*. Cambridge, Massachusetts: Ballinger Publishing Company, 1977.
Bellman, Richard. *Dynamic Programming*. Princeton, New Jersey: Princeton University Press, 1957.
Dantzig, George B. *Linear Programming and Extensions*. Princeton, New Jersey: Princeton University Press, 1963.
Dole, Stephen H. *Habitable Planets for Man*. New York: American Elsevier Publishing Company, 1970.
Dorfman, Robert, Paul A. Samuelson, and Robert M. Solow. *Linear Programming and Economic Analysis*. New York: McGraw-Hill Book Company, Inc., 1958.
Dreyfus, Stuart. *Dynamic Programming and the Calculus of Variations*. New York: Academic Press, Inc., 1965.

Fishman, George S. *Spectral Methods in Econometrics.* Cambridge, Mass.: Harvard University Press, 1969.

Gale, David. *The Theory of Linear Economic Models.* New York: McGraw-Hill Book Company, Inc., 1960.

Goldhamer, Herbert. *The Soviet Soldier: Soviet Military Management at the Troop Level.* New York: Crane, Russak & Company, Inc., 1975.

Harman, Alvin. *The International Computer Industry: Innovation and Comparative Advantage.* Cambridge, Mass.: Harvard University Press, 1971.

Hirshleifer, Jack, James C. DeHaven, and Jerome W. Milliman. *Water Supply: Economics, Technology, and Policy.* Chicago, Illinois: The University of Chicago Press, 1960.

McCall, John J. *Income Mobility, Racial Discrimination, and Economic Growth.* Lexington, Mass.: D.C. Heath and Company, 1973.

Moorsteen, Richard and Morton I. Abramowitz. *Remaking China Policy: U.S.-China Relations and Governmental Decision Making.* Cambridge, Mass.: Harvard University Press, 1971.

Park, Rolla Edward. *The Role of Analysis in Regulatory Decisionmaking.* Lexington, Mass.: D.C. Heath and Company, 1973.

Pascal, Anthony. *Thinking About Cities: New Perspectives on Urban Problems.* Belmont, California: Dickenson Publishing Company, 1970.

Pascal, Anthony H. (ed.). *Racial Discrimination in Economic Life.* Lexington, Mass.: D.C. Heath and Company, 1972.

Phillips, Almarin. *Technology and Market Structure: A Study of the Aircraft Industry.* Lexington, Mass.: D.C. Heath and Company, 1971.

Pincus, John (ed.). *School Finance in Transition: The Courts and Educational Reform.* Cambridge, Mass.: Ballinger Publishing Company, 1974.

Quade, E.S. *Analysis for Public Decisions.* New York: American Elsevier Publishing Company, 1975.

Schurr, Sam H. and Paul T. Homan. *Middle Eastern Oil and the Western World: Prospects and Problems.* New York: American Elsevier Publishing Company, 1971.

Wildhorn, Sorrell, Burke K. Burright, John H. Enns, Thomas F. Kirkwood. *How to Save Gasoline: Public Policy Alternatives.* Cambridge, Mass: Ballinger Publishing Company, 1976.

Williams, John C. *The Compleat Strategyst: Being a Primer on the Theory of Games of Strategy.* New York: McGraw-Hill Book Company, Inc., 1954.

About the Authors

Bridger M. Mitchell is senior staff economist at The Rand Corporation and Research Fellow at the International Institute of Management, Berlin. He was born in New Haven, Connecticut, in 1940. He received the B.A. from Stanford University in 1962 and the Ph.D. from the Massachusetts Institute of Technology in 1970. From 1966 to 1971 he taught at Stanford University and later served as a Brookings Economic Policy Fellow in the Department of Health, Education and Welfare. Since joining Rand in 1972 he has taught courses at Stanford University and the University of California at Los Angeles. He is the author of numerous articles in the fields of econometrics, cable television, health insurance, telecommunications, energy policy and economic regulation.

Willard G. Manning, Jr. is an associate staff economist at The Rand Corporation. He was graduated with honors in Economics from the California Institute of Technology in 1968. He received the Ph.D. in Economics from Stanford University in 1973.

From 1973 to 1975 he served on the Harvard University faculty as an assistant professor at the School of Public Health and the Kennedy School of Government. Dr. Manning has pursued research in the economics of health, energy, and telecommunications. Recently he has collaborated with Drs. Acton and Mitchell in the design and analysis of the Los Angeles experiment on peak-load pricing for residential customers.

Jan Paul Acton is a senior staff economist who joined The Rand Corporation in 1970. He received the B.A. in economics with highest honors from San Diego State College in 1966 and the Ph.D. from Harvard University in 1971. He has been principal investigator on research projects in the economics of health and several studies on various aspects of energy policy, including the Los Angeles electricity rate study. He has published several articles in the economics of health, benefit-cost analysis, energy, and pricing in regulated industries. He has testified before state regulatory bodies and before the United States Congress.